The
Macintosh
Font Book
3rd Edition

The
Macintosh Font Book

3rd Edition

Erfert Fenton

Peachpit Press

The Macintosh Font Book, 3rd Edition
Erfert Fenton

Peachpit Press
2414 Sixth Street
Berkeley, CA 94710
510/548-4393
510/548-5991 (fax)

Find us on the World Wide Web at http://www.peachpit.com

Peachpit Press is a division of Addison-Wesley Publishing Company.

ISBN 0-201-88364-3

9 8 7 6 5 4 3 2 1

Printed and bound in the United States of America

Contents

Appendices

Acknowledgments

Sincere thanks are due to the many people who took the time to help me with this book. These include Gwendolyn Ball, Danielle Beaumont, Liz Bond, Steve Brecher, Brian Blackwelder, Fred Brady, Roslyn Bullas, Ned Bunnell, Robert Koch, Luis Camus, Robin Casady, LaVon Collins, Jack Davis, Louise Domenitz, Earl Douglas, Janet Dueñas, Robert Eckhardt, Jim Felici, Jay Fenton, Kathy Forsythe, Bill Freais, Victor Gavenda, Catherine Hartley, Jim Heid, Neil and Trula Hickman, Paul Husband, Paul King, Harry Marks, Doug Nielson, Rici Peterson, Lon Poole, Caroline Pratt, Sonya Schaefer, Sumner Stone, Jim Stoneham, Karen Teague, Debra Turner, Kevin Wandryk, and John Ward.

Last, but not least, I'd like to thank Ted Nace for his encouragement.

— *Erfert Fenton*

Imagesetting by Absolute Graphics, San Jose, California

How This Book Was Made

This is a book about Macintosh fonts. It was produced entirely on an IBM PC. Just kidding. Of *course* it was produced on a Macintosh. To be more precise, the manuscript was typed in Microsoft Word, then transferred to QuarkXPress for layout. Many of the figures were created with Mainstay's Capture (now Captivate) utility and modified in Aldus SuperPaint.

Page proofs were printed on an Apple LaserWriter Pro at 600 dots per inch. Finally, the book was printed at a resolution of 1200 dots per inch on a service bureau's imagesetter.

The book's text is set in a prerelease version of Adobe Jenson, a Multiple Master font from Adobe Systems. Adobe Jenson was designed by Robert Slimbach. Chapter titles, headings, and other elements are set in Bodega Sans, from The Font Bureau, and figure captions are set in Adobe's Myriad Multiple Master font. Clip art for several illustrations is from T/Maker's Art Parts collection.

Introduction

On the day I wrote this introduction, the Smith-Corona Corporation filed for Chapter 11 bankruptcy protection. The 113-year-old company has struggled valiantly to keep an obsolescent technology alive, but it may be no match for a 10-year-old upstart called desktop publishing. Smith-Corona and other typewriter companies can blame Apple Computer for their troubles. Ever since Apple introduced its Laser-Writer printer in 1985, people have been turning to personal computers for their publishing needs, whether they're dashing off a memo or typesetting a book. I'm tempted to say that desktop publishing is here to stay, but that's probably what they said about the typewriter in 1868. At any rate, desktop publishing is going strong right now, and developers are releasing thousands of fonts a year to satisfy the public's newfound interest in type.

Introduction

Macintosh-based typography is a rich enough subject to warrant an entire book. If you're a Mac-based publisher, you need to know not only what typefaces are available, but how to use them effectively. You can no longer expect to impress people by cranking out a document with your word processor and printing it in one of the fonts that came with your laser printer. These days, you have to know enough about type to make your publications look professionally published, not just desktop published.

This book provides a centralized source of information on typefaces for the Mac, covering everything from the mechanics of installing and managing a font collection to strategies for choosing faces that work well together in a design. In addition to discussing the typefaces themselves, the book describes numerous utilities that let you organize, catalog, modify, and even create Macintosh fonts.

Like any technology, font technology is constantly changing. This edition has been revised substantially to reflect recent developments in Mac-based typography. Since the first edition came out, some types of fonts (bit-mapped and Type 3 PostScript) have pretty much faded away, others are hanging in there (Type 1 PostScript and TrueType), and others are neither here nor there (QuickDraw GX). The procedure for installing fonts has changed drastically since the previous edition was released, and many new font-related programs and utilities have been introduced.

This book is intended primarily for people who are new to Macintosh fonts. I've tried to explain things in simple language, with step-by-step illustrations of various procedures. But even if you're an old hand at Mac font management, you might learn a thing or two, whether it's how to type a special character or where to find a Cyrillic typeface.

Happy fonting!

1
Typographic Terminology

You should learn the language of typography if you're going to work with type. Of course, many Mac-based publishers think they can get along just fine without knowing the difference between italic and oblique, whether a typeface has a large x-height, or what an em dash is. The Mac's desktop-publishing capabilities have given rise to a class of instant publishers, many of whom don't know an em dash from a hole in the ground. It's pretty easy to spot their work.

If you want your publications to look professional, you have to learn more than just the mechanics of loading and printing fonts; you have to know something about typography. This chapter will help you make the most of the Mac's typographic capabilities when you create your own publication, whether it's a report, a club newsletter, or an entire book. If you want to cut to the chase and learn about Macintosh font formats, you can skip to

Chapter 4. But if you're a newcomer to the world of type, I suggest you read this chapter. Fonts are only the raw materials of typography. Without a basic understanding of typography, you'll just be typing; if you take the time to learn some background information, you'll be setting type.

Fonts and Faces

In the early days of type, a font was a set of cast-metal characters. (The word *font* is derived from the same root as *found*, as in foundry.) Back then, a separate font had to be carved and cast for each size that was to be printed. The letters, numbers, and other characters made up a *typeface*, a set of characters that share a common design. In computer-based typesetting, in which a digitally encoded master character set can be scaled to any size, the original concept of a font has become obsolete; nowadays, the terms *font* and *typeface* (or *face*) are often used interchangeably. In this book, I'll follow the convention of calling the "source" of a typeface—the characters you see on the screen, or the information the printer uses to create characters—a font. (Screen fonts and printer fonts are discussed in Chapter 4.) The printed characters generated by a computer-based font belong to a particular typeface, such as Times or Palatino. Using this terminology, you might say, "I'm going to load the Garamond font into my printer," but you wouldn't say, "What do you think of this brochure that's set in the Garamond font?" In the second case, you're referring to a page of printed type, so you'd speak of the Garamond typeface.

The Origins of Type

Clues to typography's origins can be found in many of today's typefaces. Whether the originals were chiseled in stone or penned on parchment, traces of the early letterforms that inspired some of the first typographers can still be glimpsed in many contemporary faces.

Serif Faces

Pick up any book, magazine, or newspaper and look at the typeface used in it. Chances are you'll be looking at a *serif* face, one with small counterstrokes capping the ends of each character's main strokes. The typeface you're reading now is a serif face. Serifs stem from type's predecessor, calligraphy; the word *serif* probably comes from the Dutch word *screef*, meaning "line" or "stroke." Here are some examples of serif faces:

ABCDEFGHIJKLMNOPQRSTUVWXYZ
abcdefghijklmnopqrstuvwxyz12345678

ABCDEFGHIJKLMNOPQRSTUVWXYZ
abcdefghijklmnopqrstuvwxyz123456

ABCDEFGHIJKLMNOPQRSTUVWXYZ
abcdefghijklmnopqrstuvwxyz1234567890

Shown here: ITC Charter (Bitstream), ITC Benguiat (Adobe), and Egyptian Condensed (Alphabets Inc.)

Until the fifteenth century, scribes copied books by hand. Then, around 1440, the printing industry was born. Although there is some debate among historians, a German goldsmith named Johann Gutenberg is generally credited with the invention of *movable type*. Gutenberg carved each letter in relief onto the face of a steel punch, then drove the steel into a softer metal to make a matrix. He constructed an adjustable mold to accommodate letters of different widths, arranged the matrices, and cast the letters in a molten alloy consisting mainly of lead. (If you hear the terms *hot type* or *hot lead*, they're referring to the days of molten-lead typesetting, which lasted well into this century.) The lines of cast letters, which again appeared in relief, were inked and impressed onto paper with a device adapted from wine or paper presses.

The early faces of Gutenberg and his contemporaries mimicked handwritten letters. Many of the characteristics of letters drawn with a wide-nib pen—extreme variations in stroke weight, an angular quality, and various calligraphic flourishes—were transferred to the metal letters. Like hot-metal typesetting itself, the tradition of serif typefaces has endured for centuries.

Sans Serif Faces

Despite the popularity of faces based on handwritten letters, type design hasn't evolved quite as slowly as typesetting technology. In the 1920s a new typestyle began to gain popularity. Although *sans serif* (without serif) faces had occasionally cropped up in the early 1800s, they weren't widely used until they were championed by the Bauhaus, a design school founded in Germany in 1919 by the architect Walter Gropius. The Bauhaus artists and designers applied the ideals of simplicity and functionality to painting, sculpture, architecture, furniture design—and typography. They stripped letters of old-fashioned embellishments like serifs and variable line widths, distilling letterforms to a clean, modern style made up of simple shapes and lines.

Some people felt the modern movement went too far in its attempts to reduce objects to their fundamental elements, resulting in designs that were aesthetically pleasing but of questionable functionality. Just as a chair made of steel tubing might be more beautiful but less comfy than its overstuffed counterpart, certain sans serif faces are a pleasure to look at but difficult to read. In the old days, sans serif faces were also called *grotesque* or *gothic* faces; neither is exactly a flattering appellation. Although these terms have fallen out of use, they can still be found in some sans serif typeface names, such as News Gothic or Monotype Grotesque.

Sans serif faces are rarely used for long passages of text; their uniform line weight and the similarity of many letter shapes make them less legible than serif faces. Serifs provide anchor points for the eye and help lead it from one letter to the next, making serif faces easier to read. In addition, many designers prefer the visually rich appearance of serif type to the sparse, uniform look of a page of sans serif text. For these reasons, sans serif faces are often used for relatively short blocks of text such as headlines, chapter headings, captions, or advertisements. The crisp, simple lines of sans serif letters provide a contrast to serif type, making sans serif faces ideal for accenting features such as headings or captions.

Of course, there's no law against setting a book or magazine in a sans serif face. Many people have done so, especially when they wanted to achieve a modern look. It's just that most people are accustomed to reading serif faces, and you run the risk of alienating some readers if you use a sans serif face in your publication. Here are a few examples of sans serif faces.

ABCDEFGHIJKLMNOPQRSTUVWXYZ
abcdefghijklmnopqrstuvwxyz123456

ABCDEFGHIJKLMNOPQRSTUVWXYZ
abcdefghijklmnopqrstuvwxyz123456

ABCDEFGHIJKLMNOPQRSTUVWXYZ
abcdefghijklmnopqrstuvwxyz123456

Shown here: Berthold Akzidenz Grotesk (Adobe), Bodega Sans (Font Bureau), and Futura (Adobe)

Some sans serif faces offer the best of both worlds, giving a subtle nod to serif faces by means of subtle variations in line weight and slightly flared stroke ends. Such faces are sometimes called *semisans* faces. Some examples are shown here:

ABCDEFGHIJKLMNOPQRSTUVWXYZ
abcdefghijklmnopqrstuvwxyz123456

ABCDEFGHIJKLMNOPQRSTUVWXYZ
abcdefghijklmnopqrstuvwxyz123456

Shown here: Optima (Linotype-Hell) and Rotis Semisans (Agfa)

Type Styles

As mentioned earlier, the type designers of Gutenberg's day imitated the letterforms of hand-lettered manuscripts. The ornate, angular, calligraphic style of these early faces is called *black-letter* type. Here's an example:

The Daily Planet

Shown here: Goudy Text (Monotype)

Offshoots of this style remained popular in Germany until the early twentieth century. Black-letter faces are still used today in newspaper banners, certificates, and heavy-metal album covers. However, they're so difficult to read that they're generally considered novelty faces. Don't get me wrong. There's no law against setting a book or magazine in black-letter type. But there should be.

Roman

In the mid-1400s a new typestyle was evolving—one based on a style of hand lettering that was itself inspired by the capital letters carved into the monuments of ancient Rome. Like writing with a pen, the process of carving letters into stone affected the shapes of letters; capping a stroke with a chiseled serif was the logical way to cleanly finish a letter. The new type style was called *roman*, probably after a face created around 1460 by Schweynheym and Pannartz, two Germans working near Rome. Their face was roman in form, but still had the dark, heavy look of the black-letter style.

In 1470, Nicolas Jenson, a French printer who was working in Venice, created a typeface that is considered the first true roman face. (The text you are reading now is Adobe Jenson, a digital revival of Jenson's roman face, crafted by type designer Robert Slimbach.) The roman style was adopted and refined by printers throughout Europe, gradually gaining popularity over black-letter type and evolving into the smooth, rounded letters of today's roman faces. These days, the term *roman* is also used to indicate "plain" text—that is, text without any stylistic variations such as italic or bold (these styles are described in the following sections).

Many of the letterforms used in today's roman typefaces have changed remarkably little since the original fonts were struck centuries ago. The Adobe Jenson you are reading here has been altered somewhat to make it work well in the digital medium, as well as to make it pleasing to the modern reader's eye, but Slimbach tried to remain true to the original design by keeping some of its idiosyncrasies. The result is a refined, modern-looking typeface that retains much of the character of the fifteenth-century face that inspired it.

Italic

In addition to roman type, another style based on handwriting has endured. Today's *italic* faces have their origins in a script that was popular in Italy (hence the name) in the late fifteenth and early sixteenth centuries. Italics are based on a cursive handwriting style known as *chancery script*, which was written with a flat-edged quill pen. The Venetian printer and publisher Aldus Manutius is credited with creating one of the first italic faces in the late fifteenth century. He used the face to set several books, and the style caught on and was copied by others. While the first italic faces were used to set entire books, italic type gradually assumed its current role, which is to create a contrast to roman text. Today, an italic font is often created to stylistically complement a roman font. The italics you see in this book come with the Adobe Jenson roman typeface, but the design is based on a sixteenth-century italic face by Ludovico degli Arrighi, since Jenson never created an italic face to accompany his roman design.

Italic text has many functions: it can be used to emphasize a word or phrase ("He did *what*?"), to introduce a new term, to indicate a foreign word or phrase, or to refer to an individual word or letter (many people misspell *accommodate* with one *m*). Relatively short passages—chapter or article introductions, interview questions, captions, and so on—can be set in italics to distinguish them from the main text. In addition, references to titles of books, newspapers, magazines, movies, plays, musical compositions, paintings, and other works of art are italicized.

Some typefaces have no italic complement. With digital typefaces, computer commands can create an *oblique* typeface. In this case, oblique characters are simply roman characters slanted to the right. To see an example of oblique type, turn on your Mac and start up your word processor or another program that displays text. Select the Geneva font—one of the fonts that comes with your Mac's System software—and type a word. Select the word, then choose the Italic style from your program's Font menu or dialog box. The word is now inclined to the right, or obliqued. Since Geneva has no handmade italics, the oblique version created by the computer's instructions is what appears when you print your document.

Some faces—most often sans serif ones—offer an *oblique*, rather than an italic, style. These oblique faces are not simply slanted rightward by a computer command, but are created by a type designer. The Helvetica font, which is built into many laser printers, includes an oblique style, for example. Sometimes you'll hear the term *italic* used to describe an oblique face, but in general an oblique face is a slanted version of its roman counterpart, while an italic face is a separate design that differs stylistically from its roman counterpart.

Here's an example of italic and oblique text:

Roman
Italic
Oblique

Typeface Families

You now know that a typeface is a complete set of stylistically related characters. And you've seen that a face can have both a roman and an italic (or oblique) style. A typeface *family* has additional style variations.

Weight

In addition to roman and italic styles, yet another stylistic element can be applied to a typeface: it can come in a variety of *weights*. Typeface weights range from light to bold in a series of gradations, which can include extra light, light, book, regular or medium, demibold or semibold, bold, heavy, and extra bold or black. These terms are not standardized; the medium weight of one face may look as dark as the heavy weight of another. You should look at all the members of a typeface family to see the range of weights for that particular family. Adobe's version of the Futura family, for example, comes in the following weights: light, book, bold, medium, heavy, and extra bold. Each weight is available in an oblique as well as a roman style, increasing the number of family members.

Condensed and Expanded Styles

A typeface family can be enlarged even further if it includes different character widths. Characters that are narrower than those of the basic roman face are called *condensed* or *compressed*. Characters that are wider than the roman style are called *extended* or *expanded*. Many typeface families have condensed or expanded members; these styles in turn can be combined with different weights and italic or oblique styles (condensed bold oblique, for example) to expand the family even more.

Combinations of roman and italic (or oblique), various weights, and expanded or condensed widths can swell the ranks of a typeface family. Adobe's Futura family, for example, includes 20 style and weight variations:

Light	**Extra Bold**
Light Oblique	***Extra Bold Oblique***
Book	Condensed Light
Book Oblique	*Condensed Light Oblique*
Regular	Condensed
Regular Oblique	*Condensed Oblique*
Heavy	**Condensed Bold**
Heavy Oblique	***Condensed Bold Oblique***
Bold	**Condensed Extra Bold**
Bold Oblique	***Condensed Extra Bold Oblique***

The Components of a Character

Like typefaces, individual characters have their own terminology. Figure 1.1 shows some of the major elements of a character.

Characters sit on an imaginary line called the *baseline*. The height of a capital, or uppercase, letter is called the *cap height*; the height of a small, or lowercase, letter is called the *x-height*. Since the height of lowercase letters may vary within a face, the x-height—as you may have guessed—is the height of a face's lowercase *x*, which sits squarely on the baseline (rounded letters such as *o* and *e* dip slightly below the baseline in many faces).

Parts of some characters extend below the baseline (the tail of a *g* or *y*, for example). These are known as *descenders*. The vertical strokes of letters such as *d* and *l*—which are usually the same height as uppercase letters, but are slightly taller in some faces—are called *ascenders*.

Enclosed white spaces such as those in the letters *e* and *g* are called *counterforms* or *counters*. Counterforms help the eye recognize characters and provide an even texture in a block of text.

Type Size

The standard measuring unit for characters is the *point*. For larger measurements, such as column width, a larger unit called a *pica* is used: 12 points make up a pica. There are approximately 72 points, or 6 picas, to an inch, but the

FIGURE 1.1. Some of the major character components are shown here. In many typefaces, ascenders such as d, l, and h extend higher than the face's capital letters. To give a face visually pleasing proportions, characters with rounded bottoms may dip slightly below the baseline, while characters with rounded tops may rise slightly above the face's x-height.

correspondence between points and inches isn't exact; 6 picas actually equal .996264 inches. Therefore, you should learn to measure in points and picas, rather than inches, when you're working with type.

A face's point size is measured from the top of the highest ascender to the bottom of the lowest descender. Many people who are new to typography are mystified by the apparent differences in character size among faces that are the same point size. Look at these two faces, for example:

Appearances can be deceiving

Appearances can be deceiving

The top face is Bodoni and the bottom face is Park Avenue (both of these samples are from Adobe). They're both set at 18 points. How can that be? Park Avenue is obviously much smaller than Bodoni. But if you take a pica ruler and measure the two faces—from the top of an ascender to the bottom of a descender—you'll see that both are indeed 18 points. Appearances can be deceiving. Bodoni's thick vertical strokes help make it look larger than the wispy Park Avenue. In addition, Bodoni has a relatively large x-height; its lowercase letters are much taller than those of Park Avenue, even though the ascender-to-descender measurement is the same for both faces.

Spacing

Spacing is an important part of typography. The amount of space between letters, words, and lines has a big effect on how a printed document looks.

Monospaced Type

Typewriter text is *monospaced*. Each character occupies an invisible box that's the same width as the boxes for all the other characters; the typewriter carriage moves a fixed amount of space after each character is typed. Although several typewriter-like digital typefaces exist, monospaced text is rarely appropriate for typeset material. In monospaced text, a thin letter such as *i* occipies the same space as a wide letter such as *W*, creating an uneven rhythm of white spaces between characters. To compensate for the fixed amount of space allotted for each character, thin letters such as *i* and *l* are widened with huge serifs, and wide letters such as *M* and *W* are squeezed into a narrow space. All of this makes for awkward-looking faces, which you should use only if you want your text to look like it's typewritten.

Monaco, one of the fonts included with the Mac's System software, is a monospaced font. Certain applications, such as programming tools and some communications programs, like to use monospaced fonts. You'd be crazy to use one for a newsletter or the like, however.

Proportional Spacing

Most typefaces employ *proportional spacing,* in which letters occupy differing amounts of horizontal space, depending on their shapes. Since printing devices that work with the Mac aren't hampered by the mechanical constraints of a typewriter carriage, letters don't have to occupy fixed-width spaces. In a proportional face, an *i* occupies a much narrower space than an *M*. Proportional faces create a light-dark rhythm that makes them much more readable and pleasant to look at than monospaced faces. Therefore, you should always use proportionally spaced faces for setting books, magazines, brochures, or any publications that have lengthy passages of text.

You'll find that almost all proportional faces have monospaced numbers. This apparent anomaly is easily explained: if columns of numbers are to line up, all the numerals in a face must be of equal width.

The Em space

Since a typeface can be set at a variety of sizes, certain spacing measurements must be stated as relative rather than absolute values. For example, you could specify 2 points of space between each word in a block of 12-point text, but that measurement would be inappropriate if you changed the text to 9-point or 18-point type. To avoid using absolute measurements for each size of type, a relative unit called the *em* is used. The width of an em is equal to the size of the type being used; in 10-point type, for example, an em is 10 points wide. The unit is called an em because it's generally the same width as the letter *M*, the widest letter in most faces.

Typesetters refer to *em dashes*—the punctuation marks used to set apart an explanatory phrase like this one—rather than just plain dashes. They use the term *em space* to indicate spacing in a line of text (a paragraph might be indented two em spaces, for example).

Another relative spacing unit is the *en space*, which is half as wide as an em-space. An *en dash* is a punctuation mark that is shorter than an em dash but longer than a hyphen. These punctuation marks are discussed further in the next chapter.

Word Spacing

Another type of spacing is *word spacing*. When you press the space bar while typing at the Mac's keyboard, a fixed amount of space is placed between one word and the next. Word spacing can be adjusted, however. For example, if you select *justified* text (text that lines up at both the left and right margins), some lines will have more space between words than others as lines are stretched or compressed to fit within the fixed margins. Mac word processors, page layout programs, and graphics programs offer several choices for aligning text. In most cases, you'll be setting text either justified or *ragged right* (also called *flush left*), in which only the left margin is fixed. Figure 1.2 shows some alignment options.

Justified	Ragged Right
In justified copy, each line is filled with as many syllables as possible. The remaining space is divided by the number of word spaces in the line and placed evenly in each word space. The amount of space between words thus varies from line to line in justified text, as word spaces are expanded or contracted to make each line the same width. In ragged copy, on the other hand, word spaces are the same width from line to line.	In justified copy, each line is filled with as many syllables as possible. The remaining space is divided by the number of word spaces in the line and placed evenly in each word space. The amount of space between words thus varies from line to line in justified text, as word spaces are expanded or contracted to make each line the same width. In ragged copy, on the other hand, word spaces are the same width from line to line.

FIGURE 1.2. Mac word processors and page layout programs can adjust the spacing between words to set justified text. If you use justified text, make sure your software has a hyphenation dictionary.

Whether to set a document justified or ragged right is a design decision that's up to you. Ragged right is more informal than justified; is often easier to read because of its even word spacing; and is less work to typeset, since you rarely have to hyphenate words. Many people think justified type looks more professional than ragged-right type, but keep in mind that with justified type you have to pay careful attention to hyphenation, word spacing, and letterspacing (letterspacing is described in the following section).

You should always scrutinize justified text before sending your document to the printer. Too much space between words makes a line difficult to read, preventing the reader's eye from taking in several words at a time. And wide spaces between words can form unsightly "rivers" of white space down a page. Cramped spacing can also make a line of text hard to read. Even if your software supports automatic hyphenation, you'll probably have to manually hyphenate a word here and there to fix spacing problems. (Note that placing hyphens at the end of more than three lines in a row is a typographic sin.) It's not as bad as it sounds. Most page layout programs do a good job of justifying text; just remember that you'll have to proof your layout carefully.

Letterspacing

Some Mac programs—page layout programs and graphics applications, for example—allow you to adjust the amount of space between all the letters in a word.

Tracking

Adding or subtracting an equal amount of space between all letters in a line of text is known as *tracking*. You can adjust tracking to squeeze a line of type into a narrow column, or to expand a word to fill a given space in a design. You can also tighten tracking a bit to give more subtance to a light and airy face such as New Baskerville. Here are some examples of tracking:

She stood with arms akimbo

She stood with arms akimbo

She stood with arms akimbo

Kerning

Many programs allow you to adjust the space between pairs of adjacent letters, a procedure known as *kerning*. Most Mac typefaces include built-in *kerning pairs*, two-letter combinations with the optimal amount of space between the letters. Consider the letter combination *Ty*, for example. The horizontal bar of the *T* extends some distance from the vertical stroke, and the tail of the *y* extends to the left of the letter's body. If these letters were simply placed in their own "bounding boxes," there would be quite a gap between them. But good type designers foresee such spacing problems and build kerning pairs into their typefaces. A face might include hundreds or even thousands of kerning pairs.

While Mac word processors don't recognize built-in kerning pairs, many let you manually adjust the space between letter pairs. Mac page layout programs do support built-in kerning pairs, giving them an aesthetic edge over word processors. Figure 1.3 shows an example of kerning.

As typed

With manual kerning

FIGURE 1.3. Note how tighter kerning makes the bottom word more pleasing to the eye.

Leading

The vertical spacing between one line of text and the next is as important a design element as the horizontal spacing between letters or words. The term *leading* (rhymes with *heading*) is a holdover from the days of hot-metal type-setting. When lines of type were cast in hot lead, they were placed one after another to form a page. If no space was inserted between the lines, the type was said to be *set solid*. But lines set this way are usually difficult to read; they appear cramped and dense, and ascenders from one line may nearly touch descenders from the line above. Therefore, in most cases typesetters inserted one or more thin strips of lead, each 1 point wide, between lines to make a page more readable.

Although interline spacing is now set by computer commands, the term *leading* has endured. Most Mac typefaces have a bit of space built in above each character so ascenders and descenders won't touch when text is set solid.

Leading is measured from the baseline of one line to the baseline of the next. To indicate the amount of leading for a block of text, you write the type's point size, a slash, then the baseline-to-baseline measurement in points. For example, 12-point text set solid (with no extra leading) would be 12 /12 (pronounced "twelve on twelve"); 12-point text with 2 points of leading would be 12/14; and so on. There is no set formula for the amount of leading to use, since typefaces vary widely in design. The amount of leading you use will depend on the typeface you use, the appearance you want your publication to convey, and any space constraints you might have. Some leading guidelines are presented in the next chapter.

Now that you're familiar with some basic typographic terms, you're ready to apply your knowledge to some practical typesetting examples. The next chapter offers tips for using type effectively.

2
Type Tips

The previous chapter introduced you to some of the basics of typography. In this chapter, you'll find out how to apply what you've learned to setting your own documents. While it takes a lot of practice to become a skilled typesetter, the following tips will start you on your way to creating great-looking output. In this chapter you'll learn how to avoid common typesetting mistakes, how to use accents and other special characters, and how to make your documents both readable and attractive.

The Seven Deadly Typesetting Sins

Many people who are new to publishing, desktop or otherwise, make mistakes that cause their publications to look less than professional. If you're an old-timer like me, you probably started your publishing career on a typewriter. Although most computer users have weaned themselves from hitting Return at the end of each line, some people unwittingly retain other outdated typing techniques. Other newcomers are so thrilled by their computer's typographic capabilities that they go overboard with styles or embellishments, creating documents that fairly scream "Created on a Mac by a beginner!" Some typical mistakes are discussed here.

While there are a number of ways to brand your work as that of an amateur, the following mistakes are among the most common. Once you learn to avoid these errors, you'll be ready to move on to some more advanced tips.

Extra Spaces

Perhaps the most common vestigial typing habit is leaving two spaces after a period before beginning the following sentence.

```
Placing an extra space between sentences
makes sense for typewritten text.  Typewritten
characters are monospaced; the extra space
helps the eye distinguish sentences in an
otherwise homogenous blanket of text.  By the
way, the "typewritten" text you are reading
here is actually set in a PostScript font
called Old Typewriter, which is available
from FontHaus.  Old Typewriter is meant to be
used as a display face; it doesn't have some
of the punctuation marks and other special
characters -- such as accents -- you might
need to set text.
```

Macintosh typefaces, on the other hand, are proportionally spaced, except for a few special-purpose monospaced fonts that are used for applications such as filling out forms, displaying text in telecommunications programs, or—as in the sample above—emulating typewritten text. With proportionally spaced faces, a single space between sentences will suffice. In a typeset document, the extra space is not only unneccessary but leaves unattractive gaps—especially in justified text, where software may add extra space between words to make a line fit in the space allocated.

If you find the extra-space habit hard to break, use your word processor's change function to search a document for double spaces and change them to single ones. (Some page layout programs automatically convert double spaces to single ones when you import a document.)

Double Hyphens for Dashes

Another unsightly holdover from the Age of Typewriters is the use of two hyphens to indicate a dash (an *em dash* in typesetters' terms). Few things make a Mac-produced publication look worse than a smattering of double hyphens. Typing a dash on the Mac's keyboard requires a few acrobatics, but you can eventually train yourself to simultaneously press the Shift, Option, and hyphen keys. (Incidentally, it's up to you whether to add some space around dashes. Many typesetters add space on either side of an em dash, since in some faces the dash nearly touches the adjoining letters; in this book, I've chosen not to add space around the dashes.) Again, if you're accustomed to typewriter conventions you might want to use your word processor's search-and-replace function to hunt down renegade double hyphens once you've finished typing a document. If you're placing text into a page layout program, check to see if it converts double hyphens to dashes.

Also residing in the hyphen key is the en dash, a punctuation mark about half the width of an em dash but wider than a hyphen. To type an en dash, simultaneously press the Option and hyphen keys. The en dash is used less often than the em dash and the hyphen, but when used correctly makes a document look more professional. An en dash should be used in continuing or inclusive sets of numbers, such as page numbers, times, or dates (pp. 35–43; 9:00 A.M.–5:30 P.M; April–May). The en dash is also used in compound adjectives that contain two-word or hyphenated portions (post–Industrial Revolution art; East Coast–West Coast travelers; mother-in-law–husband rivalry).

A hyphen, en dash, and em dash are shown here: - – —. (If you want to show off, you can slip in the occasional sentence containing hyphens, en dashes, and em dashes: "A self-proclaimed expert in pre–Ming Dynasty porcelains—the real experts would no doubt be amused—Larry wowed his all-too-gullible guests with his collection of Sung Dynasty ashtrays.") The length of each of these punctuation marks and its proportions in relation to the others will vary from face to face. You may find hyphens and en dashes hard to distinguish from one another in some screen fonts, but don't worry; they'll print properly. Type a sample sentence, print it, and see for yourself.

Straight Quotes

The sight of straight quotes fills my heart with loathing. They're everywhere: on book jackets, package blurbs, magazine covers, you name it. Of course, the Mac's keyboard layout doesn't make typing "curly" quotes very easy; you have to perform some fancy fingerwork to type open and close double quotes (" and "), open and close single quotes (' and '), or an apostrophe ('). The quotes you get by simply pressing the quote key (' ") aren't suitable for typeset text, especially with serif faces. You must simultaneously press Option and the Left Bracket key ([ ) for open quotes, and Shift-Option-Left Bracket for close quotes. For open and close single quotes, you must press Option-Right Bracket and Shift-Option-Right Bracket, respectively. With this setup, writing a story that contains a lot of dialogue is not a pleasant proposition.

Depending on the type of writing you do, you may need quotation marks only once or twice in a document, or you may use them on every page. Either way, you should learn how to access curly quotes when you need them. Double quotation marks are used to indicate dialogue; material quoted from another source; and titles of articles, short stories, essays, book chapters, and songs. They can also be used to indicate slang or specialized terms (the "preemies" were kept in incubators) or irony (they broke two chairs and six plates during their last "discussion"). Single quotes are used for quoted material within quotations ("If you play 'Stairway to Heaven' one more time, I'll break you and your stereo into little tiny pieces," said Bert's new roommate) or to indicate philosophical or linguistic terms (In Chinese, *ma* 'the horse' sounds similar to *ma!* 'to scold').

Many word processors and page layout programs convert straight quotes to curly ones, but if the program you're using doesn't offer quote conversion, you have several options. You can use your word processor's search-and-replace function to replace straight quotes with curly ones, but that's a pretty tedious process. First, you'll have to search for a space followed by straight quotes (chances are good that quotes preceded by a space will be at the beginning of a word) and replace all occurrences with open quotes. Then, you must search for the remaining straight quotes and replace them with close quotes. Follow the same procedure for single quotes and apostrophes. While this approach is fairly straightforward and requires no additional software, it isn't flawless. For example, with this scheme, quotes at the beginning of a parenthetical remark would be converted to close quotes, since the word wasn't preceded by a space. Likewise, a quote at the beginning of a paragraph would be preceded by a tab rather than a space, and would therefore be converted to a close quote. If you use this method, you'll have to proofread your documents carefully.

Fortunately, there's an easier way. The handy INITs described below take the drudgery out of typing curly quotes and proper apostrophes. (An INIT is a program that, when placed in the System Folder, automatically runs when you start up your Mac. Some INITs are configured as control panels; you can double-click on their icons and tweak various controls to customize them. Now, in the System 7 era, INITs are called Extensions.)

Quote Init

This shareware utility ($15) by Lincoln Stein banishes straight quotes from your documents, automatically creating curly quotes for you as you type. (If you ever need straight quotes, you can toggle Quote Init on and off with a kestroke combination.) Because it's an INIT, it's automatically activated when you start up any program; once you get used to seeing curly quotes magically appear as you type, you won't even know it's there.

Quote Init creates open quotes if you type quotes after a space, and close quotes if the quotes follow another character. Unlike some similar utilities, it's smart enough to place open quotes after a tab or return; it places close quotes after a dash, however, so be careful if you put a quotation between em dashes; also, watch out for situations like "Class of '76," where you need a single close quote. (Even though Quote Init works very well, it's always a good idea to proof your work.)

Quote Init is a multitalented utility. It not only converts quotes, but can also eliminate the bad typing habits described earlier; if the appropriate Control Panel buttons are checked, it converts double hyphens to dashes and double spaces to single ones.

SmartKeys

SmartKeys is a free Control Panel by Maurice Volaski. When you check the appropriate settings, it converts straight quotes to curly ones, double hyphens to a dash, and double spaces to a single space as you type. It also corrects another common typo by converting the second of two consecutively typed capitals to a lowercase letter if the second capital is followed by a lowercase letter.

Laser Quotes

Deneba Systems' Laser Quotes is a public-domain INIT that converts straight quotes to curly quotes as you type. Like Quote INIT, Laser Quotes can be toggled on and off if you don't need curly quotes or other special characters (certain applications, such as programming tools and communications programs, don't recognize curly quotes).

While Laser Quotes doesn't convert double hyphens to dashes or double spaces to single ones like Quote INIT and SmartKeys do, it does give you access to "hidden" characters such as the Apple symbol () if a font includes them.

To find utilities such as Laser Quotes, Quote Init, and SmartKeys, check with your local Mac user group or subscribe to an online service such as CompuServe or America Online.

Rather than using one of the utilities just described to access curly quotes or other special characters, you might want to assign certain characters to keys that you choose. Several utilities allow you to customize the Mac's keyboard; these are described in the next section.

MacQWERTY

MacQWERTY's main claim to fame is reconfiguring your keyboard to the Dvorak layout, a keyboard layout that many fast typists prefer to the standard "QWERTY" arrangement. As a sideline, however, this utility from Nisus lets you reassign any keys on the keyboard. MacQWERTY is not for the fainthearted; you have to create a text-only file called "reconfig.file" with a word processor.

In the word processor, you type the character you want to replace, press Return twice, and type the new keystroke. For example, if you wanted to type open quotes with the < key, you'd type the quote character, press Return twice, then type Shift-comma-<. You then save the file, run a keyboard-customization utility, and install your new keyboard layout. You can return to your original keyboard layout by running another utility.

QuicKeys

QuicKeys is a versatile control panel from CE Software. It has many uses, but its main function is creating macros—series of keystrokes, mouse movements, menu choices, and so on—and evoke them with the keystroke of your choice.

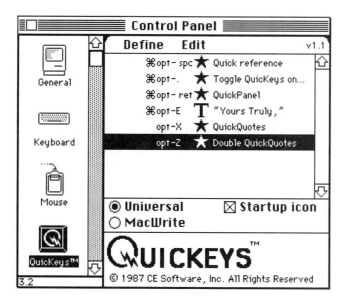

While QuicKeys is too expensive to purchase just to simplify the process of typing curly quotes and other special characters, it's a useful program that you might want to have around to speed up a variety of tasks—including typing.

You can use QuicKeys to manually assign open and close quotes—or other special characters—to the keystrokes of your choice, or you can simply activate the utility's automatic quote-insertion feature, which works much like the quote-conversion utilities just described.

To turn on the auto-quotes feature, click the QuicKeys icon in the Control Panel's dialog box. A list of shortcuts appears. In a submenu under the Define menu are two options, QuickQuotes and Double QuickQuotes. To install either shortcut, choose it from the list and assign it a keystroke; I chose Option-z for double quotes and Option-x for single quotes. When you type, press these key combinations and QuicKeys inserts open quotes after a space, left parenthesis or left bracket, return, or tab, and close quotes after any other characters.

EZQuotes

Yet another way to simplify typing curly quotes is to install a new keyboard layout. I downloaded a handy keyboard layout called EZQuotes (free, from HyperSTUff) from America Online's Desktop Publishing area.

To install EZQuotes, you simply drag the keyboard-layout icon into your System folder, which installs a resource in your System file. Open the Keyboards control panel (in the Control Panels folder, which is in the System folder) and select the EZQuotes keyboard layout.

With the EZQuotes layout installed, you can use the left and right bracket keys for single curly quotes, and Shift plus these keys for left and right double curly quotes (you can still access the brackets characters by typing Option-[or Option-]). In addition, pressing the single-quote key creates a proper apostrophe, rather than a straight quote. EZQuotes also simplifies typing an em-dash, allowing you to type it by pressing Shift-hyphen rather than Shift-Option-hyphen.

If you want to stop using the EZQuotes layout, just double-click the System file icon and drag out the unwanted keyboard layout.

Picking Up the Tab

Ironically, the one typewriter habit that should be carried over to Mac publishing is often abandoned by typesetting novices. Some newcomers try to line up items of text by repeatedly pressing the space bar, in the vain hope that what they see will be what they get. Unfortunately, elements that are positioned using the space bar may appear to be aligned on the screen, but rarely line up correctly on the printed page. If you need to line up text elements, use tabs, not spaces. And when you need to line up columns of numbers, such as dollar amounts, use your program's decimal-tab feature.

Style Mania

Many new Mac owners are so thrilled with the Mac's typographic versatility that they go hog-wild with style options. They make a heading bold, then underline it for emphasis. That's not enough. So they choose the Outline style option. Then, just in case the heading still doesn't stand out enough, they add the coup de grace: the Shadow option. You may think I'm exaggerating, but I've actually seen bold-underlined-outlined-shadowed text. It is not a pretty sight. If you must use outlined or shadowed text, use it in headlines, ads, signs, and so on—not in body copy.

Bold

Italic

<u>Underline</u>

Outline

Shadow

<u>*All of 'em*</u>

All Capitals

While some typesetting newcomers use underlining for emphasis, others choose an equally unacceptable method: setting a word, sentence, or even an entire section in all capitals to make it stand out.

THIS SECTION STANDS OUT, ALL RIGHT, BUT IT SURE LOOKS OBNOXIOUS. NOT ONLY THAT, BUT IT'S HARD TO READ. AS ALWAYS, THERE ARE EXCEPTIONS; FOR EXAMPLE, YOU MIGHT WANT TO SET AN IMPORTANT WARNING ("DO NOT USE THIS ELECTRICAL DEVICE WHILE YOU ARE IN THE BATHTUB") TO MAKE SURE THE READER SEES IT. BUT AS A GENERAL RULE, YOU SHOULD AVOID SETTING BODY COPY IN ALL CAPITALS.

If you want to make sure the reader sees an important warning, it's OK to use all caps, but you might want to place the warning in a box instead, or perhaps set it in boldface or large type, or type that's a different color than the surrounding text.

An even worse sin—and I have seen this, or I wouldn't bring it up—is setting a script face in all capitals.

(WARNING: AESTHETICALLY SENSITIVE READERS MIGHT WANT TO SKIP THE NEXT EXAMPLE.) Look:

DON'T TRY THIS AT HOME!

Ouch! I hope I've made my point. In a text passage, italics, rather than uppercase letters, should be used for emphasis. (Script faces generally don't include italics, but you shouldn't set long passages in ornate script anyway; it's meant for shorter items such as invitations, announcements, and the like.)

Squash-and-Stretch Overkill

Many Mac programs give you the ability to stretch type vertically or horizontally. I'm sorry to sound like your mom here, but just because you can do something doesn't mean you should. On the other hand, sometimes you'll want to alter a font to achieve a particular effect. If you can't afford to buy dozens of fonts, you can get extra service from the ones you have by altering them. You might want to vertically stretch a bold face to create an elegant headline font, for example. That's fine—in moderation. Here are some guidelines for altering fonts.

In this example, I've used the Horizontal Scale command in QuarkXPress to condense the Gill Sans Bold font:

Normal **Time for coffee!**

80% **Time for coffee!**

30% **Time for coffee!**

Type Trivia

The terms *uppercase* and *lowercase* come from the days of hot-metal type. In those days, printers arranged the letters of each typeface in a wooden case, capital letters in one case and small letters in another. To make the characters easy to reach, the cases were placed one on top of the other, with the capitals in the upper case. Like the word *leading,* the words *uppercase* and *lowercase* have endured, even though the technology has changed.

Condensing this face to 80% of its regular width isn't too bad, but notice how, even at that percentage, character shapes start to distort (the dot over the *i* is no longer perfectly round, for example). At 30%, the distortions are obvious. Note how the dot over the *i* is a squashed oval, while the *T* is a ponderous crossbar resting on a spindly stem (the dreaded "meatloaf-on-a-toothpick" effect).

Similar character distortions occur when you use Horizontal Scale to make characters wider:

Time for coffee!
Time for coffee!
Time for coffee!

It's OK to alter characters a little bit to create custom faces. But be aware that too much squashing, stretching, or other distortion can compromise a face's design and make your work look amateurish. In Chapter 4, you'll learn about Multiple Master typefaces, which are specially designed to be condensed or extended without losing their design integrity.

Special Characters

That last section was so *negative!* Now that you know what *not* to do, let's look at some things you *should* do to make your documents look like they were created by a typesetting pro. Mac typefaces have a wealth of special characters that are often overlooked by beginners, who may not even know these characters exist, catching glimpses of them only when their cat strolls over the keyboard or they hit the Option key by accident.

Accents

Let's say you're using your Mac to create that most common of documents, a résumé. Do you know how to place the accents over the *e*'s? Many people don't, and simply compensate for their naïveté by avoiding those pesky foreign words. Mac typefaces contain numerous accents, also called *diacritics* or *diacritical* marks, which can be accessed by pressing the Shift key, the Option key, or a combination of these keys. It's not that hard to type accents, once you know where they're hiding.

To type an acute accent (´) over an *e*, hold down the Option key and press the *e* key, then let up on the Option key and type *e* again; the *é* character appears on your screen. Similarly, to place an acute accent over an *a*, hold down the Option key and press *e* (the trigger for the acute accent), then let up on Option and type *a*. An accented *á* will appear. To place a grave accent (`) over a letter, hold down Option and press the upper lefthand key on the Mac's keyboard (or the key to the left of the spacebar on some keyboard models), release both keys, and type the letter to be accented. Voilà! An accented letter appears.

Table 2.1 shows the keystroke combinations that let you type accents and some other special characters, which are discussed in the following sections.

Ligatures

Combined letter pairs such as the *æ* in *æsthetic* or the *œ* in *œuvre* are called *ligatures*. Although they're not used as often now as they were in the old days, ligatures can add a touch of refinement to your publication. In Gutenberg's day, type founders had to cast each ligature as a separate unit, since the mechanics of movable type prevented typesetters from fusing existing letters. Fortunately, it's a little bit easier to produce ligatures on your Mac—if you can remember the right keystroke combinations. Press Option-apostrophe for *æ* and Option-q for *œ*.

Another pair of ligatures, although invisible to the untrained eye, can make a document more attractive. Although you may never have noticed it while you were reading, typesetters commonly join the letter pairs *f i* and *f l* into the more aesthetically—or æsthetically, if you prefer—pleasing *fi* and *fl*.

$$\text{fi} \;—\; \text{fi}$$
$$\text{fl} \;—\; \text{fl}$$

TABLE 2.1
Key Combinations for Special Characters (System 7 and later*)

Accents			**Quotes**	
Option-e, *letter*	á, é, etc.		Option-[	"
Option-i, *letter*	ê, î, etc.		Shift-Option-[	"
Option-`, *letter*	à, è, etc.		Option-]	'
Option-n, *letter*	ñ, ã, etc.		Shift-Option-]	'
Option-u, *letter*	ü, ï, etc.			
Opt.-*key* + Shift-*letter*	Ì, Ü, É, etc.		**Punctuation**	
Option-c	ç		Option-;	…
Option-a	å		Option- -	–
Option-o	ø		Shift-Option- -	—
Shift-Option-y	Á			
Shift-Option-a	Å		**Ligatures**	
Shift-Option-m	Â		Option-'	æ
Shift-Option-s	Í		Option-q	œ
Shift-Option-d	Î		Shift-Option-5	fi
Shift-Option-f	Ï		Shift-Option-6	fl
Shift-Option-h	Ó			
Shift-Option-l	Ò			
Shift-Option-j	Ô			
Shift-Option-;	Ú			

*Under System 6, some keystroke combinations are different from the ones shown in this table. If you're using System 6, consult your Key Caps desk accessory for the proper keystrokes.

To produce the *fi* ligature, select an adjoining *f* and *i* and press Shift-Option-5, or simply press Shift-Option-5 as you type—if you can remember the combination. (You might be able to remember that Shift-Option-5 produces the fi ligature because the word *five* starts with the letters *f-i*; how you remember the Shift-Option part is up to you.) To create the *fl* ligature, press Shift-Option-6.

Of course, you'd have to be insane to press Shift-Option keystroke combinations to produce ligatures while you're typing a document. Use your word processor's find-and-replace function to convert letter pairs to ligatures on a completed document. Alternatively, you can use a utility like SmartKeys or Quote Init to create ligatures as you type. (These utilities were discussed earlier in this chapter, in the "Straight Quotes" section.) If you use one of these utilities, I suggest you turn on only the *fi* and *fl* ligatures; if you activate the *æ* and *œ* ligature option, you might be surprised by the occasional outlaw ligature, as in *dœsn't*.

Fractions

Even the lowly typewriter has a few built-in fractions, but this feature is sadly lacking in most Macintosh typefaces. Fortunately, you won't have to resort to using decimals; there are several ways to produce good-looking fractions.

Type Your Own Fractions

If you don't mind a little work, you can type passable fractions in just about any typeface. Let's say you want to type "1⅔ cups" in 12-point Times. First, type "12/3" with no spaces between the characters. Although you can use a regular slash (the character found on the same key as the question mark) for fractions, Macintosh fonts provide a slash that's specially designed for fractions. The special slash (⁄) has a less steep angle than the regular slash (/). To type the fraction slash, press Shift-Option-1.

To complete the do-it-yourself fraction, select the 2 and change it to a 9-point superscript. Finally, select the 3 and change its size to 9 points. You now have a 12-point numeral followed by a fraction. Although this method is somewhat cumbersome, you don't need to use any additional software or special fonts.

Fraction Fonts

If you have access to an online service such as America Online or CompuServe, you can download a number of freeware or shareware serif and sans serif fraction fonts.

Here are some fractions from Helvetica Fractions, a freeware font:

½ ⅓ ¼ ⅘ ⅔ $\frac{2}{3}$ $\frac{3}{4}$ $\frac{2}{5}$

Here's a sample from the shareware font Times Fractions:

½ ⅓ ¼ ⅘ ⅔ $\frac{2}{3}$ $\frac{3}{4}$ $\frac{2}{5}$

All of these fonts let you type a set of fractions with diagonal or horizontal slashes. The fractions are designed to match the Times and Helvetica faces that come with the Mac, or similar serif or sans serif faces.

These fraction fonts can be useful, but they offer only a limited set of predefined fractions. If you're setting text that includes a lot of fractions, you might consider a font that lets you create your own custom fractions by typing a numerator and a denominator.

Expert Character Sets

Some font vendors offer expanded character sets that complement selected faces with fractions and other special characters. These *expert sets* include a set of common fractions (¼, ½, ⅛, ⅜, etc.), as well as superior and inferior numerals that let you type your own fractions. Therefore, if you need a custom fraction such as $^{15}/_{256}$, you can use the expert set's superiors for the 15 and its inferiors for the 256, creating a perfectly proportioned fraction that matches your typeface.

Unfortunately, not all faces include expert sets. If you're setting a document that includes lots of fractions, consider choosing a face that has an expert set. The expert set costs extra, and is a bit cumbersome to use since you must switch from the regular font to the expert-set font to access special characters—but it's worth the trouble if you want your documents to look professional.

Math Fonts

If you need to set not just fractions but equations as well, you might consider a mathematical font.

• Automated Graphics' MathFont series is designed for elementary-level math equations. The characters are positioned so you follow a chart and type them, rather than manually adjusting kerning or baselines to create equations.

• Linguist's Software sells LaserTech, a set of four fonts for typing equations in a word processor, page-layout program, or drawing program.

• Nisus Software offers Laser TechFonts, a collection of nine fonts for typing fractions, equations, and circuit diagrams.

• Blue Sky Research offers symbols and math extensions for its Computer Modern typefaces, which can be used with implementations of the TeX typesetting system or with Macintosh drawing or publishing applications.

Build Your Own Fractions

If you're really ambitious, you can use a font-creation program to create your own fractions and add them to a font. Fontographer, for example, lets you make fractions out of the numbers in an existing font. Here's how:

1. Open a font in Fontographer.

2. Find a character you're not likely to need (say, a foreign-currency character or an accented character or symbol you never use). Delete the unneeded character, then copy the numbers for the numerator and denominator and paste them into that character's slot.

3. Choose Select All from the Edit menu to select both numbers, then choose Scale Uniformly from the Transform menu and shrink the numbers to the appropriate size (say, 60%).

4. Position the numerator and denominator correctly, then copy and paste a slash character. You've now created a fraction.

Small Caps

Small caps are used for abbreviations such as A.M., P.M., B.C, and A.D. They can also be used for typographic elements such as captions, subheads, table titles, or the first line of a book chapter.

Some programs offer a Small Caps option in a Style menu or dialog box:

The characters produced when you select this option aren't true small caps, however; they're simply a reduced version of a face's regular capitals. Professional typesetters turn up their noses at these jury-rigged small caps, since their weight doesn't match the weight of the face's normal capital letters. Fortunately, the expert sets mentioned earlier in this chapter offer small caps that are specially tailored to match their corresponding face.

In the following example, the top line shows small caps created by a page layout program's Small Caps option. The bottom line shows true small caps from a font's expert set.

ONCE UPON A TIME, there was a little sea cucumber named Billy.

ONCE UPON A TIME, there was a little sea cucumber named Billy.

Old Style Numbers

As mentioned in the previous chapter, the numbers in a typeface are mono-spaced; each number takes up the same amount of horizontal space so columns of figures can be lined up. In keeping with their regimented appear-ance, most numbers sit squarely on the baseline, allowing them to fit neatly into charts and tables. But if you include numbers in a page of text, their rigid spacing conventions will create little pockets of monotony in the otherwise rhythmic flow of ascenders, descenders, and proportionally spaced charac-ters. If you care about the appearance of your body copy, you should use *old style numbers.* Old style numbers are usually proportionally spaced rather than monospaced. They're smaller than conventional numbers, and some of them dip below the baseline (1234567890), making them line up with the x-height and descenders of the corresponding face. In short, old style num-bers are designed to look like text, rather than numbers.

Compare the following blocks of text. The first example uses Adobe Jenson's regular numbers, while the second employs the face's optional old style numbers:

• From 1979 to 1995, more than 402 Elvis sightings were reported in the lower 48 states. In Alaska, only 13 sightings were reported in that period, perhaps because of the relative rarity of fried peanut-butter-and-banana sandwiches in that state's regional cuisine. In Hawaii, on the other hand, 67 sightings were logged.

• From 1979 to 1995, more than 402 Elvis sightings were reported in the lower 48 states. In Alaska, only 13 sightings were reported in that period, perhaps because of the relative rarity of fried peanut-butter-and-banana sandwiches in that state's regional cuisine. In Hawaii, on the other hand, 67 sightings were logged.

As you can see, the numbers in the second example blend in with the text, while those in the first example stick out like spats at an Iowa picnic. In this book, I've used Adobe Jenson's old style numbers in the body copy.

Ellipses...

Those of us who grew up pounding out prose on typewriters grew accustomed to typing three periods in a row to indicate missing text. Typing them was bad enough, but then you had to remember whether or not you were supposed to add spaces between the dots. Fortunately, Mac typefaces let you type three dots in one fell swoop by pressing Option-semicolon. These *ellipses* have just the right amount of spacing between them (…), alleviating the cramped look of periods with no spaces (...) or the airy look of periods separated by spaces (. . .). Also, the three dots that make up the ellipsis character won't get separated if they fall at the end of a line, as three periods sometimes do.

The ⌘ Symbol

The Chicago font, which is always present since it's one of the Mac's built-in fonts, includes the Command key character (⌘), which is useful if you're writing a Macintosh manual, book, how-to article, or the like.

If your keyboard has a Control key, simply choose the Chicago font and press Control-q. If you have the original Mac keyboard, which lacks a Control key, you can access the ⌘ character using Deneba's Laser Quotes utility (this utility was described earlier, in the "Straight Quotes" section of this chapter). With Laser Quotes installed, you must select the Chicago font and press Shift-Option-⌘-z to type the ⌘ symbol.

Locating Special Characters

Now for a pop quiz. Without referring to the preceding sections, how do you type an em dash? Ellipses? The *æ* ligature? You've probably forgotten, haven't you? Don't worry. You're not alone. Most people have better things to do with their already overloaded brains than remember obscure keystroke combinations. That's why Apple includes a handy desk accessory (DA) called Key Caps with every Mac.

The Key Caps DA

Key Caps is automatically installed when you install your Mac's System software. It's available under the Apple menu while you're in any application. When you select Key Caps, a map of your keyboard appears on the screen and a Key Caps menu, which lists all installed fonts, appears in the menu bar.

When you open the Key Caps DA and choose a font from the Key Caps menu, the letters on the on-screen keys are displayed in the font you chose. Press a key on the Mac's keyboard or click a key on the displayed keyboard, and the character you type appears in the sample text box at the top of the Key Caps display:

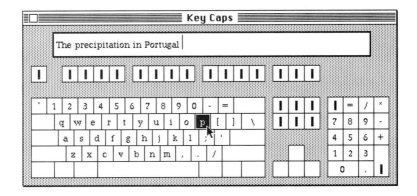

If you press Shift, Option, or both, the resulting characters appear on the displayed keyboard's keys:

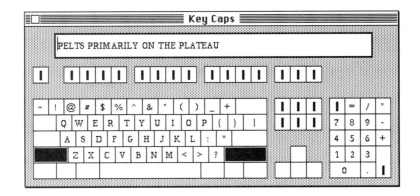

With System 7's version of Key Caps, the keys you use to type accents are outlined in gray. When you press one of those keys—on the screen or on your physical keyboard—and then let up on the Option key, the display shows which letters the selected accent can be applied to by outlining those keys in black. Press the Shift key and you'll see which Shifted keys work with the accent.

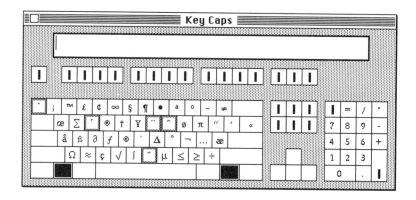

Note: If you see a rectangle on a key in Key Caps, that means the font you're looking at doesn't have the special character that's usually associated with that key. Look at the Chicago font in Key Caps, for example, and press Shift-Option to see a sea of rectangles. When you press one of these keys, the rectangle appears on the screen, but it will turn into a blank space in a printed document.

Once you've found the character you're looking for, you can select it in the sample text box, copy it with the Copy command (⌘-C), and paste it into your document. This approach certainly beats trying to remember the convoluted keystroke combination that produced the character, then typing it when you return to your document. (You might want to type a whole string of special characters in Key Caps, then copy them all to your document. Unfortunately, the characters you paste into your document won't appear in the font you chose in Key Caps; you'll have to change them to the correct font from the application's Font menu or dialog box.)

Key Caps allows you to find keystroke combinations for special characters without leaving the application you're using or digging out a manual, but you might prefer a printed reference card to on-screen help. If you're an old

Mac hand, your first inclination might be to make your own Key Caps reference cards by making a screen shot: simultaneously pressing the ⌘, Shift, and 3 keys to capture the image on the screen. Unfortunately, this feature doesn't work with Key Caps; pressing that combination of keys doesn't allow you to capture Shift, Option, or Shift-Option combinations. Don't worry; there's a way to take a snapshot of each Key Caps layout. It's a little tricky, but you can do it by following these steps:

1. First, you'll need a background for your snapshot. Open a new document in a word processor, graphics program, or any program that gives you a blank page. (Alternatively, you can select New Folder from the Desktop's File menu, and open an empty folder for your background.)

2. Select Key Caps from the Apple menu. When the Key Caps keyboard display appears, position it over the white background you just set up. (Placing the keyboard on a white background will save you the trouble of cleaning up on-screen garbage when the keyboard picture is saved.)

3. If you want to display a font on the Key Caps keyboard, select one from the Key Caps menu.

4. While pressing the Shift key, place the arrow pointer on the title bar (the striped bar at the top) of the Key Caps window and hold down the mouse button.

5. Release the Shift key, but keep holding down the mouse button. Simultaneously press the ⌘, Shift, and 3 keys—the "snapshot" combination—then release these keys (keep the mouse button held down).

6. Press the keystroke combination you want to display (none, Shift, Option, or Shift and Option), let up on the mouse button, and whisk the pointer out of the title bar so it won't appear, like a wayward thumb, in your snapshot.

7. Your snapshot is saved as a PICT-format document called "Picture 0." If you can't find the snapshot on the Desktop, use the Find command (in the Desktop's File menu) to locate it.

BigCaps

An alternative to KeyCaps is BigCaps, a desk accessory that's included with Dubl-Click Software's MenuFonts utility (MenuFonts is described in Chapter 5). Like Key Caps, BigCaps displays keyboard layouts for plain, Shift, Option, and Shift-Option keystrokes. Unlike Key Caps, however, Big Caps can display fonts in any installed size and style (bold, italic, and so on). Although BigCaps isn't free, like Key Caps, you might be tempted to spend some money in the interest of preventing eyestrain.

PopChar

Another alternative to Key Caps is PopChar, a freeware Control Panel created by Günther Blaschek, who was perhaps motivated by a desire to make it easier for people to type his first name. With PopChar installed, you simply place the pointer in the upper left corner of the screen and hold down the mouse button to see a window that contains all the characters in a font. Select a character, and it appears in your document, in the correct typeface.

TypeTamer

Another way to quickly view and insert special characters is with Type-Tamer, a utility from Impossible Software. Like PopChar, TypeTamer displays a window that contains all the special characters in the curently selected font. You click on a character to insert it into your document.

Unlike PopChar, TypeTamer costs money. However, TypeTamer performs several other type-management tasks. For further information on TypeTamer, see Chapter 6.

Readability

So far, this chapter has dealt mostly with individual characters: how to find them, type them, and use them correctly. Once you start putting characters together into words, however, and words together into sentences, you'll need to learn a few more tricks for making your printed text look good.

Spacing Tips

Spacing can be divided into two basic categories: letterspacing (the amount of space between individual letters in a word) and word spacing (the amount of space between each word in a line of text). The following tips will help you make the most of your applications' spacing capabilities—and prevent you from making some common spacing mistakes.

One Good Kern

Most Mac word processors don't support built-in kerning pairs (although some allow you to kern letter pairs manually). For the best-looking letterspacing, you should use a page layout program.

Good kerning is essential in headlines, titles, and other large type, where a poorly-kerned pair is more noticeable than in body copy. Even in a well-crafted typeface, a kerned pair that looks fine at 12 points might need to be manually tightened up when text is set at a larger size, such as in a headline. When setting headlines, professional typesetters strive for "TNT" (tight, but not touching) letterspacing.

Since you can't tell what your kerning adjustments will look like by viewing them at the coarse resolution of the Mac's screen, you'll have to print a sample of your headline to see how it looks. To save time—and paper—you might want to make several copies of your headline, try different amounts of kerning on each copy, and print a sample page. Once you've looked at the printed version, keep the headline that looks the best.

Once you develop an eye for type, you may occasionally come across a face that has some kerning pairs that just don't meet your standards. Rather than manually adjusting the offending kerning pairs in every headline, you can—if your application allows it—adjust kerning pairs to your liking and add your new kerning pairs to the font. QuarkXPress, for example, lets you edit any font's kerning information, or *kerning table*. Check your page layout program's documentation and see if it lets you edit kerning tables.

The Right Tracking

Tracking, as you learned in the last chapter, is the ability to add or subtract a specified amount of space between all the characters in a block of text. You can use tracking to squeeze a line of text into a small area or expand it to fill a space.

While tracking can come in handy, keep in mind that extremes in tracking can make text hard to read. Many people overuse tracking to make lines of text fit in narrow columns, or to eliminate "widows" or "orphans." Look at the following example:

> Slim perched at one end of the bar, which had fallen as silent as the prairie sky after his thoughtless remark. He was a tough old buzzard, but he knew when to keep his head low in the herd. "Sorry, boys. I didn't know this was cattle country," he said sheepishly.

Don't try to fit justified text into an extemely narrow column. Using tracking may make your text fit, but it won't do wonders for its readability.

If possible, edit the text or hyphenate some words to make lines fit, rather than stretching or squashing the heck out of a line by adjusting tracking. Better still, use a wider column, if possible.

Word Spacing

If you set a page of justified text, your word processor or page layout program automatically adjusts the amount of space between each word to create lines of equal length. You should always proof justified text carefully to check for the following problems:

- "Rivers" of white space running down a block of text
- Lines spaced so tightly they're hard to read
- Lines spaced so loosely they're hard to read
- An excessive number of hyphenated words

As a rule, you shouldn't justify narrow columns. What constitutes a narrow column? There's no simple answer. The optimum column width for justified text depends on factors such as the typeface used, point size, and even average word length. Your best bet is to use common sense: a justified column that's wide enough to hold an average of only three or four words per line will almost certainly cause spacing problems.

The following rules of thumb will also help you decide how to adjust word spacing:

- Use less word spacing for condensed type; **more for** expanded type
- Use more word spacing for small or large type
- Add extra word spacing to make reversed type (white type on a dark background) easier to read

If your word processor doesn't let you adjust word spacing, you can still have some control over it using the following technique. (A trick like this is known in computer parlance as a *kludge*; if you find yourself resorting to many such tricks, you should probably save up for a better word processor.) Say you've typed a 24-point newsletter headline and printed a proof on your laser printer. You feel the words are spaced a little too far apart. Open the document and select the space between the first and second word. Use your word processor's type-size command to convert the space to a smaller point size, say 18 points. Do the same to the remaining spaces between words; when you print the document again, the word spacing will be reduced. Keep in mind that this tip works best for subtracting space; if you convert a space to a larger point size, the word processor will automatically add leading above the line of text.

Weight

A face's weight has an impact on legibility. A light face, for example, may be too weak to use in long passages, while a bold face could obscure the letters' counterforms (the empty spaces in letters such as *o* or *g*), making your text hard to read. In most cases, you'll want to use a medium or book weight for body copy.

Size

Type size affects readability as well. As a general rule, body copy is easiest to read if it's set at 9, 10, 11, or 12 points. It's difficult for most people to read long passages of 7- or 8-point type, even if it's set at a crisp 2540 dots per inch; the difficulty is compounded if the text is printed at 300 dpi. Some faces look better than others at small sizes; if you need to set a passage in a small size, print a sample to make sure the face you want to use is readable at that size.

Consider a face's x-height when you're deciding what size to use; a face with a large x-height can usually be set at a smaller size than a face with a small x-height, with no loss of legibility.

Leading

One of the most common mistakes made by novice publishers is failing to use enough leading. Many word processors offer a default leading that's the same as the selected point size: 10 points of leading for 10-point type, and so on. If you dash off a document with a word processor and print it without adding any leading, the printed result will be much too dense. Insufficient leading not only gives a page a dark, unappealing color, but also makes reading more difficult. If a page has lines of tightly packed text, readers may find themselves reading the same line twice (doubling) rather than making an effortless transition from one line to the next. The eye needs a little room to scan lines comfortably. (On the other hand, if you add too much leading, the page will not only look light and insubstantial, but the reader's eye may have trouble making the giant leap from one line to the next when reading a page of text.)

The appropriate amount of leading to use depends on a number of factors, including type size, the characteristics of the typeface you're using, and the kind of publication. You might need to cram a lot of information into a catalog or ad, for example, in which case you'd want to use a minimum of leading. In a book or magazine, however, you should give the text some breathing room. The following guidelines will help you decide how much leading to apply. For the best results, however, you'll have to print some samples and see what looks good for your particular project. There are no hard-and-fast rules for how much leading to use.

• As a basic rule of thumb, leading should be at least 20% of the face's point size. More precisely, 9-, 10-, or 11-point type should have at least 2 points of leading (9/11, 10/12, or 11/13); 12-point type should have at least 3 points of leading; and 14- through 18-point type should have at least 4 points of leading.

• In general, faces with large x-heights, bold faces, faces with a strong vertical emphasis, and sans serif faces require a bit of extra leading.

• The greater the line length, the more leading you should use. A page of long lines will look less dense and more inviting if you add a little leading.

• Reversed type should have more leading than dark type set on a white background.

Figure 2.1 shows several examples of leading.

Line Length

Because the eye scans groups of words when reading, the length of a line of text affects readability. Most readers scan groups of three or four words at a time. Therefore an extremely narrow column of text is hard to read, since the eye's reading pattern is disrupted. Likewise, the eye can become tired while traversing a long line of text. Optimal line length varies, but the following rules should help you pick the right line length for your publication.

• In general, lines should be between one-and-a-half and two times the length of a face's lowercase alphabet.

• Another popular formula says that line lenght (in picas) should be about two times the face's point size (a line of 12-point type should be 24 picas long, for example).

• Lines of about 40 to 60 characters, or nine or ten words, are generally easy to read.

If you exceed these limits, make sure to add a little leading to make your text easier to read. As always, these are general guidelines; you may want to

It was a dark and stormy night. A wave of melancholia
engulfed me as I gazed with clouded eyes upon the pages
that spewed forth from the bowels of my laser printer.
Page after page of dark, dense type confronted me,
the lines stacked one on top of another like cordwood.
As my weary eyes traversed the dense blanket of prose,
a revelation came to me: I could make the book much
more inviting — not to mention readable — simply by
increasing the amount of leading!

11/11 (set solid)

It was a dark and stormy night. A wave of melancholia
engulfed me as I gazed with clouded eyes upon the pages
that spewed forth from the bowels of my laser printer.
Page after page of dark, dense type confronted me,
the lines stacked one on top of another like cordwood.
As my weary eyes traversed the dense blanket of prose,
a revelation came to me: I could make the book much
more inviting — not to mention readable — simply by
increasing the amount of leading!

11/13

It was a dark and stormy night. A wave of melancholia
engulfed me as I gazed with clouded eyes upon the pages
that spewed forth from the bowels of my laser printer.
Page after page of dark, dense type confronted me,
the lines stacked one on top of another like cordwood.
As my weary eyes traversed the dense blanket of prose,
a revelation came to me: I could make the book much
more inviting — not to mention readable — simply by
increasing the amount of leading!

11/15

FIGURE 2.1. Three leading alternatives for 12-point Times are shown here. The top sample not only looks too dark, but is hard to read as well.

vary them for different projects. Remember that readability is your goal; don't make your reader's eyes stumble through rows of short, choppy lines or crawl across the vast expanses of extremely long ones.

Copyfitting

If you need to calculate how many characters of a given face, at a given point size, will fit on a line, use the following formula:

> • Measure the width of the face's lowercase alphabet, in points. Divide this number into 342 to get the number of characters per pica, or *character count.*

Let's say you need to know how many characters will fit in a line 20 picas wide. We'll use 12-point Helvetica (a face that comes with your Mac) to illustrate the formula. The face's lowercase alphabet, when set at 12 points, measures 155 points across. Divide 342 by 155 and you'll see that 12-point Helvetica has a character count of 2.2. Therefore, you can fit about 44 characters of 12-point Helvetica on a 20-pica line (20 × 2.2 = 44).

If you need to know how many words will fit on the 20-pica line, use the following formula:

> • One word averages five characters, plus one character for the space that follows it, for an average of six characters per word.

Continuing with the 12-point Helvetica example, you'll find that you can fit about 7.3 words on a 20-pica line (44 characters per line × 6 characters per word = 7.3 words).

Visual Placement

Computers are wonderful devices. With the right software, you can precisely align elements to within a fraction of a point. Select a command and two lines of type are impeccably centered in the blink of an eye. Computers may have us beat in the speed and precision departments, but humans still have an edge when it comes to aesthetics. The same eye that was blinking while the computer centered the two text elements can tell that although the elements are aligned with mathematical precision, they still don't look centered.

As you can see in the example below, lines of text may have to be optically aligned, rather than simply mechanically aligned, to appear centered. As shown here, your eye doesn't necessarily perceive quotes as part of a word; a good designer will move type elements to compensate for such optical quirks.

"Beauty is only skin deep."

Centered by software

"Beauty is only skin deep."

Optically centered

Reversed Type

If you want maximum impact, you can print white text on a black background. But if you're shooting for maximum readability, stick to black text on a white background. If you do print white text on a black, gray, or colored background, make sure you use a large point size, preferably in a simple, legible face such as a sans serif. Add a little word spacing and leading to improve readability. Whatever you do, don't reverse a face that has hairline strokes or wide variations in stroke width. In general, make sure the face you use can hold its own against the background, or your readers may give up.

The same warnings apply if you set black text on a gray, colored, or patterned background. Make sure that the background isn't so dark or complex that it makes the text hard to read.

ELVIS IS ALIVE!

Right

Residents of Kalamazoo, Michigan, reacted with a mixture of joy and disbelief when it was revealed to them this week that Elvis Aron Presley had been secretly living among them for nearly seven years.

Wrong

Enough already. By now you're undoubtedly tired of learning rules. You'll thank me in the end for making you use old style numbers and type proper ellipses, but right now you'd probably like to get your hands on some actual typefaces and start playing with them. The next chapter will help you decide which faces to buy to start your own typeface library.

3
Building a
Typeface Library

At last count, there were more than 20,000 typefaces available for the Macintosh. And more are appearing every month. These faces cost anywhere from a few dollars for a shareware face to more than a hundred dollars for a family from an established vendor. With so many fonts to choose from, how do you go about finding high-quality typefaces at good prices? This chapter will help you find the faces you need as you build your type library. It will introduce you to the basic categories of faces, show you how to recognize some of the most popular faces, provide guidelines on when to use certain kinds of faces, and present type samples from some of the top digital foundries. With the information you learn here, you'll be able to amass a well-rounded typeface collection, rather than falling prey to the latest typeface fad or bargain-basement font sale.

Types of Type

When you're deciding which faces to buy for your collection, first consider the kinds of publications you'll be producing. Typefaces are generally grouped into four catgories: text, display, decorative, and specialty. Each kind of type is appropriate for a different job. The categories are not hard and fast (a somewhat ornate text face might be used for either text or display, for example), but the following descriptions will give you some guidelines to use when selecting different types of faces. Depending on the kind of work you do, you might find that most of the faces in your collection fall into one of the categories. If you create advertisements, for example, you might find that your type library is heavy on decorative faces. But whatever type of publications you produce, you'll probably want to start with a foundation of text faces to relieve the overworked faces that came with your laser printer.

Text Faces

Text faces are the foundation of most type libraries. Whether you're printing a book, a newsletter, or a business report, you'll need a face that's legible in the main part of the text, or *body copy*. To the uninitiated, many text faces look alike. In fact, many text faces are quite similar to one another. A good number of today's popular faces can trace their roots to a limited set of designs created by the master type designers of yesteryear. These faces are readable, pleasing to the eye, and familiar, so people feel comfortable reading them. That's why they've been around so long. While a traditional text face might not turn any heads, it's not likely to put off any readers, either. An ornate or offbeat face might make a publication more visually exciting, but if the eye has to slow down periodically to decipher a letter, the reader's concentration is disrupted and the typeface may actually become an obstacle to understanding the material. Don't get the idea that text faces have to be boring; if you take the time to study text faces, you'll find that each has a distinct character, and that even subtle variations in letterforms can make a big difference in a face's personality.

By convention, text faces are usually serif, although many readable sans serif faces exist. Sans serif conveys a modern look, while serif faces are generally regarded as the safe, traditional way to go. When in doubt, it's better to err on the conservative side; if you use a sans serif face for long passages of text (a book or magazine, for example), you run the risk of taxing the reader's eyes. On the other hand, if you're striving for a clean, contemporary look, a sans serif face might be appropriate. You might choose a sans serif for practical reasons, as well. For example, if you're setting a catalog, directory, or other publication that consists of small, tightly packed text, all those serifs can get in the way, making the material busy and hard to read. Serif faces also tend to have more variation in stroke weight than sans serif faces; at small sizes, thin stems or other character components can drop out.

Before you run out and buy hundreds of dollars' worth of typefaces, take a good look at the ones in your own back yard. If you own a laser printer, several perfectly good text faces are built into its read-only memory (there's no place like ROM). The following text faces are built into many laser printers, including Apple's LaserWriter series. Other laser printers offer these fonts or a similar selection. (For more information on printers, see Chapter 6.)

Times. It's not a glamorous face, but Times Roman is highly readable, making it one of the most popular typefaces around. Times New Roman was created for the London *Times* in 1931 by Stanley Morison; Times has been cropping up ever since in newspapers, books, ads, and almost every kind of publication imaginable. Times is somewhat condensed, making it a good choice for fitting a lot of copy into a small space. Its large x-height and bold strokes allow it to hold up even under poor printing conditions, such as newspaper printing. If you want a good, solid, workaday face, you can't go wrong with Times. But don't use this ubiquitous face if you want your publication to stand out from the crowd.

Hevetica. This sans serif face was designed in Switzerland in 1957 by Max Meidinger. It's probably the most widely read typeface in the world. Helvetica's letters and numbers are simple, compact, and readable, making this face a good choice for text, headlines, ads, signs, reports—you name it. Like Times, Helvetica is short on personality but long on versatility. Its neutrality makes it a popular choice for headings that accompany a serif face.

Bookman. ITC Bookman (ITC stands for International Typeface Corporation), which was created by Ed Benguiat in 1975, is more casual than Times. Like Times, it has a large x-height and moderate variation in stroke weight, but it's less compact than Times and a little harder to read in long passages. Bookman is strong, straightforward, and friendly, and would be a good choice for an ad, brochure, or similar publication consisting of short blocks of text. It's also ideal for headlines and other display applications (display type is discussed later in this chapter).

New Century Schoolbook. In 1924, Morris Fuller Benton developed a face called Century Schoolbook. A 1982 revival by Linotype added several weights to the earlier design. Like Times and Bookman, this sturdy, legible face stands up under poor printing conditions. As you may have guessed from its name, New Century Schoolbook is appropriate for lengthy text applications such as books. It's a little stodgy for some tastes, but it's a strong, no-nonsense face that works well in many types of publications.

Palatino. This face is dignified, elegant, classical, and formal. Palatino's lineage includes the chiseled letters of ancient Roman monuments and the calligraphy of sixteenth-century scribes. Designed by Hermann Zapf, Palatino combines some of the best traits of Renai-sance and twentieth-century type design. Use this face for books, magazines, brochures, and the like, or employ it to add a touch of class to a report or a prospectus. Palatino is an attractive face, but make sure you don't miscast it in documents that might be better served by a face with a different character (like when Meryl Streep played the Jewish housewife in the movie *Heartburn*—it just didn't work).

Avant Garde. ITC Avant Garde was created in 1970 by Herb Lubalin and Tom Carnase. This sans serif face shows the influence of the Bauhaus school of design: letterforms consist of simple elements such as circles and straight lines. Although hardly avant-garde by today's standards, ITC Avant Garde still conveys a modern look. This face works well for both text and headlines, although its minimalist, geometric letterforms make it the least readable of the laser-printer lot for long passages of text.

In addition to the built-in fonts just described, your laser printer may come with additional text fonts that you can send to the printer for output. Apple's LaserWriter Pro, for example, comes with the built-in fonts just described, as well as the following additional text fonts:

Garamond Narrow. Claude Garamond was a sixteenth-century type designer. Numerous variations on his typefaces exist today, including this condensed version, which is Apple Computer's corporate typeface. Now you don't have to use a page layout program or other software to artificially compress Garamond to give your copy that Apple-esque look.

Lubalin Graph. Designed in 1974 by Herb Lubalin, Antonio DiSpigna, and Joe Sundwall, this square serif, or Egyptian, face can be used for text or headlines. Square serif faces first appeared in the early 1800s. They were originally used as attention-grabbing faces in advertisements, then gained popularity as text faces in the early 1930s.

Lucida Bright. In 1985, Charles Bigelow and Kris Holmes released their Lucida typeface family. Designed to be legible both on screen and in printed form, Lucida also holds up very well when faxed. Lucida Bright is a lighter, more refined version of the original Lucida face.

Finally, there are two additional text fonts that come with your Mac's System software:

New York. The original New York was a bitmapped font, while the version that comes with the current Mac System software is a TrueType font (see the next chapter for descriptions of these font formats). Ignore all those warnings you've heard for years about not printing fonts with city names on your laser printer: the new New York, created by Charles Bigelow and Kris Holmes, looks just fine.

Geneva. Like New York, Geneva is a retooled version of one of the Mac's original bitmapped fonts. It's been given a new lease on life by Charles Bigelow and Kris Holmes, who designed a new font that's loosely based on the old Geneva.

If none of the fonts that come with your Mac or printer is quite what you're looking for, you'll have to get the font you need from a third party. Many companies sell text faces. One of the premier sellers of Macintosh typefaces is Adobe Systems. Adobe's faces are built into Apple's LaserWriter printers, as well as many other brands of laser printers (Adobe developed PostScript, the language that enables laser printers to print high-quality fonts; more on this in the following chapter). In addition, Adobe offers a huge font library that includes many text faces, both classics and original Adobe designs. Other good sources of text faces are Agfa, Bitstream, Linotype-Hell, and Monotype. Samples of faces from these vendors—and others—are shown later in this chapter.

Samples of text faces from several vendors are shown in Figure 3.1. For information on how to contact type vendors, see Appendix A.

Minion

ABCDEFGHIJKLMNOPQRSTUVWXYZ
abcdefghijklmnopqrstuvwxyz123456

Bitstream Arrus

ABCDEFGHIJKLMNOPQRSTUVWXYZ
abcdefghijklmnopqrstuvwxyz123456

Syntax

ABCDEFGHIJKLMNOPQRSTUVWXYZ
abcdefghijklmnopqrstuvwxyz123456

Monotype Bulmer

ABCDEFGHIJKLMNOPQRSTUVWXYZ
abcdefghijklmnopqrstuvwxyz123456

Silica

ABCDEFGHIJKLMNOPQRSTUVWXYZ
abcdefghijklmnopqrstuvwxyz123456

FIGURE 3.1. A small sample of text faces is shown here: Adobe's Minion, Bitstream's Arrus, Linotype-Hell's Syntax, Monotype's Bulmer, and Stone Type Foundry's Silica.

Display Faces

Display faces feature bold, eye-catching letters designed to capture the reader's attention or set an element off from surrounding text. Display faces are used for headlines, chapter titles, posters, advertisements, and other places where an attention-grabbing face is needed.

Display type is often sans serif, and is often bolder than the surrounding text. Not all display faces are sans serif faces, however, and not all of them are bold. Some employ stylistic extremes that would make a long passage of text virtually unreadable. Because they tend to be set at larger sizes than text faces, some display faces exhibit extremes in stroke weight: heavy or black, ultrathin (since thin strokes aren't hard to see at large sizes), or a combination of thick and thin strokes (Bodoni Poster, which is shown in Figure 3.2, combines razor-thin strokes with grotesquely wide ones). Some display faces feature exaggerated serifs, rounded or elongated characters, or calligraphic flourishes. Even if the face itself has no stylistic extremes, an otherwise mild-mannered text face might be set in an ultrabold weight or a condensed or expanded style to make it an eye-catching display face. Because display type is used for short passages, readability isn't as important a concern as it is for body copy.

The distinction between text and display faces is somewhat murky. A single typeface can overlap both categories. Souvenir, for example, is popular as both a text face and a display face (see Figure 3.2 for a sample of Souvenir). But whereas many text faces can double as display faces, the reverse is rarely true; a typeface specially designed for display purposes won't usually work well as a text face. If you're on a budget, your best bet is to concentrate on text faces first, and transform those faces into display type by adding size and weight in a word processor or condensing or expanding them in a page layout program (remember the warning in the previous chapter, however: don't condense or expand them too much).

Ideally, a display face should be neutral and flexible enough to work well with a number of text faces. Helvetica and Avant Garde, for example, are good, general-purpose display faces, with the bonus that they're built into many laser printers. Bookman, another laser printer face, is strong enough to do double duty as both a text and a display face. Figure 3.2 shows some samples of display faces.

ITC Souvenir Demi

ABCDEFGHIJKLMNOPQRSTUVWXYZ
abcdefghijklmnopqrstuvwxyz123456

Bodoni Poster

ABCDEFGHIJKLMNOPQRSTUVWXYZ
abcdefghijklmnopqrstuvwxyz123456

Industria

ABCDEFGHIJKLMNOPQRSTUVWXYZ
abcdefghijklmnopqrstuvwxyz123456

Eaglefeather Bold

ABCDEFGHIJKLMNOPQRSTUVWXYZ
abcdefghijklmnopqrstuvwxyz123456

Gill Sans Display Extra Bold

ABCDEFGHIJKLMNOPQRSTUVWXYZ
abcdefghijklmnopqrstuvwxyz123456

FIGURE 3.2. A small sample of display faces is shown here: Adobe's ITC Souvenir and Bodoni Poster, Linotype-Hell's Industria, Agfa's Eaglefeather, and Monotype's Gill Sans Display.

Your laser printer may include some display faces as well. Apple's LaserWriter Pro, for example, includes the following display faces:

- **Helvetica Black**
- **Helvetica Compressed**
- **MACHINE**
- **Onyx**

Quite a few font vendors offer display faces. These include Adobe, Agfa, Alphabets Inc., Bitstream, Carter & Cone, Castle Systems, EmDash, Emigre, The Font Bureau, The Font Company, FontHaus, FontShop, Galápagos Design Group, Image Club Graphics, Linotype-Hell, Monotype, Prepress Direct, Stone Type Foundry, Treacyfaces, URW. For information on how to contact vendors, see Appendix A.

Decorative Faces

Ah, decorative typefaces—the curse of the impulse buyer! But go ahead, have some fun; buy an Art Deco face, a script face, a rubber stamp face, or one of those newfangled faces that looks like a porcupine that's been frappéd in a blender. They may or may not be readable, but decorative faces are guaranteed to catch the reader's attention and give a page a distinctive look.

Decorative faces can add pizzazz to a letter, an invitation, or an ad. Just be careful that you don't overuse decorative faces or, worse yet, use them in inappropriate ways, like this:

With Deepest Sympathy

Expo 2000: The Cutting Edge of Technology

Shown here: Mambo (FontShop), Clairveaux (Linotype-Hell), and Fobia (Font Bureau)

There's some overlap between decorative and display faces. Although some designers use decorative faces as display type, these faces generally have so much personality that they monopolize the page design and distract the reader from the message the text is trying to convey. A decorative face in a business letter or serious presentation can stick out like a sore thumb.

Dozens of companies sell decorative faces. The companies listed in the "Display Faces" section offer a wide selection of decorative faces as well. In addition to these companies, outfits like The Electric Typographer, T-26, and Letraset offer collections of decorative and novelty faces. You can also find a great selection of decorative faces in the freeware and shareware libraries of online services such as CompuServe and America Online. If you want to look at printed samples of hundreds of free and shareware fonts before you spend time and money downloading them, I'd recommend HyperActive Software's *Font Sampler Catalog* (see Appendix A). This four-volume set provides print-outs of many of the fonts you'll find online.

ITC Zapf Chancery is built into many laser printers:

- *ITC Zapf Chancery*

Several additional decorative faces come with Apple's LaserWriter Pro printer:

- DELPHIAN
- *Nadianne Book*
- **Old English Text**
- Oxford
- *Swing Bold*

Bear in mind that decorative faces might not include the full range of characters you'd find in a text face. Some lack lowercase letters, for example, while others are missing some punctuation and symbols. Since you won't be setting a book in a decorative face (I hope), you won't need these characters.

Figure 3.3 shows a smattering of fun faces from several companies.

Jimbo

ABCDEFGHIJKLMNOPQRSTVWXYZ
abcdfghijklmnopqrstvuwxyz123456

Binner D

ABCDEFGHIJKLMNOPQRSTUVWXYZ
1234567890

A*I Chaotiqua

ABCDEFGHIJKLMNOPQRSTUVWXYZ
abcfghijklmnopqrstuvwxyz123456

Bremen

ABCDEFGHIJKLMNOPQRSTUVWXYZ
1234567890

Sophia

ABCDEFGHIJKLMNOPQRSTUVWXYZ
1234567890

FIGURE 3.3. Decorative faces are designed to be eye-catching. Shown here are Adobe's Jimbo, URW's Binner D, Alphabets Inc.'s Chaotiqua, Bitstream's Bremen, and Carter & Cone Type's Sophia.

Flourish

ABCDEFGHIJKLMNO PQRSTUVWXYZ
abcdefghijklmnopqrstuvwxyz123456

Remedy Double

ABCDEFGHIJKLMNOPQRSTUVWXYZ
abcdefghijklmnopqrstuvwxyz123456

Sloop One

ABCDEFGHIJKLMNOPQRSTU
abcdefghijklmnopqrstuvwxyz123456

Broadway Modern

ABCDEFGHIJKLMNOPQRSTUV
abcdefghijklmnopqrstuvwxyz
1234567890

Concept

ABCDEFGHIJKLMNOPQRSTUVWXYZ
abcdefghijklmnopqrstuvwxyz123456

FIGURE 3.3 (continued). Shown here are The Electric Typographer's Flourish, Emigre's Remedy, The Font Bureau's Sloop, and FontHaus's Broadway Modern and Concept.

Papyrus

ABCDEFGHIJKLMNOPQRSTUVWXYZ
abcdefghijklmnopqrstuvwxyz123456

Kipp

ABCDEFGHIJKLMNOPQRSTUVWXYZ
abcdefghijklmnopqrstuvwxyz123456

Farfel Felt Tip

ABCDEFGHIJKLMNOPQRSTUVWXYZ
1234567890

Marcus Aurelius

Kristen

ABCDEFGHIJKLMNOPQRSTUVWXYZ
abcdefghijklmnopqrstuvwxyz123456

FIGURE 3.2 (continued). Shown here are Letraset's Papyrus, FontShop's Kipp, Image Club's Farfel Felt Tip, T-26's Marcus Aurelius, and Galápagos Design Group's Kristen.

Specialty Faces

The specialty category encompasses a wide variety of faces. Perhaps the most common specialty offerings are *pi fonts*, sets of nontext characters used for specific disciplines or professions. A mathematical pi font, for example, might contain mathematical operators (addition, subtraction, multiplication, and division signs), Greek characters, large brackets, and other special characters used in mathematical expressions. A special type of pi font called *dingbats* contains pictorial characters such as arrows, check marks, check boxes, pointing hands, and decorative elements.

Other types of specialty fonts include small caps, fractions, phonetic symbols, cartographic symbols, music notation, decorative borders, chemical structures, computer keyboard layouts, typographers' ornaments, and countless doodads and thingamajigs, from dinosaurs to astrology symbols to Native American pictographs.

Figure 3.4 shows a few of the specialty faces available. More are listed in Appendix B. If you can't find just the pictorial font you need, you can make your own picture font by importing graphics into Fontographer (see Chapter 6 for a description of Fontographer).

Foreign Language Faces

A number of companies offer foreign language faces. There's enough of a selection for some faces—Hebrew and Cyrillic, for example—that you can base your buying decision on aesthetics, choosing among dozens of styles. For other languages your choices are more limited, but overall I think you'll be amazed at the number of languages supported. See Appendix C for a list of foreign language faces.

Shown here: Yaxchilan 11 sample (Ecological Linguistics)

Symbol

!∀#∃%&∋()∗+,./0123456789:;<=>?≅ΑΒΧΔΕ
ΦΓΗΙϑΚΛΜΝΟΠΘΡΣΤΥςΩΞΨΖ[∴]⊥_
αβχδεφγηιϕκλμνοπθρστυϖω∂{|}~ϒ′≤⁄∞ƒ
♣♦♥♠↔←↑→↓°±″≥×∝•÷≠≡≈…│——⌋ℵℑℜ
℘⊗⊕∅∩∪⊃⊄⊂⊆∈∉∠∇®©™∏√⋅¬∧∨⇔
⇐⇑⇒⇓◊⟨®©™∑⎛⎜⎝⎡⎢⎣⎧⎨⎩⎟⎜⎟⎞⎟⎜⎞⎠⎟⎟

Zapf Dingbats

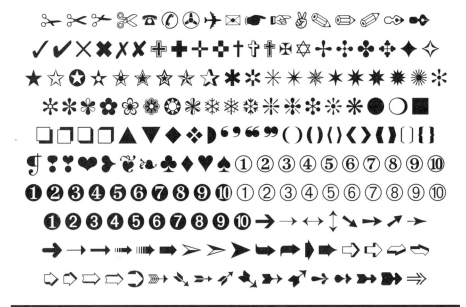

FIGURE 3.4. Specialty faces for the Mac abound. Adobe's Symbol and Zapf Dingbats are built into Apple's LaserWriter printers.

Zeal

Linotype Decoration Pi (One and Two)

FIGURE 3.4 (continued). Shown here are Apple's Zeal and Linotype-Hell's Linotype Decoration Pi.

Birds

Artifact One

FIGURE 3.4 (continued).   Shown here are FontHaus's Birds and Monotype's Artifact One.

Catastrophe

Linotype Astrology Pi Two

TF Crossword

FIGURE 3.4 (continued). Shown here are The Electric Typographer's Catastrophe, Linotype-Hell's Linotype Astrology Pi, and Treacyfaces' TF Crossword.

PIXymbols One

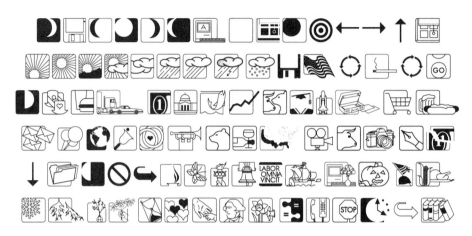

DF Incidentals

FIGURE 3.4 (continued). Page Studio Graphics' PIXymbols One and Letraset's DF Incidentals.

Starting Your Collection

If you create a lot of publications on your Mac, you'll soon find you've outgrown your printer's built-in fonts. You paste the text for a newsletter into your page layout program and find yourself staring blankly at the Font menu: Times is too mundane; Palatino's too formal; Bookman's too informal; and New Century Schoolbook is too, well, schoolbookish. It's time to buy some fonts. If you're new to Mac publishing, you may be overwhelmed by the choices that confront you; thousands of faces are available from dozens of companies. Where do you start? How do you choose?

For starters, you can listen to the pros. I asked a number of type experts—graphic designers, typesetters, publishers, and type designers—for advice on choosing some key faces to be the foundation of a typeface library.

The Experts Speak

The type experts I quizzed included type designer Sumner Stone, former *Publish* magazine editor Jim Felici, designer Kathy Forsythe (a consultant for Bit-stream), and Harry Marks, president of Marks Communications. I asked them which ten text faces they'd choose if they were starting a type collection. Not everyone chose the same ten faces, of course (type aficionados are an opinionated lot, and can rave on for hours on the merits of a favorite face or the hideous flaws of a design they despise), but there was a good deal of overlap in the faces they recommended. Ten popular text families are shown in Figures 3.5 through 3.14.

Other faces they recommended included the ITC Stone Family (designed by the aforementioned Sumner Stone; and yes, other experts besides Sumner recommended it), ITC Cheltenham, Trump Mediaeval, Gill Sans, Franklin Gothic, and the rest of the Helvetica family—condensed, light, black, and so on. Me, I'm partial to Berkeley Oldstyle (see the Adobe samples later in this chapter for a look at this face). As you learn more about type, you'll no doubt come up with your own list of favorite faces.

Of course, just because a face is popular doesn't mean it's right for your publishing project. The "top ten" list is intended to give newcomers a taste of versatile, time-honored faces. Ultimately, you'll have to decide what you need from a typeface. Should it convey a mood or message to the reader (formal, casual, lighthearted, modern, powerful, businesslike)? Should it grab the reader's eye (in an ad headline, logo, or announcement, for example), or should it be a neutral face that doesn't call attention to itself as a design element (in a textbook or catalog, for example)? Should it be readable in long passages (say, in a book, magazine, or newsletter), or would a less legible but more striking face be more appropriate (in an ad, invitation, or book jacket, for instance)? You should also consider printing conditions. You'll need a sturdy face, with no spindly stems or tiny serifs, if you're going to be printing your publication on poor-quality paper such as newsprint. You'll also need a robust face if you're going to fax your report to headquarters.

When you're shopping for type, it's a good idea to look at a sample that matches the way you intend to use the face. If you're looking for a face to use in setting a book, for example, go to a bookstore or library and see if you can find a book that's set in that face (many books include a note on the typefaces used; this information can often be found on the copyright page, the book jacket, or a colophon at the end of the book). Keep in mind, however, that the digital version you buy may not exactly match the face used in the book.

Some type vendors display passages of text in their type catalogs, but many offer such a large number of faces that they only have room for small samples. Figures 3.5 through 3.14 show a sizable chunk of text so you can get a feel for each face. The figures also show various weights and styles.

In addition to asking the experts about their favorite faces, I asked them what advice they'd give beginners on mixing faces in a document—using one face for headings and another for body copy, for example. You've probably heard this a hundred times, but I'll repeat it here just to be on the safe side: Don't use too many faces in a document. Of course, how many faces you use depends on the type of publication you're producing and the message you're trying to convey, but in general if you use more than three faces on a page you'll create a hodgepodge that will peg you as an amateur designer.

Harry Marks points out that there are no hard-and-fast rules for using one face with another. "You can't really list faces that go with other faces. You can always use Times for text and Helvetica for headlines, but it's nice to be innovative." He suggests that type neophytes read some basic books on typography (see this book's Bibliography for suggestions). Some companies that sell fonts or page layout software offer newsletters or booklets with tips on using type; see if the companies you buy from offer this type of publication.

Bodoni

Although Italian printer Giambattista Bodoni designed this typeface in 1788, it's classified as a Modern face. The Modern category includes faces with a vertical stroke emphasis, square serifs, and a strong contrast between thick and thin strokes.

When to use: Bodoni can be used as a text or display type, but should be used with care because of the immense variation in stroke weight; hairlines might fade out under poor printing conditions. Bodoni's vertical letterforms bring to mind words such as "rigid" and "formal."

Dædalus and Icarus

"I warn you, Icarus, fly a middle course:
Don't go too low, or water will weigh the wings down;
Don't go too high, or the sun's fire will burn them.
Keep to the middle way. And one more thing,
No fancy steering by sun or constellation,
Follow my lead!" That was the flying lesson,
And now to fit the wings to the boy's shoulders.
Between the work and warning the father found
His cheeks were wet with tears, and his hands trembled.
He kissed his son (*Good-bye*, if he had known it),
Rose on his wings, flew on ahead, as fearful
As any bird launching the little nestlings
Out of the high nest into thin air.
　　　　—Ovid

FIGURE 3.5. Adobe's Bodoni.

Caslon

Around 1720, William Caslon began working on a typeface that was to become one of the most enduring faces of all time. The Declaration of Independence and the Constitution of the United States were originally set in Caslon, and it's still popular today. Many variations on Caslon's design have been created over the years. You're looking at Adobe Caslon, a revival by type designer Carol Twombly.

When to use: *"When in doubt, use Caslon." That's what the typographers say. It's hard to go wrong with this sturdy, unassuming classic.*

Note: *Adobe Caslon includes an optional Expert Set, which features small caps, old style numerals, ornaments, swash italics, and other special characters.*

Dædalus and Icarus

"I warn you, Icarus, fly a middle course:
Don't go too low, or water will weigh the wings down;
Don't go too high, or the sun's fire will burn them.
Keep to the middle way. And one more thing,
No fancy steering by sun or constellation,
Follow my lead!" That was the flying lesson,
And now to fit the wings to the boy's shoulders.
Between the work and warning the father found
His cheeks were wet with tears, and his hands trembled.
He kissed his son (*Good-bye,* if he had known it),
Rose on his wings, flew on ahead, as fearful
As any bird launching the little nestlings
Out of the high nest into thin air.
      —*Ovid*

FIGURE 3.6. Adobe Caslon.

Futura

Designed by Paul Renner in 1927, Futura is one of the most popular sans serif faces. Letters are reduced to basic forms (the "o" is a simple circle, for example), unadorned by variations in line weight. Adobe's Futura family boasts 20 members.

When to use: *Futura is suitable for headlines, ads, or almost any publication that demands a modern look. Although it's very readable, you probably wouldn't want to use Futura in lengthy publications such as books or magazines. Futura is undeniably modern, but some people consider it a cold and impersonal face.*

Note: *Futura's ascenders are extremely tall in relation to the other letters in the face; you should add a little extra leading when you use this face.*

Dædalus and Icarus

"I warn you, Icarus, fly a middle course:
Don't go too low, or water will weigh the wings down;
Don't go too high, or the sun's fire will burn them.
Keep to the middle way. And one more thing,
No fancy steering by sun or constellation,
Follow my lead!" That was the flying lesson,
And now to fit the wings to the boy's shoulders.
Between the work and warning the father found
His cheeks were wet with tears, and his hands trembled.
He kissed his son (*Good-bye,* if he had known it),
Rose on his wings, flew on ahead, as fearful
As any bird launching the little nestlings
Out of the high nest into thin air.
      —*Ovid*

FIGURE 3.7. Adobe's Futura.

Galliard

Created in 1982 by Matthew Carter, Galliard is a contemporary adaptation of a sixteenth-century typeface by Robert Granjon. Carter was one of the first designers to take advantage of computer technology for font design; he made the roman and black weights by traditional means, then used a computer program to produce the bold and ultra weights.

When to use: *Galliard's calligraphic flavor makes it one of the most elegant faces around. This readable, versatile face can be called on for anything from a business document to a book or scientific paper.*

Dædalus and Icarus

"I warn you, Icarus, fly a middle course:
Don't go too low, or water will weigh the wings down;
Don't go too high, or the sun's fire will burn them.
Keep to the middle way. And one more thing,
No fancy steering by sun or constellation,
Follow my lead!" That was the flying lesson,
And now to fit the wings to the boy's shoulders.
Between the work and warning the father found
His cheeks were wet with tears, and his hands trembled.
He kissed his son (*Good-bye,* if he had known it),
Rose on his wings, flew on ahead, as fearful
As any bird launching the little nestlings
Out of the high nest into thin air.
　　　—Ovid

FIGURE 3.8. Bitstream's ITC Galliard.

Garamond

Garamond is an Old Style face, one that has little variation in stroke width, a diagonal emphasis, ascenders that are taller than the capitals, and small serifs. Claude Garamond designed his faces in the sixteenth century; since then there have been many interpretations of Garamond. Shown here is Adobe Garamond, a revival by Robert Slimbach. The italics for this face are based on the type of Robert Granjon.

When to use: *This classic face is suitable for books, magazines, and other publications with lengthy passages of text.*

Note: *There are many variations of Garamond's designs. Adobe, for example, offers Adobe Garamond, Garamond 3, Stempel Garamond, ITC Garamond, and Sabon.*

Dædalus and Icarus

"I warn you, Icarus, fly a middle course:
Don't go too low, or water will weigh the wings down;
Don't go too high, or the sun's fire will burn them.
Keep to the middle way. And one more thing,
No fancy steering by sun or constellation,
Follow my lead!" That was the flying lesson,
And now to fit the wings to the boy's shoulders.
Between the work and warning the father found
His cheeks were wet with tears, and his hands trembled.
He kissed his son (*Good-bye,* if he had known it),
Rose on his wings, flew on ahead, as fearful
As any bird launching the little nestlings
Out of the high nest into thin air.
     —Ovid

FIGURE 3.9. Adobe Garamond.

Goudy Old Style

Designed in 1915 by Frederic Goudy, this face is a favorite of designers and typographers. Typical of the Old Style faces, Goudy is reminiscent of pen-drawn letters, with subtle variations in line weight, ascenders higher than capitals, and delicate serifs.

When to use: *Goudy Old Style is a little on the delicate side, so don't use it if priting conditions are poor. This graceful, unassuming face would be an excellent choice for a book, business proposal, or brochure.*

Note: *Goudy Old Style is offered by many companies; look at samples to find the interpretation you like best.*

Dædalus and Icarus

"I warn you, Icarus, fly a middle course:
Don't go too low, or water will weigh the wings down;
Don't go too high, or the sun's fire will burn them.
Keep to the middle way. And one more thing,
No fancy steering by sun or constellation,
Follow my lead!" That was the flying lesson,
And now to fit the wings to the boy's shoulders.
Between the work and warning the father found
His cheeks were wet with tears, and his hands trembled.
He kissed his son (*Good-bye*, if he had known it),
Rose on his wings, flew on ahead, as fearful
As any bird launching the little nestlings
Out of the high nest into thin air.
     —*Ovid*

FIGURE 3.10. Bitstream's Goudy Old Style.

Janson Text

Janson was designed in the seventeenth century by Nicholas Kis. (So why isn't it called Kis?, the inquiring reader might like to know. The face was mistakenly attributed to the Dutch printer Anton Janson, and the name stuck even after Kis was found to be its true designer.)

When to use: *Janson's contrast between thick and thin strokes make it a strong, readable face for books or magazines. (The first two editions of this book were set in Janson, but then I fell in love with Adobe Jenson and decided to use it for this edition.)*

Dædalus and Icarus

"I warn you, Icarus, fly a middle course:
Don't go too low, or water will weigh the wings down;
Don't go too high, or the sun's fire will burn them.
Keep to the middle way. And one more thing,
No fancy steering by sun or constellation,
Follow my lead!" That was the flying lesson,
And now to fit the wings to the boy's shoulders.
Between the work and warning the father found
His cheeks were wet with tears, and his hands trembled.
He kissed his son (*Good-bye,* if he had known it),
Rose on his wings, flew on ahead, as fearful
As any bird launching the little nestlings
Out of the high nest into thin air.
     —Ovid

FIGURE 3.11. Linotype-Hell's Janson Text.

New Baskerville

Baskerville was designed by the English writing master John Baskerville in 1757. New Baskerville is a contemporary revival. This is a Transitional face, a style that falls between Old Style and Modern. Transitional faces show greater contrast between thick and thin strokes than Old Style faces, and have a vertical rather than diagonal stress.

When to use: *New Baskerville can be used in books, magazines, newsletters, reports, or almost any publication that calls for a pleasant, readable text face. As you can see, the face's italics are easy to read as well.*

Note: *New Baskerville is graceful, delicate, elegant…but a little wimpy. You might want to tighten up the tracking to make this face less airy.*

Dædalus and Icarus

"I warn you, Icarus, fly a middle course:
Don't go too low, or water will weigh the wings down;
Don't go too high, or the sun's fire will burn them.
Keep to the middle way. And one more thing,
No fancy steering by sun or constellation,
Follow my lead!" That was the flying lesson,
And now to fit the wings to the boy's shoulders.
Between the work and warning the father found
His cheeks were wet with tears, and his hands trembled.
He kissed his son (*Good-bye,* if he had known it),
Rose on his wings, flew on ahead, as fearful
As any bird launching the little nestlings
Out of the high nest into thin air.
    —Ovid

FIGURE 3.12. Adobe's ITC New Baskerville.

Optima

Optima, designed by Hermann Zapf, is one of the most versatile—and popular—faces around. The characters are based on classic proportions of width to height that were set by Greco-Roman and Renaissance standards. A sans serif face with just a hint of serifs in its subtly flared stroke endings, Optima mixes well with many serif and sans serif faces.

When to use: *A good all-around face, Optima is well suited for text or display applications.*

Note: *Because of its subtle gradations in stroke width, Optima is less than optimum when printed at 300 dots per inch. If you're using a 300-dpi printer for final output, think twice about using Optima.*

Dædalus and Icarus

"I warn you, Icarus, fly a middle course:
Don't go too low, or water will weigh the wings down;
Don't go too high, or the sun's fire will burn them.
Keep to the middle way. And one more thing,
No fancy steering by sun or constellation,
Follow my lead!" That was the flying lesson,
And now to fit the wings to the boy's shoulders.
Between the work and warning the father found
His cheeks were wet with tears, and his hands trembled.
He kissed his son (*Good-bye,* if he had known it),
Rose on his wings, flew on ahead, as fearful
As any bird launching the little nestlings
Out of the high nest into thin air.
    —Ovid

FIGURE 3.13. Linotype-Hell's Optima.

Univers

Univers is a good example of the virtues of family planning. Created in 1956 by the Swiss type designer Adrian Frutiger, Univers was one of the first typeface families to be planned in its entirety before production began. Adobe offers 27 styles and weights of Univers. Although it's sometimes confused with Helvetica (another Swiss sans serif), Univers offers more variation in stroke width, making it more lively and interesting than Helvetica.

When to use: *If a project has numerous elements or heading levels, the Univers family can tie the design together. It's an excellent display face, and readable in body copy as well. Use this face if you want to break out of your Helvetica rut.*

Dædalus and Icarus

"I warn you, Icarus, fly a middle course:
Don't go too low, or water will weigh the wings down;
Don't go too high, or the sun's fire will burn them.
Keep to the middle way. And one more thing,
No fancy steering by sun or constellation,
Follow my lead!" That was the flying lesson,
And now to fit the wings to the boy's shoulders.
Between the work and warning the father found
His cheeks were wet with tears, and his hands trembled.
He kissed his son (*Good-bye,* if he had known it),
Rose on his wings, flew on ahead, as fearful
As any bird launching the little nestlings
Out of the high nest into thin air.
    —*Ovid*

FIGURE 3.14. Adobe's Univers.

"Breaking the rules is fine," says Marks, "but you have to know what rules you're breaking. If you start with the basics...you get the groundwork that will then allow you to stretch out a bit." He also suggests that beginners look at good designs and emulate them. Thumb through magazines, books, or other publications to see how professional designers use type.

Publish! magazine's Jim Felici, curmudgeon that he is, advocates a conservative approach for beginners. He points out that typeface families exist to provide complementary design elements. It's hard to go wrong when you set headings in a larger, bold version of a publication's text face. "A beginner's design shouldn't be memorable," he notes. "If it's memorable, it's probably memorable for the wrong reasons." He suggests investing in a family with lots of styles and weights, such as Univers (see Figure 3.14). He also notes that Optima mixes well with many serif faces (see Figure 3.12).

Felici also suggests Adobe's Stone Family as a sure bet for novice designers. The Stone family is actually three families that are similar in design and spirit (Stone refers to it as a "type clan"). Stone's extended family includes a serif family, a sans serif family, and a charming "informal" family designed for personal communications where a traditional face might appear too formal and businesslike. (Stone also offers a serif face called Stone Print, which is available through Stone Type Foundry; see Appendix A for information.) Because the Stone superfamily was created with compatibility in mind, it's hard to go wrong mixing several members of the family in a document. Each Stone face has the same cap height and x-height, and the faces are similar enough in form to work well with each other. Figure 3.15 shows examples of several Stone faces.

Designer Kathy Forsythe agrees that there are no set rules for using typefaces. "But there are basic guidelines that one can follow for using type effectively. Judgment, taste, and appropriateness are acquired through the experience of using type regularly and through awareness of basic guidelines that can assist in the most effective use of type." When asked about combining different typefaces, Forsythe replied, "When using two or more typefaces together, contrast is the objective. You want to create different textures with type. This can be achieved in several ways: serif versus sans serif (contrast of structure), roman versus italic (contrast of form), contrast of size and weight, and caps versus lowercase. Contrast creates typographic interest and at the same time enhances and strengthens the message."

**From the Recliner of
Balso Snell, Jr.**

**1456 Della St.
San Jose, CA
95125**

Home phone: (408) 555-2379 • Work phone: NA

Dear Frank:

Would you like to come over and watch TV this
Sunday? We could drink a couple of beers and watch
the game. I think I have some crackers left over from
last weekend. Do you think you could bring over some
more of that great cheese-in-a-can like you brought
last time? It was really delicious!

I'm looking forward to hearing from you.

Cordially,

Balso

Figure 3.15. The Stone family is actually a set of three families designed to work harmoniously with one another. This example shows Bold and Bold Italic Stone Sans, Bold Stone Serif, and the regular weight of Stone informal. (The signature is in the Lettrés Eclatées face, available from FontHaus.)

As a general rule, you're asking for trouble if you team up two faces that have strong personalities. You're also living dangerously if you combine two serif faces in a document. (You wouldn't want to mix Galliard and Garamond, for example, or Bodoni and Palatino—at least *I* wouldn't.) However, all of the experts I talked with noted that they'd seen seemingly bizarre typeface combinations that worked well together. By all means, don't be afraid to experiment! But if you're new to design, keep in mind that your innovative design might be the typographic equivalent of wearing stripes and plaid.

To sum up the pros' suggestions, you should read up on typography; start out with a conservative approach, mixing different styles and weights from the same family or combining fairly bland serif and sans serif faces; and look at designs done by professionals to get ideas for your publications. But perhaps the best piece of advice was given by Kathy Forsythe, when I asked her how beginners can become more knowledgeable about type. Her reply: "By using it, primarily."

A Crash Course in Type Identification

If you follow the hallowed tradition of copying the experts, you may at first find yourself hard-pressed to identify a typeface you come across. Let's say you're thumbing through a magazine and see a face you like. If you're new to typography, chances are you won't snap your fingers and say, "Aha! That looks like Chelmsford Demi-Bold Condensed Italic." More likely, you'll mutter an expletive or two and set your document in Palatino again.

But don't despair. With some patience—and a type specimen book—you can learn to identify a typeface by first narrowing down the category it falls into and then identifying key differences between the face in question and similar faces. *Rookledge's International Typefinder*, by Christopher Perfect and Gordon Rookledge (Moyer Bell, Wakefield, R.I., 1991), can be a helpful resource. This book places 700 typefaces into 16 major design categories and numerous subcategories. Once you learn some basic design styles, you can use such a reference to ferret out a particular face.

You already know how to identify serif and sans serif faces, but that skill is right up there with the ability to distinguish between animals and vegetables. Numerous subcategories of type styles exist. Figure 3.16 shows some common design categories. If you can tell that the face you ran across is a slab

Type

Old Style. Characterized by little contrast in stroke width, heavily bracketed serifs, and a diagonal stroke emphasis reminiscent of calligraphy.

Type

Transitional. A bridge between Old Style and Modern, these faces show some contrast in stroke weight, and a vertical rather than a diagonal stroke emphasis.

Type

Modern. Characterized by extreme contrast between thick and thin strokes, square serifs, and a strong vertical emphasis.

Type

Slab Serif or Egyptian. This style originated in France after Napoleon's return from Egypt. Characterized by strong, monotone stroke weight and thick, square serifs.

Type

Script. Typefaces that imitate handwritten letters. In many script faces, the letters are connected. (Note: Never set script in all caps.)

type

Uncial. From the Latin *uncus*, for crooked. Uncials are a product of the transition from handwritten capitals to lowercase letters. Use when you're in a mediaeval mood.

FIGURE 3.16. Some of the major subcategories of type designs are shown here.

serif, for example, you'll be able to focus your search on that category and—with the help of a guide like the *Typefinder*—find the face itself, or at least one that resembles it.

After you've identified the mystery face's general design category, you can speed up your search by comparing specific letters of the unknown face to those of faces in a type specimen book or type vendor's catalog. Certain letters tend to be more distinctive than others, generally differing more than the other letters from one face to another. Among these are the uppercase *A*, *E*, *M*, and *T*, and the lowercase *a*, *e*, *g*, *r*, and *t* (these letters spell out "great TEAM," in case you're partial to memory aids). Start your comparison with one or more of these letters. *Rookledge's International Typefinder* offers tables of individual letters from different faces, speeding your search.

Try it yourself. Each of the *g*'s below belongs to one of the ten faces illustrated in Figures 3.5 through 3.14. Look at the figures and figure out which face each *g* hails from.

g g g g

Of course, you can't live on text faces alone. Figure3.17 shows samples of some of the most popular display and decorative faces. Most of these faces are faithful old workhorses from the early part of this century. A couple are newcomers that are wildly popular today and—I think—destined to become classics. (Here's Fenton's fairly foolproof typeface-identification tip: If you can't identify a typeface, just say it's Lithos and you'll have about a 90 percent chance of being right. I'm only half joking; this 1989 face by Carol Twombly is immensely popular, and shows up just about everywhere, from billboards to album covers to potato-chip bags.)

Identifying the face is only half the battle. You then have to determine whether it's available for the Mac. Fortunately, several resources are available. If you're on a budget, you can ask some of the type vendors listed in Appendix A to send you their catalogs. Or, for around $35, you can buy a book called *The Electronic Type Catalog*, by Steve Byers (Bantam, 1991). This catalog shows specimens of about 1000 popular faces from various digital foundries, in a variety of styles, weights, and sizes. For $39.95, you can order the *Precision Type Reference Guide*, a 650-page catalog of digital faces from dozens of companies. (While the *Precision Type Reference Guide* provides somewhat limited type specimens—partial character sets at small sizes—it's nevertheless a valuable resource, since you can order the fonts in the catalog from Precision Type. The guide also lists books on type, font utilities, information on foundries and type designers, and other useful font-related items.)

Whether or not you buy a reference book, it's a good idea to look at printed samples of faces from digital-type vendors before you buy a typeface. or typeface family. In some cases, when two or more Mac type vendors offer a classic face, you'll find that the faces differ widely in interpretation and execution. The following illustration shows two vendors' versions of the Goudy Old Style face:

Imitation is the sincerest form of flattery.   Bitstream

Imitation is the sincerest form of flattery.   The Electric Typographer

To further complicate matters, some companies give their own names to versions of popular faces (Image Club's Omni is based on Optima, for example). The alternate names sometimes resemble those of the original face (Hoboken for Hobo, for example, or Missive for Mistral), but not always. Because of a quirk in U.S. copyright law, a typeface's name (the name *Bembo*, for example) can be protected, but not the design of the face itself. Therefore, anyone can duplicate the characters of an existing typeface, give it another name, and legally sell their version of the face. Adobe and other type vendors license many of their faces from established type houses such as Berthold, Linotype-Hell, or ITC, and are therefore allowed to use the faces' original names. However, many smaller type companies and individual type designers have copied the letterforms of classic faces but renamed the faces to avoid trademark infringements.

While companies can take legal action if someone uses one of their trademarked typeface names, so far there has been little they can do to stop others from copying the letterforms themselves. That may change someday, however. An organization called the Typeface Design Coalition has been working for years to make U.S. copyright laws apply to typeface designs.

ITC Anna	THE FACE LOOKS FAMILIAR
Antique Olive	The face looks familiar
Arnold Boecklin	The face looks familiar
Banco	THE FACE LOOKS FAMILIAR
ITC Benguiat	The face looks familiar
Broadway	The face looks familiar
Brush Script	The face looks familiar
Cooper Black	The face looks familiar
Dom Casual	The face looks familiar
ITC Eras	The face looks familiar
Hobo	The face looks familiar
Italia	The face looks familiar
Lithos	THE FACE LOOKS FAMILIAR
Mistral	The face looks familiar
Park Avenue	The face looks familiar
Peignot	THE FACE looks FAMILIAR
Shelley Allegro	The face looks familiar
Souvenir	The face looks familiar
Tekton	The face looks familiar
University Roman	The face looks familiar

FIGURE 3.18. Some popular decorative and display faces. (All faces shown are from Adobe, except Broadway, which is from Image Club, and Shelley Allegro, which is from Bitstream.)

In 1988 the U.S. Copyright Office declared that digital typefaces were not copyrightable. But in January 1990 Adobe Systems, after many months of legal wrangling, received a copyright registration for one of its digital fonts. How? By registering it as a *computer program*, which can be copyrighted. Although the copyright applies to the programming instructions that generate the characters of a typeface, it still doesn't extend to the typeface design itself. Still, Adobe's action was a step toward recognizing digital typefaces as works of authorship.

How to Buy Typefaces

Now that you know a thing or two about typefaces, you're probably ready to buy a few. Once you've decided which faces or families you want, you have a number of ways to buy them. With the exception of Letraset's Fontek series, which are found in some art supply stores, you probably won't be able to run down to the corner store for some fonts. (A few font packages are offered in software stores, but the selection is usually limited.) Chances are, you'll call one or more of the companies listed in Appendix A and order some fonts over the phone. Or, you may prefer to order from a reseller that offers faces from many companies; Precision Type, FontHaus, and FontShop are good choices for this approach.

Many type companies offer individual faces or entire families on floppy disks. Some, such as Adobe and Monotype, offer prepackaged sets of faces; buying the package is often much cheaper than individually purchasingeach font it contains. If you think you'll be buying a lot of faces from a particular company—and if you have a CD-ROM drive—you might want to consider buying a CD full of fonts.

Font CD-ROMs

Font CD-ROMs come in two basic types: locked and unlocked. An unlocked CD contains a library of hundreds or even thousands of fonts. When you buy the CD, you have access to all the fonts on it; simply install the ones you need on your Mac and you're ready to go. Needless to say, buying a library of thousands of fonts can be expensive. (Buyer beware: If you see an ad for a CD that includes hundreds and hundreds of fonts for only a few bucks, chances are you'll get what you pay for. The fonts on these bargain-basement CDs vary in quality, but if an offer sounds too good to be true, it probably is.) Unless you think you'll need instant access to hundreds of fonts, chances are you'll use a locked CD.

A locked CD generally costs about $50 to $75 or so, and includes a number of unlocked fonts at no additional charge. You can use software on the CD to browse the company's fonts, viewing on-screen—and sometimes printed—samples and reading descriptions of the faces. When you decide which fonts you want to buy, you contact the company and pay for your fonts. A company representative contacts you by phone or fax with codes to unlock, or decrypt, the fonts you've ordered. When you've unlocked your fonts, you install them just as you would any other fonts (see Chapter 5 for information on installing fonts).

Locked CDs have several advantages: you can buy a few fonts at a time, as you need them; you can, in most cases, buy a single style or weight if you wish, saving you the expense of buying an entire family; and you can receive same-day service on your order.

Here's the ordering screen from Adobe's *Type On Call* CD:

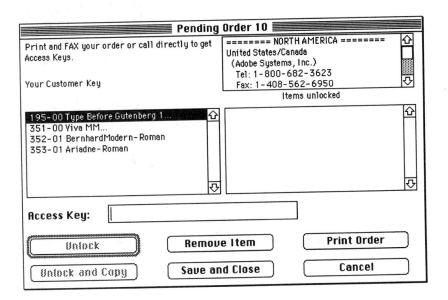

Fonts Online

A growing number of font companies are going online to provide information about their wares. Some let you preview their fonts on commercial online services such as CompuServe and America Online. A few font vendors even let you order online; if you have a CompuServe account, for example, you can order Treacyfaces fonts 24 hours a day (select the Go command and type "DTP OnLine" to enter the CompuServe DTP OnLine area).

Other vendors have made their way to the Internet's World Wide Web. If you have access to the Web, you can order fonts from more than 30 companies, including Alphabets Inc., Emigre, Red Rooster, and T-26, at the DesignOnline home page (http://www.dol.com). Through DesignOnline you can order the *International Typefounders CD-ROM*, which lets you unlock any of its more than 3000 fonts on demand, as described in the previous section. You can also order fonts online via the DesignOnline page; you can receive either the unlocking code for a font on the *International Typefounders CD-ROM*, or receive the font itself as electronic mail. (Note: If you don't know much about the World Wide Web, but would like to learn, there are plenty of good introductory books on the subject. It's all the rage these days.)

You can also peruse some of Adobe's fonts at their site on the World Wide Web (http://www.adobe.com/Type). This site also provides information on other Adobe type products. Here's a sample of some of the fonts you can view on-screen (shown here are samples from the Wild Type collection):

While you're hanging around on the Web, you should check out Will-Harris House (http://www.will-harris.com), the online domain of longtime type fiend Daniel Will-Harris. In this amusing and informative Web site, Mr. Will-Harris fontificates on various matters typographical, including tips on using type and descriptions of his favorite faces.

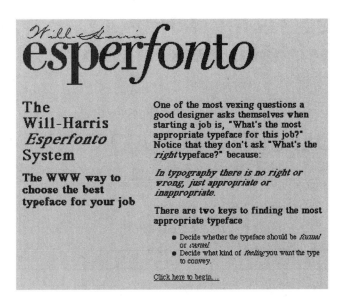

If you frequent the online world, you'll no doubt come across more type resources as time marches on. Look in your online service's desktop publishing area, or use a search utility and look for "Fonts."

Meanwhile, here's an old-fashioned paper-and-ink resource to help you start your typeface library: the following pages show samples from many of the major Mac type sellers (and some of the minor ones). The samples will give you a taste of what each vendor offers; for example, if a company offers text, display, and decorative faces, the illustration will most likely show some of each. Once you're ready to buy some fonts, you might have questions about which font format to choose (PostScript or TrueType); font formats and other technical issues are discussed in the next chapter.

Adobe Systems

Barmeno Bold

ABCDEFGHIJKLMNOPQRSTUVWXYZ
abcdefghijklmnopqrstuvwxyz123456

ITC Berkeley Oldstyle

ABCDEFGHIJKLMNOPQRSTUVWXYZ
abcdefghijklmnopqrstuvwxyz123456

Bernhard Modern

ABCDEFGHIJKLMNOPQRSTUVWXYZ
abcdefghijklmnopqrstuvwxyz123456

Caslon Book

ABCDEFGHIJKLMNOPQRSTUVWXYZ
abcdefghijklmnopqrstuvwxyz123456

Graphite

ABCDFGHIJKLMNOPQRSTUVWXYZ
abcdefghijklmnopqrstuvwxyz123456

Adobe Systems *(continued)*

ITC Isadora Bold

ABCDEFGHIJKLMNOPQRSTUVWXYZ
abcdefghijklmnopqrstuvwxyz123456

Lithos

ABCDEFGHIJKLMNOPQRSTUVWXYZ
1234567890

Lucida Sans

ABCDEFGHIJKLMNOPQRSTUVWXYZ
abcdefghijklmnopqrstuvwxyz123456

Nofret Bold

ABCDEFGHIJKLMNOPQRSTUVWXYZ
abcdefghijklmnopqrstuvwxyz123456

Trajan Bold

ABCDFGHIJKLMNOPQRSTUVWXYZ
1234567890

Agfa Division, Bayer Corp.

Eaglefeather Informal Bold

ABCDEFGHIJKLMNOPQRSTUVWXYZ
abcdefghijklmnopqrstuvwxyz123456

Garth Graphic

ABCDEFGHIJKLMNOPQRSTUVWXYZ
abcdefghijklmnopqrstuvwxyz123456

Letraset Romic Light

ABCDEFGHIJKLMNOPQRSTUVWXYZ
abcdefghijklmnopqrstuvwxyz123456

ITC Tiepolo

ABCDEFGHIJKLMNOPQRSTUVWXYZ
abcdefghijklmnopqrstuvwxyz123456

Visigoth

ABCDEFGHIJKLMNOPQRSTUVWXYZ
abcdefghijklmnopqrstuvwxyz123456

Alphabets, Inc.

Egyptian Bold Condensed

ABCDEFGHIJKLMNOPQRSTUVWXYZ
abcdefghijklmnopqrstuvwxyz123456

Fusion

ABCDEFGHIJKLMNOPQRSTUVWXYZ
abcdefghijklmnopqrstuvwxyz123456

Koch Antiqua Demi

ABCDEFGHIJKLMNOPQRSTUVWXYZ
abcdefghijklmnopqrstuvwxyz1234567890

Temerity

ABCDEFGHIJKLMNOPQRSTUVWXYZ
abcdefghijklmnopqrstuvwxyz123456

Venezia

ABCDEFGHIJKLMNOPQRS
TUVWXYZ1234567890

Bitstream

Bitstream Amerigo

ABCDEFGHIJKLMNOPQRSTUVWXYZ
abcdefghijklmnopqrstuvwxyz123456

Bitstream Carmina

ABCDEFGHIJKLMNOPQRSTUVWXYZ
abcdefghijklmnopqrstuvwxyz123456

Bitstream Cataneo

ABCDEFGHIJKLMNOPQRSTUVWXYZ
abcdefghijklmnopqrstuvwxyz123456

ITC Charter

ABCDEFGHIJKLMNOPQRSTUVWXYZ
abcdefghijklmnopqrstuvwxyz123456

Bitstream Chianti

ABCDEFGHIJKLMNOPQRSTUVWXYZ
abcdefghijklmnopqrstuvwxyz123456

Bitstream *(continued)*

Bitstream Cooper

ABCDEFGHIJKLMNOPQRSTUVWXYZ
abcdefghijklmnopqrstuvwxyz123456

ITC Galliard

ABCDEFGHIJKLMNOPQRSTUVWXYZ
abcdefghijklmnopqrstuvwxyz123456

Mirarae

ABCDEFGHIJKLMNOPQRSTUVWXYZ
abcdefghijklmnopqrstuvwxyz123456

Bitstream Mister Earl

ABCDEFGHIJKLMNOPQRSTUVWXYZ
abcdefghijklmnopqrstuvwxyz123456

Bitstream Oz Handicraft

ABCDEFGHIJKLMNOPQRSTUVWXYZ
abcdefghijklmnopqrstuvwxyz123456

Castle Systems Design

Goudy Stout

ABCDEFGHIJKLMN
OPQRSTUVWXYZ

Koloss

ABCDEFGHIJKLMNOPQRSTUVWXYZ
abcdefghijklmnopqrstuvwxyz
1234567890

Metropolis Bold

ABCDEFGHIJKLMNOPQRSTUVWXYZ
abcdefghijklmnopqrstuvwxyz123456

Rudolf

ABCDEFGHIJKLMNOP
QRSTUVWXYZ

Schneidler Initials

ABCDEFGHIJKLMNOPQRS

Judith Sutcliffe:
The Electric Typographer

Electric Hand

ABCDEFGHIJKLMNOPQRSTUVWXYZ
abcdefghijklmnopqrstuvwxyz123456

Flourish

ABCDEFGHIJKLMNO PQRSTUVWXYZ
abcdefghijklmnopqrstuvwxyz123456

Santa Barbara Electric

ABCDEFGHIJKLMNO
PQRSTUVWXYZ
ABCDEFGHIJKLMNOPQRSTUVWXYZ123456

Oldstyle Chewed

ABCDEFGHIJKLM
ABCDEFGHIJK

Emigre Graphics

Modula Bold

ABCDEFGHIJKLMNOPQRSTUVWXYZ
abcdefghijklmnopqrstuvwxyz123456

Remedy Double

ABCDEFGHIJKLMNO
PQRSTUVWXYZ
abcdefghijklmnopqrstuvwxyz
1234567890

Senator Demi

ABCDEFGHIJKLMNOPQRSTUVWXYZ
abcdefghijklmnopqrstuvwxyz123456

Totally Gothic

ABCDEFGHIJKLMNOPQRSTUVWXYZ
abcdefghijklmnopqrstuvwxyz123456

The Font Bureau

Belucian Book

ABCDEFGHIJKLMNOPQRSTUVWXYZ
abcdefghijklmnopqrstuvwxyz123456

Bodega Serif Medium Oldstyle

ABCDEFGHIJKLMNOPQRSTUVWXYZ
abcdefghijklmnopqrstuvwxyz123456

Fobia

Munich Bold

ABCDEFGHIJKLMNOPQRSTUVWXYZ
1234567890

FontHaus

Felt Tip Roman

ABCDEFGHIJKLMNOPQRSTUVWXYZ
abcdefghijklmnopqrstuvwxyz123456

Lettrées Eclatées

ABCDEFGHIJKLMNOPQRSTUVWXYZ
abcdefghijklmnopqrstuvwxyz123456

Magnesium Grime

ABCDEFGHIJKLMN
OPQRSTUVWXYZ
1234567890

Parade Script

ABCDEFGHIJKLMNOPQRSTUVWXYZ
abcdefghijklmnopqrstuvwxyz123456

FontShop

Caustic Biomorph

ABCDEFGHIJKLMNOP
QRSTUVWXYZ123456

Confidential

ABCDEFGHIJKLMNOPQRSTUVWXYZ
ABCDEFGHIJKLMNOPQRSTUVWXYZ123456

Mambo Medium

ABCDEFGHIJKLMNOPQRSTUVWXYZ
abcdefghijklmnopqrstuvwxyz123456

Priska Serif

ABCDEFGHIJKLMNOPQRSTUVWXYZ
abcdefghijklmnopqrstuvwxyz123456

Tyson

ABCDEFGHIJKLMNOPQRSTUVWXYZ
abcdefghijklmnopqrstuvwxyz123456

Galápagos Design

Kristen

ABCDEFGHIJKLMNOPQRSTUVWXYZ
abcdefghijklmnopqrstuvwxyz123456

Fontoon

**ABCDEFGHIJKLMNOPQRSTUVWXYZ
abcdefghijklmnopqrstuvwxyz123456**

Maiandra

ABCDEFGHIJKLMNOPQRSTUVWXYZ
abcdefghijklmnopqrstuvwxyz123456

Stylus

ABCDEFGHIJKLMNOPQRSTUVWXYZ
abcdefghijklmnopqrstuvwxyz
1234567890

Image Club Graphics

Choc

ABCDEFGHIJKLMNOPQRSTUVWXYZ
abcdefghijklmnopqrstuvwxyz123456

Fajita Mild

ABCDEFGHIJKLMNOPQ
RSTUVWXYZ123456

Farfel Felt Tip

ABCDEFGHIJKLMNOPQRSTUVWXYZ
1234567890

Fragile

abcdefghijklmnopqrstuvwxyz
abcdefghijklmnopqrstuvwxyz123456

Jazz Poster

ABCDEFGHIJKLMNOPQRSTUVWXYZ
1234567890

ITC Fonts

ITC Anna

ABCDEFGHIJKLMNOPQRSTUVWXYZ
Z1234567890

ITC Bees Knees

ABCDEFGHIJKLMNOPQRSTUVWXYZ
1234567890

ITC Legacy Serif

ABCDEFGHIJKLMNOPQRSTUVWXYZ
abcdefghijklmnopqrstuvwxyz123456

ITC Mona Lisa Recut

ABCDEFGHIJKLMNOPQRSTUVWXYZ
abcdefghijklmnopqrstuvwxyz123456

ITC Officina Sans

ABCDEFGHIJKLMNOPQRSTUVWXYZ
abcdefghijklmnopqrstuvwxyz123456

Letraset USA

Bergell

ABCDEFGHIJKLMNOPQRSTUVWXYZ
abcdefghij-klmnopqrstuvwxyz123456

Dolmen

ABCDEFGHIJKLMNOPQRSTUVWXYZ
abcdefghijklmnopqrstuvwxyz123456

Faithful Fly

ABCDEFGHIJKLMNOPQR
STUVWXYZ1234567890

Jazz

ABCDEFGHIJKLMNOPQRSTVVWXYZ
abcdefghijklmnopqrstuvwxyz123

Hazel

ABCDEFGHIJKLMNOP
QRSTUVWXYZ123456

Letter Perfect

Silhouette

ABCDEFGHIJKLMNOPQRSTUVWXYZ
abcdefghijklmnopqrstuvwxyz123456

Spring

ABCDEFGHIJKLMNOPQRSTUVWXYZ
abcdefghijklmnopqrstuvwxyz1234567890

Spumoni

ABCDEFGHIJKLMNOPQRSTUVWXYZ
abcdefghijklmnopqrstuvwxyz123456

TomBoy

ABCDEFGHIJKLMNOPQRSTUVWXYZ
abcdefghijklmnopqrstuvwxyz123456

Linotype-Hell

Clearface Gothic

ABCDEFGHIJKLMNOPQRSTUVWXYZ
abcdefghijklmnopqrstuvwxyz123456

Duc de Berry

ABCDEFGHIJKLMNOPQRSTUVWXYZ
abcdefghijklmnopqrstuvwxyz1234567890

Diotima

ABCDEFGHIJKLMNOPQRSTUVWXYZ
abcdefghijklmnopqrstuvwxyz123456

Herculanum

ABCDEFGHIJKLMNOPQRSTUVWXYZ
1234567890

Industria Solid

ABCDEFGHIJKLMNOPQRSTUVWXYZ
abcdefghijklmnopqrstuvwxyz123456

Monotype

Bulmer

ABCDEFGHIJKLMNOPQRSTUVWXYZ
abcdefghijklmnopqrstuvwxyz123456

Cantoria

ABCDEFGHIJKLMNOPQRSTUVWXYZ
abcdefghijklmnopqrstuvwxyz123456

Centaur

ABCDEFGHIJKLMNOPQRSTUVWXYZ
abcdefghijklmnopqrsvwxyz123456

Gill Sans Display Extra Bold

ABCDEFGHIJKLMNOPQRSTUVWXYZ
abcdefghijklmnopqrsvwxyz123456

Ellington

ABCDEFGHIJKLMNOPQRSTUVWXYZ
abcdefghijklmnopqrstuvwxyz123456

T-26

Amplifier

ABCDEFGHIJKLMNOPQRSTUVWXYZ
abcdefghijklmnopqrstuvwxyz123

Divine

ABCDEFGHIJKLMNOPQRSTUVWXYZ
1234567890

Osprey

ABCDEFGHIJKLMNOPQRS
TUVWXYZ1234567890

Tema Cantate

ABCDEFGHIJKLMNOPQRSTUVWXYZ
abcdefghijklmnopqrstuvwxyz123456

Tetsuo Organic

ABCDEFGHIJKLMNOPQRSTUVWXYZ
abcdefghijklmnopqrstuvwxyz123456

Treacyfaces

Akimbo Light

ABCDEFGHIJKLMNOPQRSTUVWXYZ
abcdefghijklmnopqrstuvwxyz123456

Hôtelmoderne Serif

ABCDEFGHIJKLMNOPQRSTUVWXYZ
abcdefghijklmnopqrstuvwxyz123456

Guestcheck Heavy

ABCDEFGHIJKLMNOPQRSTUVWXYZ
abcdefghijklmnopqrstuvwxyz
1234567890

Raincheck

ABCDEFGHIJKLMNOPQRSTUVWXYZ
abcdefghijklmnopqrstuvwxyz123456

URW

Crillee Bold Italic T

ABCDEFGHIJKLMNOPQRSTUVWXYZ
abcdefghijklmnopqrstuvwxyz 123456

ITC Fenice Bold T

ABCDEFGHIJKLMNOPQRSTUVWXYZ
abcdefghijklmnopqrstuvwxyz123456

Frutus T

ABCDEFGHIJKLMNOPQRSTUVWXYZ
abcdefghijklmnopqrstuvwxyz123456

Mariage D

ABCDEFGHIJKLMNOPQRSTUVWXYZ
abcdefghijklmnopqrstuvwxyz1234567890

Plaza D

ABCDEFGHIJKLMNOPQRSTUVWXYZ
1234567890

Keeping Track of Your Collection

After looking at all those swell samples on the preceding pages, you're probably ready to go out and collect hundreds of typefaces. When you find that your collection has grown to the point that you can't keep track of all your faces, you might want to invest in a type-specimen generator such as Agfa TypeChart or Rascal Software's theTypeBook. These programs automatically print out sample pages for all your installed fonts—or for a group of fonts you select.

Type-specimen programs let you customize your specimen sheets, offering a variety of layouts and point sizes. A page created by theTypeBook is shown here:

4

Font Basics

Now that you know some of the fundamentals of typography, it's time to familiarize yourself with Macintosh fonts. This chapter describes the different font formats you're liable to encounter on the Macintosh. You'll learn basic font terminology and be able to recognize the icons that represent the various components of PostScript and TrueType fonts. To make sure you're comfortable working with fonts, several hands-on exercises let you dissect font icons to see what's in them. By the time you're done with this chapter you'll have a solid understanding of Macintosh fonts.

Screen Fonts

No matter what kind of font you buy, it will include a *screen font*, the characters that you see displayed on your Mac's monitor. Screen fonts are also called *bitmapped fonts*, since displayed characters are made up of a map, or grid, of tiny squares (these squares are sometimes called *pixels*, which is short for "picture elements"). The word *bit* stands for "binary digit," the 1s and 0s that make up computer instructions. Each pixel on the Mac's screen holds one bit of information: if a bit is 1, or "on," the pixel is black; if a bit is 0, or "off," the pixel is white.

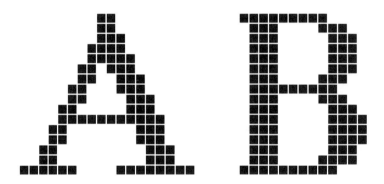

The Mac displays fonts—and everything else on the screen—at a resolution of 72 pixels per inch, more commonly called *dots per inch (dpi)*. When a document is printed on a dot-matrix printer, text is printed at 72 dots per inch; the printed characters are made up of dots that correspond to those on the screen. (Apple's ImageWriter, a dot-matrix printer that made its debut along with the first Macs, offered some improvement in print resolution by scaling down larger bitmapped fonts and printing them at 144 dpi when printing in Best-quality mode.)

When the Mac was introduced back in 1984, the only fonts available were bitmapped fonts. The Mac came with a basic set of fonts, and a number of companies sold collections of bitmapped fonts. A couple of programs, including Altsys's FONTastic, allowed people to create their own bitmapped fonts, and hundreds of homemade fonts cropped up on user-group disks and online bulletin boards.

Bitmapped fonts still exist, but nowadays hardly anybody prints directly from bitmaps. A resolution of 72 dpi (or even the 144 dpi provided by the ImageWriter's Best-quality mode) is unsuitable for high-quality printing. The notorious *jaggies*—the stair-step effect caused by the relatively large size of the dots that make up bitmapped fonts—make characters appear coarse and chunky. Also, bitmapped fonts come in a limited selection of sizes. A bitmapped font might come in 9-, 10-, 12-, 14-, 18-, and 24-point sizes, each of which was individually drawn by a font designer. If you select the 18-point size, for example, the font will display and print fine. But let's say you want to print the font at 16 points. Since that size isn't available, the Mac will do its best to scale the font by using information in the existing sizes, usually with miserable results:

Times 18 point is designed to be legible on screen.

Times 16 point has no corresponding screen font.

These days, bitmapped characters are still used for screen display—since the screen is still made up of a matrix of dots—but characters are printed using a superior technology called *outline fonts*. (Outline fonts are discussed in the following section.)

Screen fonts come packed in a suitcase icon with the letter *A* on it. In most cases, several sizes of a font will be packed into a suitcase. If you like, you can start up your Mac and take a look at some screen fonts right now; you'll understand fonts better if you know how to recognize the various icons that represent them. When your Mac's System software—the core software that enables your Mac to perform basic functions like opening applications and saving documents—was installed, several fonts from Apple were automatically placed in the System Folder (more on these fonts later).

Let's take a look at some screen fonts. (*Note:* To follow the steps below, you must be running System 7.1 or later. Font icons will be located in different places in earlier System configurations. If you're not sure which System version you're using, you can find out by choosing About This Macintosh from the Desktop's Apple menu.)

To look at some screen fonts, perform the following steps:

1. In order to see the font icons, you'll need to pull down the View menu on your Mac's Desktop and select "by Icon." (If you normally use another viewing option, such as "by Name," you can reselect it from the View menu after you finish this exercise.)

2. Locate your Mac's System Folder, which looks like this:

System Folder

Double-click on the System Folder to open it. (If necessary, select "by Icon" from the View menu to see the icons that reside in the System Folder. Depending on how your Mac's viewing preferences are set up, you may have to select "by Icon" from the View menu for each icon you open.)

3. Find the Fonts Folder, which looks like this:

Fonts

Double-click on the folder to open it. You'll see a number of icons that represent the fonts that are currently installed. For now, don't worry about what the icons look like.

4. Find the suitcase named New York. This suitcase holds the New York font, which comes with every Mac. New York was automatically added to the Fonts folder when your Mac's System software was installed.

New York

(*Note:* If you already have lots of fonts installed, you may find it easier to select "by Name" from the View menu and find New York that way.)

A suitcase is merely a place to store fonts. To see the icons that represent the fonts themselves, you'll have to look inside the suitcase. To see what's in the suitcase, double-click the suitcase icon (a tiny suitcase icon will appear next to the font's name if you're viewing by name; you can double-click this icon as well).

You should see a window that looks like this:

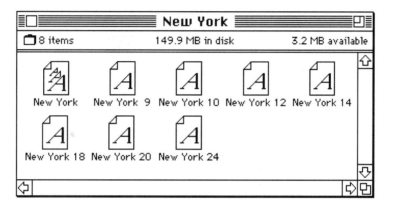

You're looking at the contents of the New York font suitcase. You'll see several icons shaped like a page with a folded corner, sporting the letter *A*. (For now, ignore the icon with three *A*'s on it; this icon will be discussed in the following section.) Each icon labeled with the name "New York" plus a number represents a particular point size of the New York screen font.

5. You can dig one level deeper into the contents of a font suitcase. Double-click on one of the screen-font icons, and you'll see a sample of the font in the selected size. The 12-point size of New York is shown here:

(*Note*: Leave this suitcase open if you want to learn more about its contents. We'll be looking at it again in the following section.)

Generally, you won't need to go poking around in font suitcases. Once a font is installed, it is automatically available to any program that supports fonts; you don't have to open a suitcase to get a screen font to appear as you type. This exercise was simply meant to familiarize you with what screen fonts look like and where they live. You'll feel more comfortable working with fonts if you know how to recognize their icons and look under the hood to see what's in them. (In this example, we looked at a screen font that was already installed when your Mac was set up; you'll learn how to install additional fonts in the next chapter.)

Here's a brief summary of screen fonts:

• Screen fonts (also called bitmapped fonts) are the characters that appear on your Mac's screen when you type some text.

• Screen fonts reside in a suitcase icon, which is located in the Fonts folder, which resides in the System Folder.

Outline Fonts

As mentioned in the previous section, bitmapped fonts are only half the equation for printing high-quality type. The 72-dpi resolution of bitmapped fonts wouldn't meet anybody's definition of typesetting. To print text at higher resolutions—from the 300 dots per inch of a low-end laser printer to the 2540 dpi of a typesetting service bureau's imagesetter—you need an *outline font*. (The folks at Apple—rebels that they are—sometimes call outline fonts *variable-size fonts* in their manuals, but we'll call them outline fonts here.)

The concept of outline fonts is unique to computer-based typesetting. In the days of hot-metal type, if you wanted to print a 12-point *g*, you'd use a piece of metal cast in the shape and size of a 12-point *g*. For a 14-point *g*, you'd use another piece of cast metal. And so on. Phototypesetting, which was popular in the 1970s and 80s, came closer to the concept of an outline font; a typesetting machine would photographically reduce or enlarge a master character to achieve the specified size. In the world of computer typesetting, an outline font is a master font that's stored as a mathematical outline made up of curves and control points. Outline fonts are *scalable*—a single outline can generate printed characters from as small as 1 point in size to more than 1000 points.

Outline fonts are also *resolution-independent*. The same outline can be used on your 300- or 600-dpi printer at home or on a service bureau's 1200- or 2500-dpi imagesetter. The outlines contain the information necessary to render the subtle curves, strokes, and line-weight variations that make up the characters of a typeface.

There are two basic types of outline fonts: TrueType and PostScript. We'll look at both types in this chapter.

TrueType Fonts

If you're new to Macintosh fonts, chances are the first fonts you'll see will be TrueType fonts. That's because Apple includes a set of TrueType fonts with the System software that comes with every Mac (System 7 and later). When you install your Mac's System software, the following TrueType fonts are automatically installed:

- **Chicago**
- `Courier`
- Geneva
- Helvetica
- Monaco
- New York
- Times
- Symbol ($\alpha\beta\chi\delta\epsilon$)

TrueType is Apple's own outline-font format, developed to loosen Adobe's grip on outline-font technology. (Adobe developed PostScript, the original format for Macintosh outline fonts; PostScript fonts will be discussed next.) TrueType came out along with the first version of System 7, which was released in 1991.

When TrueType was announced, the computer press churned out a frenzy of "Font Wars" articles, wondering which font format would predominate. As it turns out, the wars were more of a skirmish. The winner: owners of IBM PCs. TrueType fonts are immensely popular in the Windows world. Although many of the major Mac font vendors—with the notable exception of Adobe—now offer fonts in both TrueType and PostScript formats, TrueType never really caught on in a big way for Mac users.

TrueType is here to stay, however. Because a set of TrueType fonts comes with the Mac, many Mac owners don't know—or care—which font format they're using. But you, dear reader, obviously care about fonts, or you wouldn't be reading this book. Read on, and you'll learn how TrueType fonts work. Later in this chapter, after PostScript fonts are described, we'll look at the pros and cons of both formats.

Each character in a TrueType font is based on a single outline that can be scaled to any size and printed at a variety of resolutions on a variety of devices. TrueType automatically works if System 7—or a later upgrade such as 7.1—is installed. If you're using System 6.0.7—or later System 6 upgrades—you must install a TrueType System extension. (The extension is included with some of Apple's printers, such as the StyleWriter II.)

The TrueType font outline contains the information necessary to scale the font to any size for screen display as well as printing. Therefore, if you specify 32-point type in, say, a page-layout program, TrueType generates a respectable-looking 32-point font on the screen. If you change your mind and decide you want 36-point text, TrueType creates a 36-point version from the master outline and displays it on the screen. Unlike the bitmapped fonts discussed earlier, TrueType doesn't need to use a set of hand-drawn fonts, in a limited number of sizes, for screen display.

Let's take a look at a TrueType font. At first glance, you can't tell whether a font is a TrueType font or not. Like the bitmapped fonts just described, TrueType fonts reside in a suitcase icon:

New York

If you followed the steps in the previous exercise (under "Screen Fonts"), you opened up the suitcase containing the New York font and looked at some of its contents. You looked inside an icon labeled with a single *A*, which denotes a screen font (also called a bitmapped font or a *fixed-size font*; Apple calls the bitmapped fonts in a TrueType suitcase fixed-size fonts, although they're just the same as the screen fonts described earlier in this chapter). If you're a tidy sort, and closed your suitcase instead of leaving its contents strewn about, follow the steps in the previous section to open the New York suitcase again.

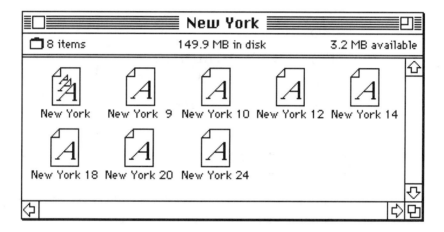

This time, we'll focus on the icon with three *A*s on it. This icon represents a TrueType font:

New York

Double-click on the icon, and this is what you'll see:

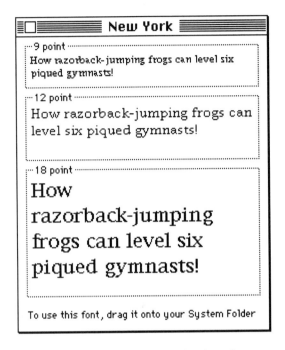

Three sizes of the New York font are displayed. You see three sample sizes, rather than just one, because TrueType fonts are outline fonts. Each of these sizes is generated from the TrueType master outline for the New York font. These are just representative samples; TrueType can create fonts of any size from the master outline. (The fonts shown here are what you'll see on the screen. They'll look much better when they're printed, because your printer will have a higher resolution than the screen's paltry 72 dots per inch.)

So, if TrueType can produce a font of any size from a master outline, what are all those other icons—New York 9, New York 12, and so on—doing in the New York font's suitcase? An excellent question. (Now you're starting to see why beginners often become confused when they're learning about Macintosh fonts.) Here's a subtle point: although TrueType fonts don't *need* a set of handcrafted bitmapped fonts for screen display, many TrueType fonts offer them anyway to provide the best possible display. While TrueType does a good job of scaling fonts from a master outline, the scaled fonts still don't look as good on screen as characters created by a human designer (see, we're not obsolete yet); therefore, a number of fixed-size fonts are included with Apple's core set of TrueType fonts.

In the following example, the top sample is a 9-point New York screen font created from a TrueType outline, while the bottom sample is the hand-made 9-point screen font that accompanies New York:

How razorback-jumping frogs can level six
piqued gymnasts!

How razorback-jumping frogs can level six
piqued gymnasts!

Note how the hand-drawn font is more readable than the TrueType-generated font, which is missing serifs on several characters. Although you don't need to have the fixed-size fonts installed, it's a good idea to keep them—they don't take up much disk space. There are three reasons to keep your fixed-size TrueType fonts (the icons with a single *A*):

Reason 1: As you can see in the example above, fixed-size fonts are more legible than screen fonts generated by TrueType, especially at small sizes.

Reason 2: Note how the line lengths are a little bit different in the 9-point New York example. If you create a document using TrueType fixed-sized fonts, then print it on another Mac that has only the TrueType scalable font (the icon with three *As* on it) installed, you'll get discrepancies in spacing and line breaks when you print your document.

Reason 3: If the fixed-size fonts are not installed, TrueType will have to use its scaling instructions to create screen fonts in those sizes from the font's outline data, taking up extra processing time (the scaling operation doesn't take up much processing time, mind you, but why waste any time when the prefab screen fonts are available?).

So, how do TrueType fonts work? Basically, each character in a font is made up of instructions that describe its shape in terms of points and curves. The "intelligence" necessary to scale the characters to any size is built into the font. The following illustration shows a letter from a TrueType font, displaying the points, lines, and curves that make up the letter, as well as some of the instructions that accompany it. The instructions specify which aspects of the character's shape should be preserved when it's scaled; a designer might want to keep stem weights consistent, for example, or eliminate serifs for screen display at small sizes.

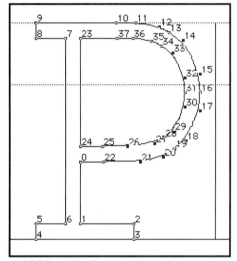

Instruction	Points
NPUSHB[0] 25	All
MDAP[1]	6
MDRP[29]	16
MIRP[13]	35, 31
SRP0[0]	6
MIRP[13]	35, 1
MIRP[13]	35, 24
IUP[1]	none
SVTCA[0]	none
MIAP[0]	1, 4
MIAP[0]	7, 9
MIRP[29]	24, 8
MDRP[4]	23
SRP0[0]	4
MIRP[29]	24, 5
MDRP[4]	1
SRP0[0]	4
MIRP[20]	30, 0
MIRP[13]	24, 24

© 1990 Apple Computer

TrueType technology allows font designers to add *hints*, instructions that tell a screen or printer where to place dots to make characters look as good as possible at any resolution. Since TrueType lets font designers use their own discretion when adding hints, some TrueType fonts are hinted better than others.

TrueType's instructions try to preserve a character's shape as closely as possible when the character is rendered at different sizes and resolutions. The process of altering an outline to approximate the character's shape when it's converted to pixels, or *rasterized*, is called *grid-fitting*.

The following illustration shows how a TrueType character would look at a low resolution (such as screen resolution) with no instructions, and how the same character appears when its instructions alter the outline so that the appropriate pixels fall within its boundaries.

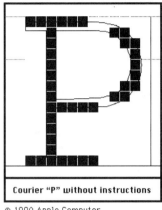 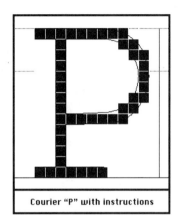

Courier "P" without instructions Courier "P" with instructions

© 1990 Apple Computer

As far as Mac outline fonts go, TrueType is the new kid on the block. Before TrueType was even a gleam in an Apple engineer's eye, PostScript outline fonts were well established in the Macintosh world. Which font format should you use? Read the following section on PostScript fonts, then the final section, which compares the two formats, and you'll be able to decide for yourself.

PostScript Fonts

Adobe Systems' PostScript is more than just a font format; it's a page-description language that handles both text and graphics. PostScript pretty much put the Macintosh on the map with the introduction of desktop publishing, which allowed regular schmoes like you and me, with little or no typesetting or graphics-design experience, to produce anything from newsletters to books with a personal computer. Although PostScript has been around for more than a decade—which makes it ancient in computer terms—it's still going strong. PostScript printers abound, and thousands of PostScript fonts are available from scores of vendors.

PostScript is the "brains" of printers such as Apple's LaserWriter series; the language is built into the printer. When you send a document to a PostScript printer, all the elements on a page—text and illustrations—are drawn by the printer's PostScript routines and then transferred to paper (see Chapter 7 for more information on printers). PostScript's ability to handle both text and graphics allows you to lay out an entire publication in a page-layout program, rather than treating type and illustrations as separate elements. (Having spent many hours of my youth pasting sections of type and graphics onto book pages using razor blades and hot wax, I was a big PostScript fan from the start.) Mapping out a whole page at a time is a memory-intensive task, but the printer itself is a powerful computer that contains a microprocessor and at least 1 megabyte (MB) of *RAM* (random-access memory) in which to store an image before printing it. These days, many PostScript printers come with at least 2MB of RAM, and you have the option of adding more RAM if you need it.

PostScript is a *device-independent language,* which means that text and graphics can be printed at the resolution of any PostScript-based output device. Many laser printers offer a resolution of 300 dots per inch, although 600-dpi printers such as Apple's LaserWriter Pro are becoming popular as prices continue to drop; some 600-dpi printers are now less than $1000. Laser printers with a resolution of 1200 dpi are available, but are not yet affordable for most home users. PostScript-based typesetting machines—usually called imagesetters because of their ability to set text and graphics—print at resolutions of around 1200 or 2500 dpi on coated paper or film. (This book was output on an imagesetter at 1200 dots per inch.)

PostScript printing devices create characters out of a matrix of dots, essentially filling in the characters' outlines. The higher a printer's resolution,

---

Type Trivia

PostScript is so named because it's a programming language that uses a syntax called *postfix notation,* which puts operators at the end of instructions (or, as they say in PostScript, operators at the end of instructions puts).

---

the better an outline font's characters will look. A resolution of 300 dpi is charitably called "near-typeset quality," while true typeset quality is achieved at 1200 dpi or higher. At 1200 dpi, the dots are small enough to produce any typographic subtleties—such as variations in stroke width or calligraphic flourishes at the ends of serifs—that a designer may have included in a face.

How do PostScript fonts work? Like TrueType fonts, PostScript fonts are outline fonts; each character is stored as a scalable outline made up of curves and control points. A single outline can generate characters of any size:

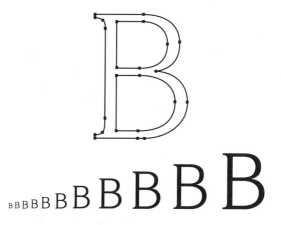

Type 1 and Type 3 PostScript

There are two subspecies of PostScript fonts: Type 1 fonts and Type 3 fonts (Type 2 was an evolutionary dead end, so you won't see any of those around). These days, almost all PostScript fonts are in Type 1 format, but you'll still see the occasional Type 3 PostScript font, so I'll briefly describe the two types.

In the beginning, there was Adobe. As the developer of PostScript, Adobe owned the proprietary technology necessary to make PostScript fonts that included hints. (Hints, you may remember from the discussion of TrueType, are instructions that make subtle alterations to character shapes, making them look as good as possible when printed at relatively low resolutions such as the original LaserWriter's 300 dots per inch.) Hints are especially helpful when type is printed at small sizes—say, 9 points or smaller—where character shapes can easily become distorted. Let's say you're printing a 7-point letter *n* on a 300-dpi PostScript laser printer. Without hints, the left-hand stem might come out wider than the right-hand stem. The hinting instructions could decide to make both stems the same width (assuming they're supposed to be of equal widths in that particular typeface). Although the overall shape of the *n* may be compromised a little by the hinting instructions' decision, the printed result still looks better than an *n* with lopsided stem weights.

Because Adobe controlled the PostScript font-making environment, other font developers pretty much had three options: 1) license Adobe's font-development technology (Linotype, Monotype, and Agfa did just that); 2) develop their own hinting techniques (Bitstream went that route); or 3) build unhinted, Type 3 PostScript fonts (anybody who couldn't afford option 1 or 2 chose this option). Fontographer, an affordable font-creation tool from Altsys, allowed designers to create Type 3 PostScript fonts. A cottage industry was born, as hundreds of aspiring font designers set up shop in their homes and offices. Unfortunately, Type 3 fonts often looked less crisp than Type 1 fonts at low resolutions.

Then, in 1990, Apple forced Adobe's hand by announcing TrueType, which was billed as an open development environment (meaning any font developer could have access to the code for creating characters and adding hints), rather than a proprietary technology like Adobe's. Adobe finally relented, and published the specifications for Type 1 PostScript. Nowadays, almost all font developers create fonts in Type 1 PostScript format. And it's not just the large digital-type foundries that produce Type 1 fonts; Fontographer now supports the Type 1 format, enabling its users to create high-quality PostScript fonts (Fontographer is discussed in Chapter 6).

Type 3 PostScript fonts haven't quite died out, since they have one advantage over their Type 1 cousins: the characters in Type 3 fonts can be more elaborate than Type 1 characters. For example, characters in a Type 3 font can contain shades of gray, graduated fills that go from light to dark, or variable stroke weights. In essence, a Type 3 font can be more like a PostScript graphic than a font.

Screen Fonts and Printer Fonts

Now let's look at the anatomy of a PostScript font. Unlike TrueType fonts, which reside in a single suitcase icon, each PostScript font consists of two separate icons. (*Note:* Just when you thought things were getting complicated enough, another variable rears its ugly head. If you've installed the QuickDraw GX component of System 7.5, the GX installer has automatically converted each of your installed PostScript fonts from two icons to a single suitcase icon. See Chapter 9 for a discussion of QuickDraw GX fonts.)

A PostScript font is made up of two components: a screen font and a printer font. The screen-font icon contains the bitmapped characters that are displayed on your monitor, while the printer-font icon contains the scalable outlines used to print the font's characters at any size.

Before we look at PostScript font icons, a couple more definitions are in order. If you own a PostScript printer, it has a set of *built-in* or *resident* PostScript fonts, which are permanently installed in its *ROM* (read-only memory). These fonts are available every time you turn on the printer (printers are discussed in more detail in Chapter 7). You won't see any printer-font icons for these fonts (unless you've added them to use with Adobe Type Manager, which is discussed later in this chapter), since the font outlines are built into the printer. You will see screen font icons for these fonts, however, since the Mac needs to display a bitmapped font on the screen. If you want to use a font that isn't included with your printer, you can buy PostScript fonts from Adobe or dozens of other vendors, or get them from Mac user groups or online services such as CompuServe or America Online. These fonts are called *downloadable fonts*, because the outline information must be loaded into the printer before the font can be printed. We'll look at downloadable fonts in the step-by-step exercise below.

Now we'll look at a PostScript font—assuming you have one installed. Since the Mac doesn't come with a set of PostScript fonts, you might not be able to follow along on your Mac, as you could with the TrueType exercise. But even if you don't look at the innards of PostScript font icons, reading this section will help you understand how PostScript fonts work. (If you're not sure whether any PostScript fonts are installed on your Mac, follow along and you'll soon find out. If you need help installing PostScript fonts, see the section on font installation in the following chapter.)

As in the earlier exercises, we're assuming that you're using System 7.1 or later (but not System 7.5 with QuickDraw GX), and that you've selected "by Icon" from the Desktop's View menu; select View by Icon, if necessary, each time you open an icon.

1. Double-click on your Mac's System Folder to open it.

System Folder

2. Within the System Folder, you'll see a folder called Fonts. Double-click on it.

Fonts

3. Inside the Fonts folder, you'll see icons for all your installed fonts, whether they're bitmapped, TrueType, or PostScript. If you have PostScript fonts installed, their screen-font components will show up as suitcase icons.

Romic

Unfortunately, you can't tell just by looking at a suitcase icon whether it contains a bitmapped font, a TrueType font, or a PostScript font's screen-font component. You'll have to open the suitcase to find out.

4. Double-click the suitcase icon to view its contents. The contents of a PostScript font's screen-font suitcase look something like this:

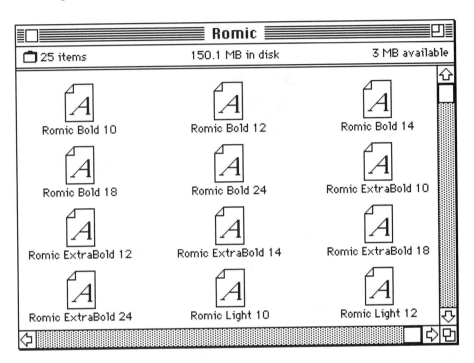

You'll see a number of screen-font icons, each labeled with a font name, followed by a weight or style description (Bold, Light, Italic, and so on) and a point size. (If you also see an icon with three *A*s on it, you'll know you've opened a TrueType font suitcase; see the previous section for details.) Each of these icons denotes a hand-drawn bitmapped font, in a particular size, that is used to display characters on the screen.

The contents will vary from one suitcase to another; certain fonts might have only one weight or style, for example, while others might have additional weights or styles (Semibold, Black, Condensed, or Oblique, for instance).

5. Double-click on one of the screen-font icons to see a sample of that font, in the particular size and style you've selected.

Now we're ready to look at the second half of a PostScript font: the printer font. If you haven't already done so, close the windows from the screen-font suitcase you were just looking at.

1. If you've just finished looking at screen fonts, you should still be in the Fonts folder. If you're starting from scratch, open your Mac's System Folder, then the Fonts folder. Finally, make sure you've selected "by Icon" from the View menu.

If any PostScript fonts are installed on your Mac, you'll see some icons in the Fonts folder that aren't suitcases. Now, that's a roundabout way to describe something (does she tell people, "When you go to the zoo, you'll see a lot of animals that aren't giraffes"? you may be thinking). But I have my reasons. Font companies give their printer fonts all manner of different icons, so I can't say that a printer-font icon looks like such-and-such. Here are a few examples of printer-font icons:

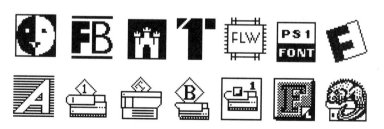

PostScript fonts from Adobe Systems are very popular (Adobe developed PostScript, you'll recall). Their printer-font icons look like this:

ParkAve

Unlike screen-font suitcases, which show a font's full name, printer-font icon names are generally abbreviated versions of the font's name and weight or style.

If you see a strange-looking icon in your Fonts folder, chances are it's a PostScript printer-font icon. If you have any doubts about a strange icon you find in your Fonts folder—or anywhere else on your Mac—you can easily see whether it's a printer font.

Birds

2. Click once on the mystery icon to select it. It will become highlighted to show it's selected. Press the ⌘ and I keys—the keyboard shortcut for the Get Info command—and you'll see an Info window that indicates that you're looking at a PostScript font.

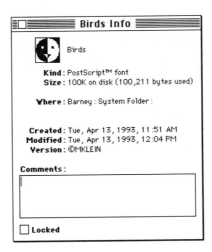

There's another way to tell whether an icon represents a PostScript printer font. I've been telling you to view your Font folder's contents by icon so you can see what the different types of font icons looks like. But if you select "by Name" from the View menu, you'll get the following view of your Font folder's contents.

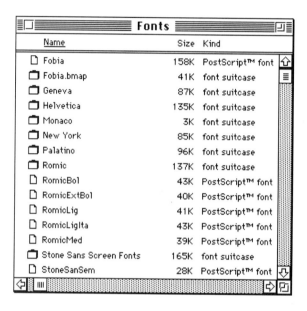

This view isn't very helpful for identifying suitcase icons; they're simply labeled "font suitcase," whether they contain TrueType fonts or screen fonts for PostScript fonts (some font vendors are kind enough to attach handy labels like "bmap" or "Screen Fonts" to their screen-font suitcases, but you can't count on that). Printer fonts are conveniently labeled "PostScript™ font" in this window, however.

There. Now you know how to recognize the screen fonts and printer fonts that go together to make up a PostScript font. To recap, a PostScript font is a scalable, or outline, font, which means it will look good when printed at any size. You can print downloadable PostScript fonts on a PostScript printer with the screen-font and printer-font components just described. But to make the most of PostScript fonts, you need one more component, an add-on utility called *Adobe Type Manager.*

Adobe Type Manager (ATM)

When PostScript fonts were introduced, they had some limitations. For starters, they had a limited number of sizes that could be displayed clearly on the screen. If you refer to the description of screen fonts above, you'll see that each PostScript font comes with a set of hand-drawn bitmapped fonts (also called screen, fonts), in a certain number of sizes.

A program's Font menu indicates which screen-font sizes are installed by highlighting those sizes:

```
✓ Other...    ⌘⇧\
  7 pt
  9 pt
  10 pt
  12 pt
  14 pt
  18 pt
  24 pt
  36 pt
  48 pt
  60 pt
  72 pt
```

As described earlier in this chapter, in the section on screen fonts, if a particular size isn't available, the Mac's System software will do its best to create a screen font, but the results usually aren't pretty. (In the menu shown above, if you choose the 48-point option—a screen-font size that isn't available—you'll get characters with the jaggies.) Since PostScript fonts also include an outline font, output from a PostScript printer looked fine at any size, but reading uninstalled sizes on the screen was no fun. Enter Adobe Type Manager (ATM).

ATM is a utility from Adobe that creates legible screen fonts of virtually any size for Type 1 PostScript fonts. ATM takes the information in a PostScript font's outline—the printer-font component—scales the characters to any size you specify, and rasterizes the characters, converting the outline data to dots for screen display or printer output.

Here's an example of some screen fonts without ATM installed:

Scaling away

Scaling away

Scaling away

Here are the same screen fonts created by ATM:

Scaling away

Scaling away

Scaling away

As you can see, ATM does a good job of creating screen fonts at various sizes, freeing you from the limitations of hand-drawn screen fonts. In fact, ATM does such a good job of creating screen fonts that many people save hard disk space by installing only a couple of screen-font sizes (usually 10 and 12 points) and letting ATM create the rest on the fly. (You'll learn how to install fonts in the next chapter.) Unless you're really short on disk space, however, I'd recommend leaving all your screen fonts tucked away in their suitcases. For one thing, screen fonts don't take up *that* much disk space; they typically run from 8K to 20K per size. Installing selected sizes (or throwing away sizes that are already installed) takes time, and—according to an Adobe representative—you run a slight risk of corrupting a suitcase file's data if you open it and add or remove screen fonts. More important, ATM takes some time to perform the scaling calculations necessary to display screen fonts, whereas fixed-size screen fonts display right away. Why waste time waiting for

ATM to create an 18-point screen font if you can have a prefab one immediately available?

In addition to providing readable screen fonts at virtually any size, ATM has another advantage. It lets you print PostScript fonts on non-PostScript printers such as Apple's StyleWriter. A PostScript printer, remember, has the powerful PostScript language built into it. The printer possesses the "intelligence" that's used to scale the fonts and graphics it prints. A non-PostScript printer (sometimes called a *QuickDraw printer* because it uses the Mac's built-in QuickDraw routines to create text and graphics) has no built-in page-description language, no built-in fonts, no "intelligence." It takes its orders from the Mac, printing whatever information is sent to it. Its main advantage is that it's much cheaper than a PostScript printer. Since such a printer has no font-scaling capabilities, it can't print downloadable PostScript fonts. It can, however, print PostScript fonts that have been scaled by Adobe Type Manager. ATM, remember, is a rasterizer—a program that converts outline data to dots. You've already seen how this works for screen display. But ATM also rasterizes font outlines to whatever resolution a printer supports. Therefore, if a QuickDraw printer outputs pages at 300 dpi, a font rasterized by ATM will print at 300 dpi, producing printed text that looks just as good as output from a 300-dpi PostScript printer.

(*Note:* ATM doesn't work with your PostScript printer's built-in fonts. Because the printer's resident fonts are built into its ROM, ATM has no way of accessing their outlines; ATM works only with downloadable PostScript fonts. If you want to use ATM to scale PostScript printer fonts such as Times and Helvetica, you can install the printer fonts that come with the ATM package. Also, if you buy a PostScript laser printer such as the Laser-Writer Pro from Apple, you won't need to use ATM to scale the screen fonts that correspond to the printer's resident fonts. That's because Apple includes a set of TrueType fonts for screen display, allowing TrueType to do the on-screen font scaling—the printer still prints PostScript fonts, however. If you find the thought of using TrueType fonts with a PostScript printer confusing, I don't blame you; see Chapter 9 for an explanation of how this works.)

ATM is a Control Panel. You can use the installer program that comes with ATM, or you can simply drag the ATM icon onto your System Folder, and it will be automatically placed in the Control Panels folder.

To see the ATM Control Panel once ATM is installed, perform the following steps.

1. Double-click the System Folder to open it.

System Folder

2. Double-click on the Control Panels folder. (Or, you can choose Control Panels from the Apple menu, then choose ATM from the submenu.)

Control Panels

3. Double-click on the ATM icon; click on it once if you have System 6.

~ATM™

You'll see the following Control Panel:

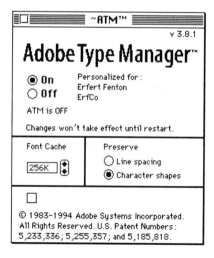

You can customize ATM in a number of ways.

• The Font Cache determines the amount of memory that's available for the data ATM creates as it's building fonts. The default amount is 256K. If your applications scroll at a glacial rate or take a long time to display characters on the screen, try increasing the font cache by clicking the up arrow. Adobe recommends at least 50K for each PostScript font you use frequently. Of course, you don't have an unlimited amount of RAM in your computer; you'll have to adjust your font cache in relation to how much RAM you have, and how much of that is being used by other applications. (From the Desktop, choose About This Macintosh from the Apple menu to see how much unused RAM your Mac has.)

• Choose "Preserve line spacing" if you want the line spacing (leading) on your screen to approximate that of your printed output. With this option selected, accented characters may be compressed on the screen so they fit in the same space as unaccented characters. (This option affects only displayed characters, not printed ones.) If you choose "Preserve Character shapes," extra space will be added between lines so accented characters will display without any distortion. This option may affect line and page breaks, however, so you may not want to use it.

• The "Substitute for missing fonts" option will be gray—the Mac's way of telling you an item isn't available—unless you've installed Adobe's Super ATM utility. Super ATM is discussed in Chapter 8.

Installing ATM is easy. If you buy the ATM package from Adobe, you simply run an installer program and ATM installs automatically, along with 30 fonts that come with the package. ATM is also included with other Adobe font collections (Adobe Type Basics and Adobe Value Pack, for example) or font families. If your copy of ATM comes as an ATM icon, rather than rolled into an installer program, simply drag the icon into your System Folder to install it, then follow the instructions above to open the ATM Control Panel and adjust the settings if you wish. (*Note:* ATM, like many other programs, is often updated. Be sure to check the Read Me file that accompanies the version of ATM you're installing.)

OK. Now you know how to recognize the screen and printer fonts that together make up a PostScript font. And you've learned how ATM uses a font's outline data to create scaled fonts that you can display on the screen and print on a PostScript or non-PostScript printer. Before we go on to a quick comparison of PostScript and TrueType fonts, let's look at one more type of PostScript font: Adobe's Multiple Master format.

Multiple Master Fonts

Digital fonts have many advantages over their precursors—you never end up spilling hot lead all over your lap, for one—but they have some drawbacks as well. Alas, some of the niceties of fine typesetting were lost in the transition from metal to silicon. Among these was a feature called *optical scaling*, or *visual scaling*.

When a computer creates a font by scaling a master outline, the proportions of the character stay the same, whether it ends up being printed at 6 or 60 points. In the days of metal type, a 6-point *a* might look considerably different than its 60-point counterpart. Sure, hinting might alter the outline's shape a bit to accommodate the resolution of different output devices, but the characters are all derived from the same master outline.

If you've ever set PostScript type at a small size—say, at 6 or 7 points for a footnote—you might have been impressed at the clarity of the characters, but vaguely disappointed in the footnote's readability. A passage of 6-point text somehow looks too light and wispy; hairlines and serifs may be barely visible, or may drop out entirely because they're so small, and characters may appear cramped and too close to one another. On the other hand, letters set at large sizes for headlines might appear too beefy and loosely spaced. These visual flaws are by-products of using the same outline for characters of vastly different sizes.

In the days of metal type, designers didn't simply make large and small versions of the same master design; they realized that letterforms had to be specially tailored to be readable and aesthetically pleasing at different sizes. In those days, a distinct font was made for each point size within a typeface. The shape, weight, and proportions of a given character might vary considerably, depending on its size. Here's an example of how characters might differ from one size to another:

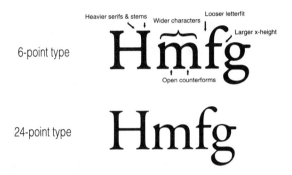

When digital fonts made their debut, optical scaling was seen as a necessary casualty of the technology. Then came *Multiple Masters*. In 1991, Adobe introduced a new font technology that brought optical scaling—and a number of other variable characteristics—to digital typographers. Multiple Master fonts are a type of PostScript font, but unlike the regular PostScript fonts we just looked at, Multiple Masters generate fonts from a number of master outlines, rather than just one (hence their name).

Depending on the design, a Multiple Master font might let you adjust character attributes such as weight, width, optical size, or even character style (one face offers subtle gradations between a serif and a sans serif face, for example). These attributes are called *design axes*, and they exist within a conceptual space called a *design matrix*. Uh oh. I'm starting to get metaphysical here. Let's look at an example.

Let's say a Multiple Master font has a design axis for character weight. There would be a light character at one end of the design matrix and a bold one at the other. Multiple Master technology allows you to choose not only the light or the bold weight, but any weight in between, allowing hundreds or thousands of weight variations, rather than the six or eight weights you might find in a traditional typeface family. This type of Multiple Master font is called a *single-axis design*, because it has only one design parameter: weight.

Got that so far? Now let's move on to a slightly more complex example. A Multiple Master font can let you change more than one design attribute at once by offering more than one design axis. You could, for example, change character weight and width, going from a light condensed face to an ultrabold expanded one. In this case the font would have two design axes: weight and width. Imagine a square with a master design at each corner: light condensed, light expanded, ultrabold condensed, and ultrabold expanded. The design matrix for this two-axis Multiple Master font would contain a series of characters that increased in both weight and width as the design progressed.

light condensed   light expanded

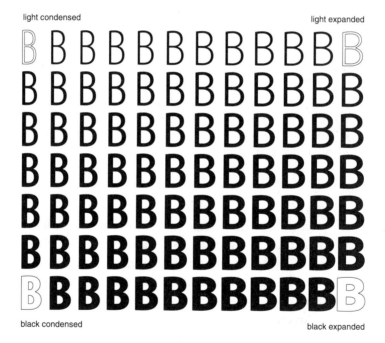

black condensed   black expanded

Now add a design axis for size, and you'll see the emergence of optical scaling. If you increase weight and width as characters in the design matrix get smaller, somewhere in the design matrix you'll get wide characters with thick stems, which are suitable for printing at small sizes. Somewhere else in the design matrix will be narrower, thinner characters suitable for printing at large sizes. Automated optical scaling may not rival the designs of sixteenth-century typographers, but it's a step in the right direction.

The "corners" of a Multiple Master's design matrix are defined by the font's designer. This precaution prevents aestheticall challenged users from squashing, stretching, or otherwise manipulating a font beyond the bounds of legibility as we know it.

The face used to set this book, Adobe Jenson, is a Multiple Master design that includes design axes for weight and optical scaling. Other Multiple Masters have design axes for weight and width. One Multiple Master face, Penumbra, lets you slide between a serif and a sans serif design. Here's a sample of Nueva, which has design axes for weight and width:

Captain of our fairy band,

Helena is here at hand;

And the youth, mistook by me,

Pleading for a lover's fee.

Shall we their fond pageant see?

Lord, what fools these mortals be!

Multiple Master fonts include a *base font,* which is the set of outlines used to create variations in weight, width, or any other design axes the font's designer has supplied. These variations are called *instances.* The set of preset styles and weights that come with each Multiple Master font are called *primary instances.*

You can adjust the design axes of Multiple Master fonts to create *custom instances* with Font Creator, a utility that comes with every Multiple Master package. Font Creator is automatically placed on your hard disk by an installer utility that comes with Multiple Master fonts. Double-click on the Font Creator icon to start it up.

Font Creator

You'll see the following window:

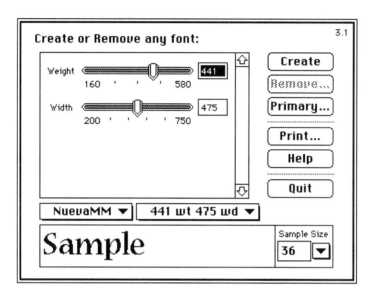

Font Creator's slider bars let you adjust design axes such as weight or width, and preview the results on the screen or click the Print button to print a specimen page showing various sizes. Other buttons let you remove an instance if you don't need it, or restore a primary instance that you've removed. Once you've created a custom instance that you like, click the Create button to save that instance. Your custom font will now appear in your applications' Font menu, just like any other font. Well, OK. Multiple Master screen fonts are not just like other fonts; they have horrendously cryptic names, like

AJenMMIt_348 RG 12 OP
AJenMMIt_348 RG 72 OP
AJenMMIt_348 RG 8 OP
AJenMMIt_556 SB 12 OP
AJenMMIt_556 SB 72 OP
AJenMMIt_556 SB 8 OP
AJenMMIt_684 BD 12 OP
AJenMMIt_684 BD 72 OP
AJenMMIt_684 BD 8 OP

I'll admit it. These names are not, shall we say, intuitive. But with a little practice, you can learn what the abbreviations mean. In this example, you're looking at the Myriad (Myria), Multiple Master (MM), Italic (It) font, in various weights (the numbers don't mean much unless you look at Font Creator's Weight slider bar, which for this font goes from 215 to 700 units), including light (LT), regular (RG), semibold (SB), bold (BD), and Black (BL). Myriad also has a design axis for width (again, the numbers refer to Font Creator's Width slider), which goes from condensed (CN) through normal (N), to semiextended (SE).

The menu above shows the primary instances, which come with the font. If you create some custom instances with the Font Creator, your menu might look something like this:

```
MyriaMMIt_215 LT 300 CN
MyriaMMIt_215 LT 600 NO
MyriaMMIt_215 LT 700 SE
MyriaMMIt_320 wt 340 wd
MyriaMMIt_320 wt 476 wd
MyriaMMIt_320 wt 636 wd
MyriaMMIt_400 RG 300 CN
MyriaMMIt_400 RG 600 NO
MyriaMMIt_400 RG 700 SE
MyriaMMIt_535 wt 700 wd
MyriaMMIt_565 SB 300 CN
MyriaMMIt_565 SB 600 NO
MyriaMMIt_565 SB 700 SE
MyriaMMIt_658 wt 348 wd
MyriaMMIt_658 wt 612 wd
MyriaMMIt_700 BD 300 CN
```

Custom instances that you cook up with Font Creator don't have weight or width abbreviations such as BD or CN; instead, they show numerical values for weight and width, and generic lowercase abbreviations for weight (wt) and width (wd).

You don't have to create custom instances to use Multiple Masters; each Multiple Master font comes with enough primary instances to suffice for many typesetting projects. But you're missing out on a great technology if you don't create your own custom styles and weights.

Despite the need for a secret decoder ring for font names, I love Multiple Master fonts. For less than the price of a traditional type family, you can create the weights, widths, or styles you need. If I'm going to set some reversed type (white type on a black or colored background), for example, I can use a Multiple Master font and add a little weight so stems and serifs don't drop out. Or if I want a custom demibold weight or condensed width for a book heading, I can use a Multiple Master to create it. A lot of people are intimidated by Multiple Masters, however, for one reason or another. With any luck, the previous discussion has presented the basics of Multiple Masters in a non-scary fashion. Remember, Multiple Masters are just PostScript fonts that include additional capabilities.

Which Format Should You Use?

Now that you understand the basics of TrueType and PostScript fonts, you may be wondering which format you should use. Actually, you can use both formats if you wish. I've successfully printed many documents that contain both TrueType and PostScript fonts on my PostScript laser printer. To avoid confusing both yourself and your Mac's System software, however, you should avoid having a TrueType font and a PostScript font with the same name on your Mac.

When it comes to the quality of printed output, it's a toss-up between PostScript and TrueType fonts. Some people say that TrueType's hinting creates better-looking characters than PostScript's at small sizes. I can't tell the difference with my naked eye. Both formats print just fine on a PostScript or QuickDraw printer (PostScript fonts require ATM if they're printed on a non-PostScript printer). PostScript and TrueType fonts generally cost about the same (some type vendors include fonts in both formats on their CD ROMs), so pricing probably won't affect your decision. It may simply come down to a matter of personal preference.

Each format does have some pros and cons, however. The following observations may steer you toward one format or the other.

TrueType Pros and Cons

Pros:

• Availability. A set of TrueType fonts comes with your Mac's System software. They're automatically installed and ready to use when you install the System.

• Convenience. A TrueType font comes in a single suitcase icon, whereas a PostScript font requires three components: a screen font, a printer font, and (for on-screen scaling or printing to non-PostScript printers) ATM.

• Printing ease. With TrueType fonts, you don't need an add-on utility like ATM to print documents on a non-PostScript printer.

Cons:

• Many service bureau operators don't like them. If you intend to print your documents at a typesetting service bureau, I'd advise you not to use TrueType. The imagesetters at service bureaus are PostScript-based, and the people who work there are accustomed to working with PostScript. Many service bureau operators have had trouble printing TrueType fonts, in part because some of the TrueType fonts from early collections were poorly made. In addition, TrueType uses the Mac to process fonts—rather than an image-setter's built-in PostScript routines—so printing can be slow.

I'm not saying that you can't take TrueType fonts to a service bureau; I'm just saying that many service bureau operators would prefer that you didn't. The situation has been gradually improving as service bureau personnel become accustomed to TrueType font, and as TrueType technology matures and font quality improves. As one service bureau manager told me, "Well, TrueType fonts are less of a nightmare than they used to be." Hardly a resounding endorsement. If you want to use TrueType fonts, check with your service bureau and find out its policy on TrueType.

• System software compatibility. You must install the TrueType System extension to use TrueType fonts with System 6.0.7 or 6.0.7. And you can't use TrueType at all with earlier versions of System 6.

PostScript Pros and Cons

Pros:

• Availability. Although many companies offer both TrueType and PostScript fonts, there are more PostScript font designs to choose from.

• Familiarity. Many Mac-based graphic designers and typesetters are accustomed to working with PostScript fonts, since these fonts have been around for a decade. If you plan on collaborating with someone on a publishing project, you may find that PostScript is the preferred format.

• Service bureau operators like it. Typesetting service bureaus use PostScript-based imagesetters. They're used to working with PostScript fonts, and have extensive PostScript font libraries. If you plan on printing documents at a service bureau, I'd strongly recommend PostScript fonts.

• Multiple Masters. Until QuickDraw GX is supported by more applications (see Chapter 9), TrueType fonts can't offer the versatility of Multiple Master fonts, which can create hundreds of weights, widths, and styles (as well as optical scaling) from a single set of outlines.

Cons:

• Multiple components. PostScript fonts require three components (screen fonts, printer fonts, and ATM), while TrueType fonts come in a single suitcase. This setup may change someday, but for now PostScript fonts are more of a chore to install and keep track of.

• ATM is needed for non-PostScript printers. You need to install ATM to print PostScript fonts on a non-PostScript printer, whereas TrueType fonts will print on a PostScript or non-PostScript printer with no software add-ons.

Now that you've looked under the hood of both TrueType and PostScript fonts, you should be ready to use them. The following chapters discuss installing and managing PostScript and TrueType fonts.

5
Font Installation
&
Management

The previous chapter introduced you to the iconography of PostScript and TrueType fonts. In this chapter, you'll learn what to do with those icons to put your Mac's fonts to work. You'll find out how to install PostScript and TrueType fonts, how to manage a large font collection, and how to spot and solve common font-related problems.

The good news: the basic procedure for installing fonts has gotten a lot easier since the early days of the Macintosh. The bad news: there are now enough variables—from different font formats to various versions of the Mac's System software—to bewilder anyone who's new to fonts. Don't worry; once you've read this chapter you should be able to install fonts—of any kind—on a Mac running just about any version of the System software.

Before you start, you should know which version of the System software—the core software that allows you to start up your Mac and run any program—your Mac is running. If you're not sure which version of the System you're using, here's what you do:

• From your Mac's Desktop—the screen you see when you turn on the computer—select About This Macintosh (or About the Finder, if that's what appears) from the Apple menu. A window that tells you, among other things, which System version you're running will appear:

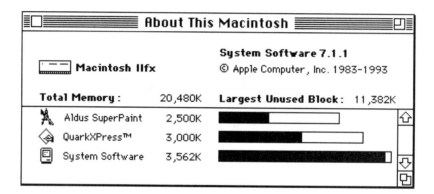

This window tells you what model of Mac you have, how much memory is installed, how much memory the System and your currently open applications are gobbling up, and what version of the System software is installed (version 7.1.1 in this example).

Installing Fonts

Once you know which version of the System you're using, turn to the appropriate section below. The procedure for installing fonts differs from one System version to another, so make sure you're reading the section that corresponds to your System.

Before you install any fonts, you should be familiar with the font icons and terminology presented in the previous chapter.

System 4

If you're using System 4, you must have strayed from the "Antiques" section of your local bookstore to the "Computers" section and picked up this book by mistake. If you want to run any current Mac software, you should upgrade your System to at least System 6.

System 6

If you're running any version of System 6—6.0, 6.0.1, and so on—you'll need to use a utility called the *Font/DA Mover* to install your fonts. (Allow me to take this opportunity to encourage you to upgrade your System software to System 7. It's much easier to install fonts under System 7; read the following sections if you're curious.)

Because installation instructions for PostScript fonts and TrueType fonts differ slightly, each format will be described separately.

Installing PostScript Fonts

The Font/DA Mover is included with the System 6 software disks. In the old days, it was included with some companies' fonts. Most people use some version of System 7 these days, however, so you won't necessarily find the Font/DA Mover included on a disk of fonts you buy.

Here's what the Font/DA Mover icon looks like:

Font/DA Mover

Cute, huh?

It may have a cute icon, but the Font/DA Mover is one of the least-loved pieces of software around, in part because it actually makes you do some work—locating files, clicking buttons, and so on. The Font/DA Mover isn't the most intuitive utility in the world, but it's not *that* bad. The following instructions should help demystify its operation.

To install a PostScript font in System 6, double-click on the Font/DA Mover icon to open it. The following window will appear:

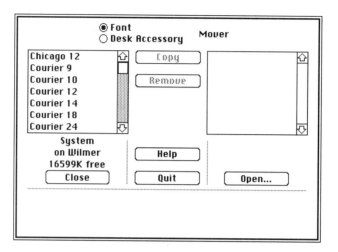

Make sure the Font button at the top is selected, or you'll be looking at a list of desk accessories instead of fonts.

In System 6, fonts are installed in the Mac's System file. In the Font/DA Mover, fonts that are already installed in the System appear in the left-hand column (the number following each font's name indicates the font's point size). Note that the left-hand column is labeled "System on *name of the current startup disk*." At this point, the right-hand column is empty.

To install some fonts, click on the Open button beneath the Font/DA Mover's right-hand column. A dialog box appears, asking you to locate the fonts you want to install:

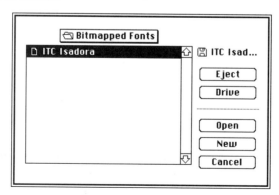

The fonts you want may be on a disk you've inserted, or you may have copied them to your hard disk. Click on the Drive button, if necessary, to find the font file you're looking for. (At this point, you're looking for bitmapped fonts, which, as you'll recall from the last chapter, reside in a suitcase icon; we'll get to printer fonts in a minute.) Once you've found the right font file, click on the Find dialog box's Open button. The fonts in the selected suitcase will appear in the right-hand column of the Font/DA Mover:

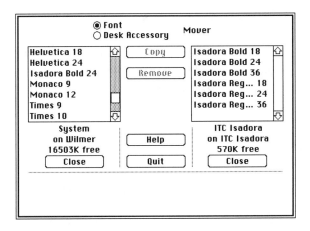

To install a font, first click on its name. The name will be highlighted, showing it's selected:

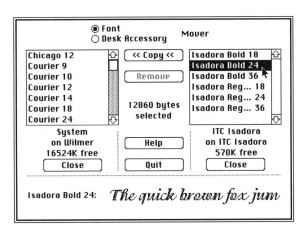

When you select a font, its name, its point size, and a sample sentence appear at the bottom of the Font/DA Mover window. The size of the font file, in bytes, appears in the center of the window.

You can select more than one font at a time if you wish. To choose several fonts, sweep the cursor down the list of font names. Or, to select several nonadjacent fonts, hold down the Shift key and click on each name you want to select. If you select more than one font at a time, the total number of bytes selected is displayed, but no sample text is shown.

To install the selected font or fonts in the System file, click on the Copy button. Note that the arrows on the Copy button point toward the left, indicating that the fonts in the right-hand column are being moved to the left-hand column (the System file).

Once a font is copied to the System file, its name appears in the left-hand column:

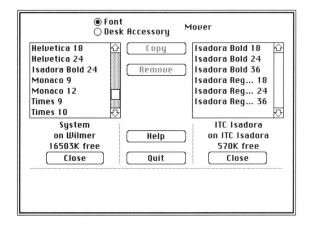

If you prefer, you can open a font suitcase first, then select the System file and install the fonts. In this case, the System file's contents appear in the right-hand column, and the fonts to be installed appear in the left-hand column. In the interest of not confusing yourself, however, I suggest you stick to the method just described.

You can also use the Font/DA Mover to remove unwanted fonts from the System file. (You might not need every style, weight, or size of a particular font family, for example.) To remove a font, select its name in the System-file column, then click on the Remove button. As with installing fonts, you can select several fonts at once for removal. But be careful when removing fonts: once you hit that Remove button, your fonts are gone forever. Make sure you have backup copies of all your fonts. That way, if you remove a font by accident, or if your System file bites the dust, you'll be able to reinstall all your fonts.

The Font/DA Mover can install up to 500 fonts. To the Font/DA Mover, a "font" is a particular typeface in a given size; 10-point Helvetica and 12-point Helvetica are treated as two separate fonts.

If you're using Adobe Type Manager (this utility was described in the previous chapter), you may want to save disk space by installing just a few sizes of each font family member. ATM will do the on-screen scaling for you, so you won't need every size available. If you know you're going to be using a font at a particular size, however, you might want to install the hand-drawn bitmap for that size. Keeping the number of installed fonts down is especially important in System 6, given the Font/DA Mover's 500-font limit and the fact that you don't want a bloated System file (it has to hold desk accessories too, remember).

The Font/DA Mover offers a way to help keep your System file slim. You can install fonts in an application—or even a document—rather than in the System. (Unlike fonts installed in the System, which are available to all applications, these fonts are available only in the specific program or document where you installed them.) To do so, double-click on the suitcase that contains the font or fonts you wish to install. The Font/DA Mover window will appear. Hold down the Option key, click on the Open button beneath the empty column, and select the disk or folder that holds the appropriate application or document. Follow the font-installation procedure just described to install the fonts; the only difference is their destination. This technique not only keeps the System file down to size, but it allows you to reduce clutter in font menus as well. For example, if you use a special architect's font in a drafting program, you can install the font just in that program, rather than having it intrude on the Font menu of every program you open.

The Font/DA Mover also lets you pack suitcases with customized collections of fonts. Let's say you use a particular set of fonts for everyday work, but occasionally need a specialized set for your monthly newsletter. If you can't comfortably fit both sets in your System file, you can place each set into its own suitcase icon, keeping each collection in a neat package rather than rummaging through a pile of floppy disks or searching your hard disk when you need to change font collections.

To create a custom suitcase, open the Font/DA Mover and find the first font you want to place in the suitcase; it can be in a suitcase or in the System file. Click on the Open button beneath the empty column, and the following dialog box will appear:

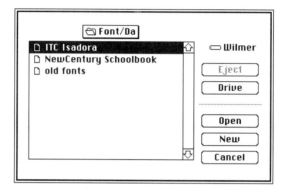

Instead of clicking on Open, as described earlier, click on the New button. A dialog box appears, asking you to name your new suitcase. Give it a descriptive name and click on the Create button.

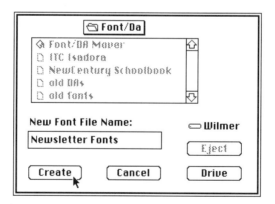

You can now transfer fonts to the new suitcase, just as you would to the System file. Insert disks, if necessary, to load fonts from different sources. The next time you need a set of fonts for a particular job, you can delete unnecessary fonts from the System file and install a set from your custom suitcase. (Although custom suitcases can come in handy for that monthly newsletter, you shouldn't use them to remove and reinstall fonts on a daily basis; constantly moving fonts to and from the System can eventually damage the System file.)

Well, after that lengthy discourse on the Font/DA Mover, you've only installed half of the files you need for PostScript fonts. You still need to install the printer fonts (if you don't know what a printer font is, review the previous chapter). When you buy a PostScript font, it comes with both screen and printer fonts. The printer fonts may be in their own folder, labeled "Printer Fonts" or "Outline Fonts," or they may be sitting in plain view when you insert the disk.

Fortunately, installing printer fonts in System 6 is much less of a chore than installing screen fonts. To install a printer font, you simply drag its icon into the System Folder. That's all there is to it.

Remember to install a printer font for every style and weight you wish to print. Eventually, you may find your System Folder awash in printer font icons. You may be tempted to tidy things up and put them in their own folder. Don't do it. System 6 requires printer font icons to be "loose" inside the System Folder.

Note: Your PostScript font disk also includes a file called "Metrics" or "AFM" (Adobe Font Metrics). You don't need to install this file; very few Mac applications require AFM files. (Of course, if an application's manual says you should install a font's AFM file, by all means install it.)

Installing TrueType Fonts

The original Font/DA Mover worked with PostScript and bitmapped fonts, since TrueType fonts didn't exist when the utility made its debut. If you're planning to install TrueType fonts under System 6, you need version 4.1 of the Font/DA Mover, as well as the TrueType INIT.

These items were released with Apple's pre–System-7 LaserWriter LS and StyleWriter printers, and can nowadays be downloaded from online services such as CompuServe and America Online.

To install TrueType fonts under System 6, place the TrueType INIT in the System Folder. Then, open the Font/DA Mover (version 4.1) and use it as described in the previous section. There's a slight difference between Post-Script and TrueType fonts when they're listed in the Font/DA Mover; unlike PostScript fonts, TrueType fonts don't display a point size after a font's name (they're scalable to any size, as you probably remember from the last chapter).

There's one more difference between installing PostScript and True-Type fonts: with TrueType, you don't have to install any printer fonts, because one icon takes care of everything.

System 7

Installing fonts in System 7 is a piece of cake. The following sections describe how to install PostScript and TrueType fonts. Well, OK, it's not quite as piece-of-cakey as all that; System 7.0 and 7.0.1 handle fonts in a slightly different manner than System 7.1 and later versions. The installation procedure is the same, but the font icons end up in different places. Here goes.

Installing PostScript Fonts

To install the screen-font component of a PostScript font, simply drag a suitcase icon—which contains a number of screen fonts—or a fixed-size font icon onto the (closed) System Folder:

Adobe Caslon   or   ACaslon Regular 14   →   System Folder

In System 7.0 and 7.0.1, screen fonts are automatically placed into the System file when you install them:

System

If you open the System file by double-clicking on its icon, you can see the screen fonts it contains. (You can drag font icons out of an open System file and into the Trash if you want to remove them.)

In System 7.1, 7 Pro, or 7.5, screen fonts are automatically placed in a folder called Fonts when you install them:

Fonts

If you open the Fonts folder by double-clicking on it, you can see the screen fonts it contains. (You can drag font icons out of the Fonts folder and into the trash if you want to remove them.)

To install a PostScript font's printer-font component, you drag its icon onto the (closed) System Folder.

MetroBol   System Folder

In System 7.0 and 7.0.1, the printer fonts are automatically placed in the Extensions folder.

Extensions

If you open the Extensions folder by double-clicking on it, you can see the printer fonts it contains. (You can drag font icons out of the Extensions folder and into the Trash if you want to remove them.)

In System 7.1, 7 Pro, and 7.5, printer fonts are automatically placed in the Fonts folder, along with the screen fonts.

Note: Your PostScript font disk also includes a file called "Metrics" or "AFM" (Adobe Font Metrics). You don't need to install this file; very few Mac applications require AFM files. (Of course, if an application's manual says you should install a font's AFM file, by all means install it.)

RomicMed.AFM

Installing TrueType Fonts

The procedure for installing TrueType fonts is the same as the procedure just described for installing PostScript fonts, with one exception: there are no printer fonts to install—and no AFM files to not install.

Font-Installation Tips

Now you know the basics of installing fonts. Rather than simply dragging every font file in sight into the System Folder, you may want to refine your font-installation strategy. That way, you'll save disk space, reduce your System's workload, and reduce the risk of font-related problems. Here are some factors to consider.

How Many Fonts Should You Install?

For starters, let's look at how many fonts you *can* install. (The following discussion assumes you're using System 7.1 or later.) Once you start installing fonts, it's easy to get carried away, dragging suitcase after suitcase into your System Folder. Sooner or later, however, you'll hit the wall; you'll see a dialog box that tells you you've reached the maximum number of fonts that can be installed. You may be dismayed, at first, to learn that you can install only 128 fonts. How can a person live with a paltry 128 fonts! Don't worry. This scary dialog box doesn't really mean you can use just 128 fonts at a time; what it should say is that you can install only 128 font *suitcases* at a time. As you'll soon see, that's another story entirely.

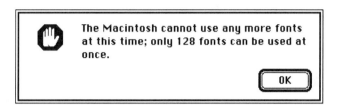

According to an Apple representative, a font suitcase (which, as you'll remember, can hold TrueType fonts and/or the screen-font component of PostScript fonts) can theoretically hold up to 16,381 fonts. (That number, by the way, represents the total number of fonts the System can handle.) Don't try this at home! The Apple spokesperson also said that if you try to put that many fonts in a suitcase, "your System will eventually choke." I don't doubt it. Not only that, but you might find yourself choking back tears if you placed several thousand fonts in a suitcase and that suitcase somehow became damaged, causing you to have to reinstall all those fonts. I'd suggest a more moderate approach. (For one chapter of this book, I placed 340 fonts in a single suitcase, but I consider even that number to be living dangerously.)

Here's my strategy for installing a safe and sane number of fonts. This method allows you to use a relatively large number of fonts, while still conserving disk space and System resources.

Font Installation Strategies

To install a large number of fonts without taking up a lot of space, follow the steps below. If you're using PostScript fonts, you should have Adobe Type Manager installed so screen fonts will be scaled properly.

1. Pick a suitcase. Any suitcase. As you learned in the last chapter, a suitcase is just a place to store fonts. While a font suitcase initially comes with one or more fonts packed inside it, the suitcase is not irrevocably tied to those

fonts; you can open the suitcase and move fonts in and out at will. You can even change the name of a suitcase icon to reflect the font collection it contains. (*Note:* While it's OK to change the name of a suitcase icon, you should *not* change the name of a printer-font icon.)

2. Give the suitcase a descriptive name, such as "Decorative Fonts," "Newsletter Fonts," or "Chapter 3 Fonts." In this example, we'll call the suitcase "My Fonts."

3. If you want to keep the fonts that are already in the suitcase, fine. If you want to remove them and start with an empty suitcase, double-click on the suitcase icon to open it, then drag the fonts it contains into the Trash; if you throw some fonts away, make sure you have a backup copy somewhere. (*Note:* If you want to keep the original suitcase intact and work on a copy, click on the suitcase to select it, then choose Duplicate from the File menu.)

Now you're ready to fill your suitcase with fonts.

4. Find a suitcase that has some fonts you'd like to put in the My Fonts suitcase. It can be on a floppy disk you've inserted or somewhere on your hard disk. Double-click on the suitcase to open it and view the fonts it contains:

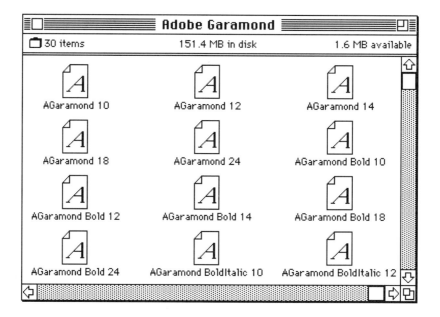

5. Drag one or two sizes—I like to use the 10- and 12-point sizes—of each style or weight you want into the My Fonts suitcase. (You could drag the fixed-size fonts directly into the Fonts folder, without putting them in a suitcase, but personally I don't like to have hundreds of loose font icons rattling around in my Fonts folder.) Since you have ATM installed, you need only one size of each (having two sizes produces slightly better on-screen fonts).

Although your Mac's System software can create facsimiles of italic or bold screen fonts by slanting or beefing up the plain style, respectively, it's best to install the bold, italic, and bold italic styles if you plan to use them. Doing so provides a closer match between the look of the displayed and printed page than does allowing the Mac's software to create fake bold or italic screen fonts. Besides, the Mac can't create versions of weights or styles other than the basic three (bold, italic, and bold italic), so you absolutely have to install screen fonts for demibold, light, extra bold, and the like.

6. If you're installing PostScript fonts, make sure you install a printer font for each style or weight you intend to use.

7. Repeat the procedure to place additional fonts in your My Fonts suitcase. You can add hundreds of fonts if you wish, but you might want to limit the size of the suitcase if you plan to place a backup copy on a floppy disk. (Also, keep in mind that installing hundreds of fonts makes your applications open more slowly.)

8. Make sure the My Fonts suitcase is located in the Fonts folder, which is in the System Folder. Make additional suitcases for other projects if you wish. If you're not using the fonts in a particular suitcase, you can drag the suitcase out of the Fonts folder to free up System resources. Place it back in the Fonts folder when you need it again.

That's all there is to it. Now, when you pull down an application's Font menu, you'll see the names of all the fonts you placed in the My Fonts suitcase. If you've installed hundreds of fonts, your Font menu may be pretty long. It may seem like an epic journey from Aachen to Zapf Chancery. And you may question the wisdom of installing hundreds of fonts when you find the members of font families dispersed, residing several inches—or even feet—away from one another on the menu. That's because, in order to fit font names in the limited width of a dialog box, font manufacturers abbreviate the names of styles or weights other than plain. Here are some common style and weight abbreviations:

- B (Bold)
- Bk (Book)
- Blk (Black)
- C (Condensed)
- D (Demibold)
- I (Italic)
- L (Light)
- M (Medium)
- O (Oblique)
- XB (Extra Bold)

These abbreviations can be combined into atrocities such as CXBO for Condensed Extra Bold Oblique. (*Note:* Don't confuse the style and weight abbreviations just described with the two-letter abbreviations you sometimes see after a font's name. These abbreviations show which foundry produced the font. Examples of these foundry abbreviations include BT for Bitstream and MT for Monotype.)

Selecting Styles and Weights

After traversing the Font menu a few times, you may be tempted to simply select the Plain style of a font—especially if its name starts with a letter that falls early in the alphabet—and select a style such as Bold or Italic from a Style menu or submenu. Easier still, you can select some text and use a keyboard shortcut, such as ⌘-Shift-B for Bold or ⌘-Shift-I for Italic. This generally works fine, but I'd advise you to make a habit of selecting styles by selecting the style name from the Font menu. Why? If you haven't installed a particular style or weight (or if it doesn't exist) and select Bold, Italic, or both from the Style menu, the Mac will go ahead and create a computed bold or italic screen font, as described earlier. You'll be in for an unpleasant—and time-consuming—surprise when you print your document and discover an artificially obliqued or bolded (all right, so *bolded* isn't a real word; I couldn't quite bring myself to say *emboldened*) face staring back at you from the page.

To be fair, I should point out that there's another school of thought that says you should choose styles via the Style menu or a keyboard shortcut, rather than from a Font menu. Why? Let's say you've typed a book chapter in the Galliard font. The chapter contains dozens of bold headings and italicized terms, also in Galliard. At the last minute you decide to make a design change and print the chapter in New Baskerville. You'd like to select the entire chapter and change the font to New Baskerville, keeping the bold and italic styles intact. If you selected B Galliard Bold and I Galliard Italic from the Font menu when typing the original chapter, however, the entire chapter will reappear in New Baskerville plain (a.k.a. roman); your style designations will be lost. If, on the other hand, you made the bold and italic style selections using the Style menu or keyboard commands, the style formatting will remain intact when you make the global font change. Your revised document will include New Baskerville bold and italic text, saving you a lot of trouble.

It's up to you to decide which method you prefer. Just try to be consistent, so you don't end up confusing yourself. You can cause problems if you accidentally employ both methods. For example, if you select I Goudy Italic from the Font menu, the italic style of the Goudy font appears on the screen. So far, so good. But if you forget what you're doing and later select a section that's in italics, then use the Style menu to italicize the section, you've italicized a section that's already in italics. Doing so obliques the italic screen font, which could potentially cause spacing problems or confuse a printer, which could end up printing italic-italic or bold-bold. You might want to try an experiment or two and see this phenomenon for yourself. You'll see that it's hard to tell just by looking at the screen whether you've double-bolded or double-italicized a font.

Speeding Up Font Menu Scrolling

This is small consolation, I know, but you can increase the speed at which the Font menu scrolls, which will help you get to the style or weight you need more quickly. All you have to do is position the arrow pointer correctly. Pull down the Font menu and try it. If you place the point of the arrow right on the center of the little triangle at the bottom of the scrolling Font menu (or slightly above, to the left, or to the right of it), scrolling chugs along at a leisurely pace. If, however, you place the point of the arrow on the bottom point of the triangle (or slightly below it), scrolling revvs up to a respectable speed.

If you want to stop scrolling without selecting a font, move the arrow pointer to either side of the Font menu. (Keep the mouse button held down, or you'll have to take it from the top.)

Scrolling faster is well and good, but there are better ways to tackle a lengthy Font menu. If you don't mind spending a little money, it's time to throw some utilities at the problem. We're now entering the area of font management.

Font Management

From shortening your Font menu to selectively installing the fonts you need, a number of utilities can help you maintain control over a large font collection. We'll start with some add-on programs that can make your Font menu much easier to navigate.

Font Menu Organizers

The tradition of preceding a font name with a style or weight abbreviation (B for Bold, BI for Bold Italic, XBO for Extra Bold Oblique, and so on) can make even a medium-size Font menu hard to navigate. And if you have hundreds of fonts installed, scrolling to the style you need can be a major expedition. (These days, some font vendors place style abbreviations after their font names, which makes finding fonts a little easier but doesn't make your Font menu any shorter.) Instead of hunting around for the various members of a large font family, you can use a Font menu organizer to consolidate font families under a single heading. Font menu organizers include Adobe Type Reunion, Dubl-Click Software's MenuFonts, Eastgate Systems' Fontina, and

Impossible Software's TypeTamer. These utilities place font family members together under a single font name, then let you access the various styles and weights via a submenu.

Try to find some members of the Futura Condensed family in the left-hand menu below. Ugh! Now, look at the menu on the right, which has been consolidated by TypeTamer. That's more like it!

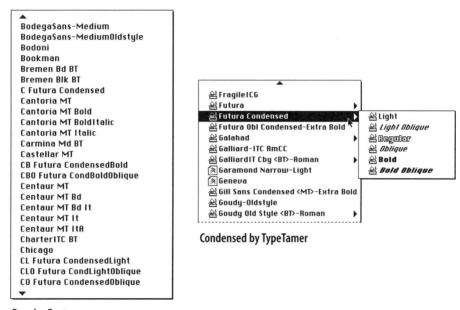

Condensed by TypeTamer

Regular Font menu

TypeTamer

In addition to consolidating font families into submenus, TypeTamer has several other talents. The program's SpeedFonts feature lets you type the first few letters of a font's name to zip to that font in the menu. And its TopFonts feature places the names of the fonts used in a document at the top of the Font menu, allowing you to select a font quickly when you use it again.

TypeTamer provides other information as well. It places an icon beside each font in the menu, showing whether it's a PostScript (including Multiple Master), TrueType, or bitmap font. (This information can come in handy if you've forgotten to install the printer-font component of a PostScript font—

the bitmap icon will appear next to the font's name, indicating that it won't print correctly.) Place the pointer on an icon to display a font's character set; letters and numbers are the default, but you can customize the sample text if you wish.

If you're like most people, you can't remember all the Option and Shift-Option combos for special characters. TypeTamer can display a font's special characters, allowing you to simply point to a character to insert it in a document, rather than typing Shift-Option combinations until you hit it right or opening Key Caps to find the proper combination.

Finally, TypeTamer lets you create your own font categories for the Font menu, based on the way you work with fonts. If you're a designer, for example, you might want to place all your sans serif fonts together, allowing you to try out several in a sample layout without hunting for them. Or you might want to place all pictorial or symbol fonts in one category, or perhaps divide fonts up by vendor. (A font can appear in more than one category; for example, a particular font might fit both your Display and Sans Serif categories.) Whatever categories you choose, you can add or delete fonts at any time.

A utility like TypeTamer or Type Reunion can help you manage an unwieldy Font menu, but you might want to have more control over installing your fonts. That's where a *font-management utility* can come in handy.

Font-Management Utilities

Symantec's Suitcase and Alsoft's MasterJuggler are both font-management utilities. Their basic functions will be described here. For the gory details on using these utilities, I suggest you read Robin Williams's helpful book, *How to Boss Your Fonts Around* (Peachpit Press, 1994).

In a nutshell, font-management utilities let you shuffle sets of fonts in and out of circulation as you need them for a particular job. They let you activate or deactivate sets of fonts without going through the tedious process of using the Font/DA Mover (System 6) or dragging font icons in and out of the System Folder (System 7). System 6 users get the added bonus of being able to install more than 500 fonts, the limit set by the Font/DA Mover. In addition, these utilities offer a number of font-compression and trouble-shooting capabilities.

Suitcase and MasterJuggler operate in a similar manner, but differ enough to warrant separate discussions. You should consider using one of these utilities if you use a lot of fonts, especially if the fonts you need differ from project to project.

Suitcase

Suitcase lets you create groups, or *sets*, of font suitcases, placing them outside your System Folder and activating only the sets you need for a particular job. When you use Suitcase, you don't have to wrestle with a long Font menu, and your applications will launch more quickly because the System file won't be bogged down by hundreds of fonts.

With Suitcase installed, you can open and close font sets with a few keystrokes. Organizing the sets takes some work up front, but it will be worth your trouble once you start shuffling fonts in and out of use.

Suitcase is an extension, so you install it by simply dragging its icon into the System Folder. You can then choose Suitcase from the Apple menu whenever you want to customize your font sets. Most people choose to have a permanent set of fonts that's open all the time, then open or close other sets as needed (in some programs, you can even open a set while you're working on a document, without quitting the application).

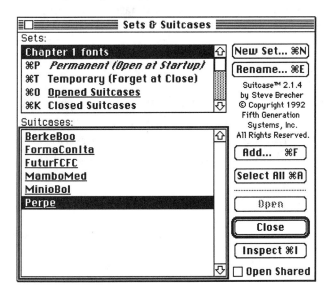

Suitcase also lets you compress screen-font files to save disk space (it automatically decompresses them when they're needed), allows you to display fonts in their own typefaces (I find this distracting, but some people like it), and provides ways to track down the dreaded font ID conflicts (these are described in the "Troubleshooting" section below).

MasterJuggler

Like Suitcase, MasterJuggler is a font-management utility that lets you store fonts outside the System Folder, conserving System resources and letting you create your own font-management scheme. With MasterJuggler, you can create groups of fonts that are always open, and open and close other groups at will.

MasterJuggler is an extension; to install it, you simply drag its icon into your System Folder. MasterJuggler is then available in the Apple menu. In MasterJuggler's window, you find the font suitcases you need for a particular job, then open those suitcases to create a font list. You can open fonts permanently (they'll still be available when you shut down and restart your Mac) or temporarily (they'll be available only until you turn off your computer).

MasterJuggler lets you view a list of fonts in their actual typefaces, helps you spot and correct font ID conflicts (these are described in the next section), and compresses fonts and automatically decompresses them when you need them.

Troubleshooting

So far, you've learned how to install and organize your font collection. In theory, all your fonts should print just fine and you should be happy. In reality, you may run into problems. This section describes some of the most common font problems and gives tips on how to solve them.

Font ID Conflicts

Unlike people, who identify typefaces by name, the Mac uses numbers to identify fonts. When the Mac was introduced, Apple, in its infinite wisdom, allocated a grand total of 256 font ID numbers to identify all the fonts that would ever be used on the Mac. Who knew? It soon became apparent that this desktop publishing thing was a hit, and in later years Apple upped the pool of font ID numbers to 16,381 (alas, that's still not nearly enough numbers to dole out a unique number to each font that's available today).

If the Mac encounters two fonts with the same ID number, strange things can happen. What usually happens is that you think you're printing Font A, but Font B appears when your document rolls off the printer. Or, you might open an application and find that an installed font doesn't appear in the Font menu, or that it's listed in the Font menu but another screen font shows up when you type. Needless to say, this can drive you crazy.

Various safeguards have been put in place to prevent font ID number conflicts (increasing the number of available ID numbers was a start; Apple also assigned a range of numbers to various font vendors and encouraged application developers to ask for fonts by name instead of ID number), but they still crop up from time to time.

If you're using System 6, the Font/DA Mover does its bit to avoid ID number conflicts; if you install a font that has the same ID number as a font that's already installed, it will renumber the second font so there's no conflict. That's fine, as long as you use your fonts on only one Mac. If you print your document on another Mac, however, you may run into problems. (*Note:* Check your fonts' licensing agreement; some companies allow their fonts to be used on only a single computer or a single printer.) Let's say you install Adobe's Glypha Bold, which has ID number 161, for your publication's head-lines. So far, so good. A few weeks later, you buy Adobe's Hobo, which also has ID number 161, and install it with the Font/DA Mover. Since a font with ID number 161 has already been installed, the Font/DA Mover gives Hobo a new ID number. All this goes on behind the scenes; you don't have to worry about how the Mac identifies fonts in your documents.

If you simply print your documents on your own Mac, everything should be fine. But if you take your document to a typesetting service bureau, for example, you might be in for a shock when you pick up your output. Your Glypha headlines have turned into Hobo—not exactly the look you origi-nally had in mind.

What happened? A simple case of mistaken identity. In this example, the document you gave to the service bureau contained a font identified by the number 161. If the version of Hobo on the service bureau's Mac still had its original ID number, 161 (the number that's now assigned to the Glypha font in your document), the service bureau is going to print the font with ID number 161—in this case, Hobo.

Most service bureau operators have ways to minimize font ID conflicts. Talk to your service bureau's manager before you bring a document in, and find out how he or she would like you to deal with the fonts in your document. Service bureaus are discussed further in Chapter 7.

If you're just printing documents from your own Mac under System 6 or System 7, your chances of font ID conflicts are minimal. The Font/DA Mover or the System software will resolve ID conflicts. Suitcase and Master-Juggler also renumber fonts, if necessary, to prevent conflicts. It's when you transfer a document from one Mac, with its own set of fonts, to another Mac, with *its* own set of fonts, that problems are likely to occur.

You may encounter the occasional font ID glitch on your Mac, however. Here are a couple of precautions you can take to help avoid problems:

• Don't install two fonts with the same name. This includes a TrueType and a PostScript version of the same font, or two fonts with the same name from different vendors.

• Don't put copies of the same font into more than one suitcase.

The bottom line: If anything weird happens to your fonts when they're printed or displayed, you may have to reinstall them. That's no fun—but neither is wrestling with font conflicts.

Damaged Suitcase Files

If you created a font suitcase while your Mac was running System 6, when you upgrade to System 7 and try to open the suitcase, you may see a message telling you that the suitcase is damaged. There are a few things you can try in order to salvage the fonts it contains:

• Try dragging the suitcase into the System Folder. Sometimes the fonts in it will be installed correctly.

• Use Font/DA Mover 4.1 to copy the contents of the damaged suitcase file into a new suitcase.

On occasion, you may try to open a font suitcase that's in your Fonts folder (under System 7.1 or later), only to see a message that the suitcase is damaged (usually System error −39 or "Command could not be completed because the file is damaged"). You'll probably want to remove the damaged suitcase file by dragging it into the Trash. If you try to move the damaged suitcase from the Fonts folder to the Trash or to another folder, however, the Macintosh displays an error message informing you that the file can't be moved.

Here's how to remove a damaged suitcase from the Fonts folder:

1. Drag the Fonts folder out of the System Folder and onto the Mac's Desktop.

2. Create a new Fonts folder in the System Folder.

3. Drag your undamaged fonts from the old Fonts folder to the newly created Fonts folder.

4. Restart your Macintosh.

5. Drag the Fonts folder you placed on the Desktop (the one with the damaged font suitcase) into the Trash.

6. Reinstall the fonts that were in the damaged suitcase, either from a backup copy or from the original font disk, by dragging them into the closed System Folder.

(*Note*: System 7 considers a font to be damaged if its name is longer than 31 characters. System 6 allowed fonts to have longer names, but System 7 doesn't. You should contact the font vendor and request a System 7–compatible version of the font.)

theFONDler

For one-stop font diagnostics, you might try a utility called theFONDler, from Rascal Software. The Fondler is named after the *FOND* (font family descriptor) resource, which is part of the information contained in a font. (A *resource* is a chunk of data that is shared by all programs.) This utility scans your hard disk and analyzes all the fonts on it, identifying problems such as font ID conflicts, missing printer fonts, and damaged font files. Where possible, it corrects the problems it encounters.

If you're often stumped by font problems and can't figure out the cause, theFONDler may be just the thing for you.

The Acid Test

If you want to learn a lot about font management, try writing a book about fonts and printing it on a service bureau's imagesetter. The fact that you're reading this book, which includes hundreds of typeface samples, shows that it can be done.

I'll close this chapter with the most common font problem of all, as related to me by a beleaguered Adobe technical-support staffer.

☞ The Most Common Font Problem of Them All ☜

If you're using PostScript fonts, you may sometimes run into problems when you print a document that looked fine on the screen. If a printed font ends up as a bitmapped font or is converted to Courier, chances are you haven't installed the printer font. Check to see that the correct printer font (that means the correct style or weight if necessary—not just the plain style) is installed in the Fonts folder (if you're running System 7.1 or later). The printer font must be in the Fonts folder; it won't be recognized if it's sitting somewhere else in the System Folder, on the Desktop, or in another folder.

Pointing hands are from the Handsome font (Castle Systems)

6
Creating &
Modifying Fonts

Even if you have a large collection of typefaces, you may not find exactly the face you need for a certain job. In pre-Mac times, you would have had to hire a designer or a typesetter to add special effects to type. But with a Mac and the right software, you have many options for modifying type yourself. You can do anything from condensing or expanding a face in a page layout program to creating your own typeface from scratch. If you don't have the time or energy to create your own typeface, you might want to spice up some of the faces in your collection using a graphics program or type special-effects program.

In addition to modifying the letters themselves, you can alter other aspects of a font: change its format (PostScript, True Type, Mac, IBM PC), for example, or add special characters such as small caps or old style figures. This chapter will show you how to enhance your fonts in a number of ways.

Font Special Effects

If you're like many Mac publishers, you've already shot a good portion of your budget on a basic set of typefaces and a word processor. You may not have much left over for fancy special-effects programs. The following tips show you how to add special effects to type if you own only a bare-bones word processor. In this section, we'll go from low-budget effects using programs you may already have, to those created with font special effects programs.

Word Processors

If you're on a budget, you can create some decent type effects with just a drawing program and a word processor. Word processors have improved dramatically since the last edition of this book, and many of the new models let you do some or all of the following: automatically create drop caps, flip and rotate text, import EPS graphics, kern headlines, condense and expand text, and even create drawings from within the word processor. If you have a word processor of recent vintage, you won't need many of the following tips. However, if you're still using Old Faithful, you might be able to use one of the following tips.

Do-It-Yourself Drop Cap

If your word processor doesn't let you automatically create a *drop cap* (a large capital letter that extends into the text of an opening paragraph), you can make one yourself.

1. Type your opening paragraph.

2. Select the first letter in the paragraph and choose a large point size and the bold style from the appropriate menu or submenu. From the Style menu or submenu, make the character a subscript.

3. Return to the main document window and place a tab stop in the document's ruler, so you can place a few lines of the opening paragraph's text to the right of the drop cap.

4. Print a test page. You may have to adjust the drop cap's size or adjust the amount of subscripting to raise or lower the letter to the proper height.

Low-Budget Condensed or Expanded Type

If you have a drawing program like Canvas or SuperPaint, you can add condensed or expanded headlines to a word processor document.

1. Type a line of text in the drawing program. (Make sure you're using a drawing program that supports outline fonts, and not a bitmapped painting program.)

2. Select Copy from the Edit menu to copy the text.

3. Open your word processor document and paste in the text.

4. Click on the text to select it. The word processor will treat the text as a graphic element, surrounding it with "handles" that you can drag.

5. Hold down the Shift key and drag the bottom handle downward to condense the text, or the right-hand handle to the right to expand it:

Pasting EPS Artwork into a Word Processor

EPS (Encapsulated PostScript) is a graphics format that lets you see a picture, rather than just a box with a few words describing the picture, when you import a PostScript graphic into a program. Some word processors—especially older ones—support only PICT, the Mac's native graphics format. If you need to paste an EPS image into a word processor that doesn't support EPS import, here's what you do.

1. Open a drawing in a PostScript graphics program such as Macromedia FreeHand or Adobe Illustrator.

2. Select the image and hold down the Option key while you select Copy from the Edit menu. This transfers PostScript as well as PICT information to the Clipboard.

3. Open your word processor document and choose Paste from the Edit menu to add the illustration to the document.

Graphics Programs

If the tips just described are too low-budget for your tastes, you might consider spiffing up your fonts with a PostScript graphics program. You can use Adobe Illustrator or Macromedia FreeHand to add striking special effects to text. These programs let you alter the shapes of the characters in a PostScript font, which are made up of a series of lines and curves. In addition, these programs let you skew, rotate, shrink, and expand letters, as well as apply more sophisticated effects such as text on a path and pattern fills.

Adobe Illustrator

You can add a variety of graphics special effects to type with Adobe Illustrator. A few examples are described here.

Illustrator lets you treat a line of text as a graphic object, applying PostScript effects such as skew, rotate, mirror, and scale. You can even alter a text selection's stroke (outline) or fill (interior shade). Here's how:

1. Type a letter, then select it.

2. Use the program's Stroke and Fill commands to thicken the letter's outline and add a gray fill.

3. You can now import the modified letter into a document created with a word processor or page layout program, where it will appear as a graphic.

Illustrator's text-enhancement capabilities go far beyond simple stroke and fill assignments. For example, you can use the program's Paste In Front menu option in conjunction with fill and stroke variations to create an inline effect like the one shown in Figure 6.1. You can also add scanned textures or patterns to text with Illustrator's masking function.

As you become more proficient in Illustrator, you'll discover ways to combine text and graphics to create spectacular effects. If you have a scanner, you can import your own textures and add them to fonts. If you don't have a scanner, you might want to buy a collection of scanned textures or clip art. Go ahead, experiment! Figure 6.2 shows a decorative initial cap created in Illustrator by artist Jack Davis.

To create an inline effect with Illustrator, perform the following steps:

1. Open a new Illustrator document and type some text.

2. Select the text and open the Paint Style palette. Set the text's fill and stroke to black, and enter a line weight (8 points in this example).

3. Copy the text, then choose Paste In Front from the Edit menu. Set the fill and stroke to white. This time, enter a smaller line weight (6 points here). Close the paint attributes window.

4. Copy the text again, choose Paste In Front, set the fill and stroke color to black, and enter a smaller line weight (4 points here). The result will be perfectly aligned inline text.

You can use Illustrator's masking function to add a pattern or scanned texture to text:

1. Open a new Illustrator document and type some text.

2. Place a pattern or texture into the document; this example uses a scanned marble texture saved in EPS format.

3. Position the texture over the text, then select Send To Back from the Arrange menu.

4. Select both the text and the texture, and choose Make Mask from the Object menu.

FIGURE 6.1. Special effects created in Adobe Illustrator.

Macromedia FreeHand

FreeHand's forte has always been precise text positioning. The program not only allows you to adjust text attributes such as kerning and tracking, but also lets you attach a line of text to a path of any shape, a handy feature for logos, maps, signs, and other graphics (see Figure 6.3).

FreeHand's snap-to grid and cursor-position readout help you align text with graphic elements in a design. The program's ability to precisely position text in relation to graphics can save you time and trouble when you're creating logos, letterheads, and other designs that mix text and graphics.

FreeHand lets you transform a line of text into condensed or expanded type by selecting the text and dragging the handles of its selection box. Keep in mind that text altered in this way is treated as a graphic when you place it into a page layout program; you can't use the layout program's text-editing features on a block of type condensed or expanded in this manner. (Progress is being made in this department, however; see Chapter 9 for a look at the flexible editing options future font technologies will offer.)

Type Special-Effects Programs

While graphics programs let you alter text in a variety of ways, you can buy a program that specializes in typographic special effects. These programs let you accomplish, with the click of a button, what it might take you hours to do in Illustrator, FreeHand, or another graphics program. Several type-effects programs are described in this section.

LetraStudio

Letraset's LetraStudio lets you reshape text to create dozens of novel effects with your PostScript or TrueType fonts, from rippled letters to curves, arches, perspective views—you name it. Type a line of text, then select one or more of the program's effects to reshape or reposition a word's baseline, skew or distort a word, create a drop shadow, overlap letters, scale or rotate a selection, change stroke weight or fill color, and more. As you work, you can adjust text attributes such as kerning, tracking, and font size, viewing your work-in-progress on the screen and periodically printing proofs to see how your project is coming along.

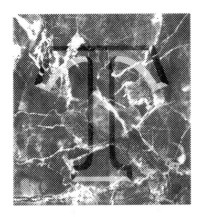 

FIGURE 6.2. Decorative initial caps created in Adobe Illustrator.

FIGURE 6.3. Special effect created in Macromedia FreeHand.

LetraStudio even lets you select one letter in a word and apply an effect, as shown here:

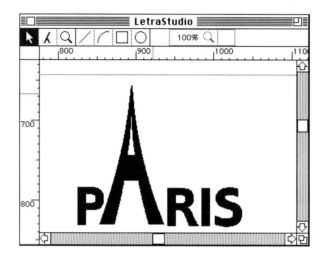

You select effects from submenus in the program's Effects menu. The Text submenu lets you skew, rotate, condense, or expand a text selection. The Line submenu allows you to reshape a word's baseline into an arch or a free-form curve. Finally, the program's Envelope menu lets you surround a block of text with one of 18 shapes. These shapes have movable "handles" attached to them; drag one or more envelope handles to bend, stretch, shrink, curve, or slant the enclosed text.

LetraStudio also includes some basic drawing tools—line, circle/oval, square/rectangle, and arc—which you can use along with the program's text effects. Don't mistake LetraStudio for a drawing program, however; the drawing tools merely augment the program's many special effects.

Once you've created an effect you like, you can save it in EPS or PICT format and incorporate it into a document created with a graphics program or page layout application.

TypeStyler

Brøderbund's TypeStyler offers more than 30 predefined special effects. You type in the text you wish to modify; select a font, size, and style; and choose the effect you want from a scrolling list. Text appears in an "envelope;" drag the envelope's handles to change its shape. Although the effects themselves are canned, you can modify aspects of each one, adding your own artistic signature to letters or words.

With TypeStyler, you can resize, reshape, mirror, distort, skew, and rotate text selections. You can do anything from making a word look as though it would through a fish-eye lens to stretching it like a piece of taffy. You can also alter a selection's stroke weight and fill color, adding grays, colors, patterns, or gradient fills to letters. The program also offers a number of shadow options, allowing you to adjust a shadow's color, angle, and position. Like LetraStudio, TypeStyler lets you adjust kerning, letterspacing, and word spacing. Here's an example of an effect that combines several of TypeStyler's capabilities:

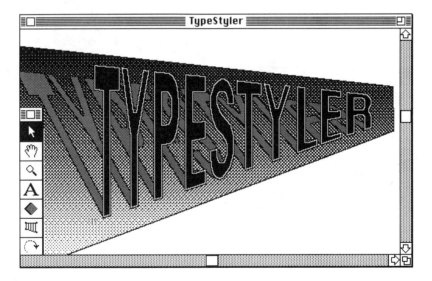

TypeStyler's effects can be printed directly from the program or saved in one of several standard graphics formats and incorporated into other documents. You can also import graphics into TypeStyler and superimpose text on a picture.

Type Twister

Adobe's Type Twister offers 50 built-in designs. You can use them as-is, or customize them to make your own designs. You can use the 20 fonts that come with the program, or apply Type Twister's effects to your own TrueType or PostScript fonts.

A preview of your text effect appears in Type Twister's window. Grab a handle and drag it to stretch, resize, rotate, or skew the text. You can also customize various attributes of the design, such as its perspective and shadows.

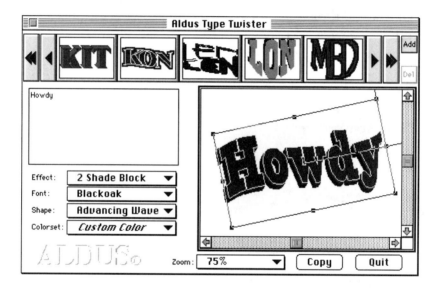

When you finish your type effect, you can transfer it to another application for printing. TypeTwister copies a 300-dpi embedded PostScript image to the Clipboard (you can increase the resolution, if necessary, using the program's Preferences dialog box), allowing you to easily transfer your image to another application.

TypeTwister is somewhat less sophisticated than LetraStudio or TypeStyler; it doesn't let you work on a single letter in a word, for example, or adjust kerning or tracking. On the other hand, it's considerably cheaper than the other two programs. If you need a simple, inexpensive type-effects program, TypeTwister may do the trick.

Letraset Envelopes

This plug-in for Adobe Illustrator and Macromedia FreeHand lets you condense, stretch, slant, scale, rotate, flip, resize and reshape text and graphics. You can use one of the utility's 200 built-in distortion envelopes, or create your own envelopes by manipulating Bézier curves.

StrataType 3d

Add three-dimensional effects to your PostScript or TrueType fonts with Strata's 3-D effects program. StrataType 3d transforms text into 3-D shapes, then lets you add textures (marble, wood, chrome, and other textures are included with the program, or you can create your own textures from scanned PICT images), adjust the size and shape of beveled edges, position text (on an arc or in a circle, for example), rotate letters, set a vanishing point, add a background, and position a light source. Then, sit back while the image renders. You can save the image as a PICT, TIFF, or EPS file and transfer it to a graphics application or page layout program.

Pixar Typestry

Like StrataType 3d, Pixar Typestry makes PostScript or TrueType fonts into three-dimensional objects, allowing you to add textures (glass, gold, marble, and so on), lighting (19 light sources are available), rotation, and other effects. It's the "other effects" that make Typestry stand out. For example, you can animate a block of text (either as a series of frames or a QuickTime movie), making it rotate, scroll, or zoom toward the viewer, complete with professional effects such as motion blur.

Typestry is not only impressive, but fun to use as well. How many other programs (outside of games, that is) offer controls such as Particle Life Span and Ejection Speed? One more plus: Typestry is one of the few programs out there that support QuickDraw GX fonts (see Chapter 9 for a description of GX font technology).

Creating and Editing Fonts

If you can't achieve the look you want by using one of the special-effects programs just described, you might want to try your hand at designing your own font. Before you rush out and buy a font-design program, however, you should realize that type design is an art; some people devote their entire lives to it. Don't expect to produce professional-quality typefaces your first time around. On the other hand, these programs are relatively affordable and easy to learn, so why not give font design a try? You don't have to create an entire font; you might want to use Macromedia's Fontographer, for example, to create a logo or some decorative initial caps, or to alter some characters of an existing font to make your own custom creation.

Creating New Fonts

These days, two programs—Fontographer and URW's Ikarus-M—let you create fonts from scratch. Both of these programs, which are in the same price range, let you produce high-quality fonts that include professional features such as kerning and hinting.

A Font That Modifies Itself

If you get tired of modifying fonts, you can always have PostScript do the job for you. A unique font family called Random Beowolf has a life of its own (the BeoSans face is shown here). Built-in PostScript commands make subtle changes to the shape of each letter each time the font is printed. Depending on how random you feel, you can choose among three levels of modification. Beowolf was designed by Erik van Blokland and Just van Rossum, and is available from FontShop (see Appendix A).

Q: What did the Zen master say to
    the hot dog vendor?

A: Make me one with everything.

Fontographer

Fontographer was the first outline-font editor ever released for a personal computer. But the granddaddy of personal font-design tools isn't showing its age; it's been conscientiously upgraded over the years, and has been significantly improved with every new version. Originally developed by Altsys, Fontographer is now sold by Macromedia.

With Fontographer, you can create TrueType and PostScript fonts, including Multiple Master fonts. These fonts work just like the fonts you buy from commercial vendors; you can print them at any resolution on a PostScript or non-PostScript printer. You create characters by drawing your own Bézier-curve outlines or by scanning hand-drawn letters and using the program's automatic outlining feature (keep in mind that auto-traced outlines often require a lot of fine-tuning). You can also import EPS artwork from a PostScript drawing program like FreeHand or Illustrator, and turn the images into characters in a font.

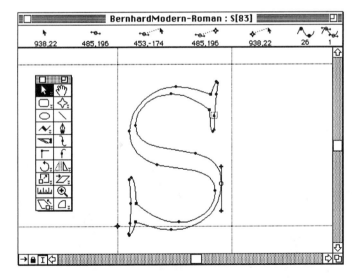

The beauty of Fontographer is that it's easy to use, so beginners can get right to work. You can import an EPS graphic and turn it into a character with little trouble. Or you can import an existing font and modify it for your own use (just don't try to sell it, or you could get into trouble).

While Fontographer is fun for beginners, it has enough advanced features to satisfy professional type designers. Many of the fonts you buy from commercial vendors were created in Fontographer, which offers precise control over not only the shapes of characters, but also over typographic features such as font metrics and kerning pairs.

The latest version offers several new features, including the ability to blend two existing fonts to create a hybrid font, a Change Weight command that instantly makes a font bolder or lighter, a 3-D rotation tool, and the option to accept input from a pressure-sensitive tablet to create calligraphic faces that look like they're drawn with a pen.

Ikarus-M

For years, professional type designers have been using the Ikarus type-production system to create digital typefaces. A Macintosh version that offers much of the functionality of the original program is available from URW (which stands for Unternehmensberatung Karow Rubow Weber, if you must know). Ikarus-M lets you create faces from scratch or convert Ikarus-format fonts into PostScript format.

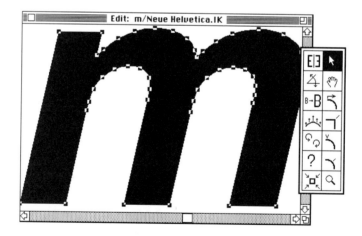

Unlike Fontographer, which lets you draw on the screen using the Mac's mouse, Ikarus-M makes use of a special digitizing tablet and a four-button mouse for entering character data. You place a paper-based drawing of a character—with control points for corners, tangents, and curves marked on it—on the drawing tablet, then trace the character with the mouse, which has a crosshair sight for precise positioning. As you press the appropriate mouse button for each type of control point, the outline of the traced character appears on the screen. (You also have the option of placing a PICT-format character in a background drawing plane and tracing the character.)

Once the character is entered, you can zoom in on it and move control points until it looks right. The program displays numerical information describing curves, distances, and cursor position; you can read the values as you move the mouse, or type in values to position a control point.

Ikarus-M lets you rotate, scale, mirror, and skew character outlines. Batch processing of functions such as rotate or oblique can be applied to a group of characters to save you time. Another tool that can save you time and effort is an add-on module that interpolates between one weight and another, automatically creating an intermediate weight. Another add-on program, Linus-M, auto-traces scanned artwork to produce character outlines.

Unlike Fontographer, Ikarus-M isn't a program that encourages beginners to noodle around with fonts. But it's a good tool for serious font designers, and is suitable for large-scale font-production environments.

Modifying Existing Fonts

A number of programs let you modify the characters of an existing font, creating a condensed or expanded face, for example, or creating special characters such as old style figures or small caps.

Someday, a single font will be able to contain thousands of characters. (See Chapter 9 for a discussion of Apple's new QuickDraw GX font technology, which does just that.) Meanwhile, a typical Macintosh font includes around 230 characters—not nearly enough for professional typographers, who like to augment their fonts with additional characters. Adobe and other font vendors have obliged sophisticated type users by providing expert collections, supplemental fonts that include characters such as small caps, old style figures, fractions, ligatures, swashes, and ornaments. Expert collections provide a workable solution, but are still far from ideal, since you have to select a separate font to type the characters in the expert set. Fortunately, you can use font-modification programs to take characters from one font and place them in another font, creating a hybrid font with special characters such as ornaments or old style figures.

You can also use Fontographer to place characters from one font into another, as described below.

Creating a Composite Font with Fontographer

Many text families include expert sets, complementary faces that offer additional characters such as fractions, extra ligatures, small caps, old style figures, swash capitals, and ornaments. I prefer old style figures (several of which dip below the baseline, as you may recall) to modern figures (which rest on the baseline) in long passages of text, since modern figures create unsightly pockets of uniformity in the color and rhythm of the page. However, it's a bother to select the expert-set font just to add old style figures, so I sometimes forgo them if I'm in a hurry. Fortunately, it's possible to replace seldom-used characters in a font with useful characters from an expert set, saving you the trouble of switching from one font to another.

If you own Fontographer, which was described earlier in this chapter, here's how to replace unneeded characters with characters from an expert set. (*Note:* Be sure to use a copy of the font you're going to alter; you may need the original someday.)

1. First, you need to figure out which characters are expendable. Use the Key Caps desk accessory to look at your original font. To make it easy to remember where your new characters are positioned, try to pick an adjacent group of expendable characters. In my case, I almost never use the accented characters that are accessed by holding down the Shift and Option keys and typing the third row of keys (a, s, d, etc.).

2. Start up Fontographer and choose Open Font from the File menu. Open the font to which you wish to add characters (the base font). The Font Window appears, displaying the font's character set.

3. Choose Open Font again, this time choosing the expert-set font that has the characters you wish to add. Position the two Font Windows so you can access them both.

4. Click on the base font's Font Window and type the key combination for the first character you wish to replace (in this example, Shift-Option-a). The Å character is highlighted.

5. Click on the expert-set font's Font Window and find the character you wish to add (in this case, the old style figure 1). Click on the character to select it, then choose Copy from the File menu.

6. Click on the base font's Font Window again (the Å is still highlighted) and select Paste from the File menu. The Å is replaced by the 1.

7. Repeat this procedure to replace the other nine unneeded characters with old style figures.

8. Choose Generate Font Files from the File menu, and follow Fontographer's instructions for creating a font.

9. Place your new font in the Fonts folder in your System Folder, and it's ready to use. When you type the Shift-Option key combinations, the old style figures you added will appear.

FontMonger

FontMonger, from Ares Software, is a multitalented utility that, among other things, lets you convert PostScript fonts to TrueType and vice versa. It also allows you to modify an existing font to create oblique characters, superscript and subscript characters, fractions, and composite characters made up of pieces of several existing characters.

You can also use FontMonger to merge the characters of two or more fonts, creating a composite font that has the characters you need. You might want to add a set of typographer's ornaments to a font, for example, or add some phonetic symbols or other special characters for a particular project.

FontMixer

Monotype's FontMixer allows you to mix characters from different fonts, creating a composite font that includes the special characters you need. FontMixer lets you replace unneeded characters in a PostScript Type 1 font with characters from one or more additional fonts, including expert collections. Let's say, for example, that you want to add fractions to Monotype's Perpetua font. You first open the Perpetua font with FontMixer, creating the base font for your new, composite font. You then open the Perpetua expert collection font, which offers numerators and denominators for fractions. Choose ten expendable characters in the original Perpetua font to replace with the numerators from the expert collection, and another ten to replace with the denominators.

When you're finished mixing your custom font, you select Make Font to create screen and printer versions of the new font, which you install and use like any other PostScript font.

FontHopper

One more utility is worth mentioning here. Ares Software's Font-Hopper converts IBM PC fonts to Macintosh format and vice versa. It works with both TrueType (for PCs running Windows) and PostScript fonts.

With the programs described in this chapter, you should be able to create exactly the character, logo, typeface, or typographic special effect you need. You should also be able to combine characters from several fonts into a single, composite font, saving yourself the trouble of switching between fonts to access special characters. With any luck, you won't have to build your own composite fonts for long. Apple's QuickDraw GX fonts (see Chapter 9) have the ability to include thousands of characters per font. I'm confident that someday QuickDraw GX fonts—or something like them—will be universally accepted by Macintosh program developers, making life easier for you, the font user.

For now, let's take those new, composite fonts you've created and make sure you know how to print them. The next chapter covers printing basics.

7

Printing Options

By now you've mastered the fundamentals of typography, amassed a giant font collection, and learned how to manage it. You've laid out a document with the right amount of leading, aesthetically compatible text and headings, and fancy touches like drop caps and ligatures. But you're not done yet. You still have to print the thing.

In this chapter, we'll look at the basics of printing documents on the Macintosh, whether it's on a home or office laser printer or on a service bureau's high-resolution imagesetter.

Types of Printers

On the whole, printers that are used with the Mac come in two species: "smart" and "dumb." Dumb printers (that is, QuickDraw printers) get their printing instructions from the Mac, while smart printers (i.e., PostScript printers) have their own built-in instructions for printing. When it comes to printing fonts, you can get good-looking results from either a QuickDraw printer or a PostScript printer. How good the printed output looks will depend, in part, on the printer's *resolution*, the number of dots per inch (dpi) it prints. Resolution typically ranges from 300 dpi to 1200 dpi, depending on the model you buy. Your buying decision may come down to price, or it may hinge on whether you want to take advantage of PostScript graphics.

First, let's look at the basics of PostScript and QuickDraw printers.

QuickDraw Printers

QuickDraw printers are a lower-cost alternative to their more sophisticated relatives, the PostScript printers. These printers use QuickDraw, the Mac's built-in set of graphics routines, to print text and graphics. If you can live without PostScript niceties like text on a path, halftones, and EPS (Encapsulated PostScript) graphics, you may find that a QuickDraw printer, coupled with the font-scaling talents of Adobe Type Manager (ATM) or TrueType, meets your printing needs just fine. (See Chapter 4 for descriptions of ATM and TrueType.)

Unlike PostScript laser printers, which have Adobe's PostScript page-description language built in, QuickDraw printers let the Mac run the show. QuickDraw commands are sent from the Mac to the printer; since the Quick-Draw printer has no PostScript interpreter built in, you can't print PostScript graphics on a QuickDraw printer (you can, on the other hand, print Quick-Draw-based graphics on a PostScript printer). If you plan on using your printer to print proofs of pages that will later be set on a service bureau's high-resolution PostScript imagesetter (more on service bureaus later in this chapter), I'd suggest spending a bit more and getting a PostScript printer.

PostScript Printers

Many brands of printers have PostScript built into them. These printers use the PostScript page-description language to image and print an entire page of text and graphics, giving you precise control over text and image scaling, positioning, and special effects. Apple's popular LaserWriter-series printers use PostScript. The PostScript interpreter (the software routines that convert PostScript instructions to the patterns of dots that make up text and graphics) in a given printer may be licensed from Adobe, or it may be a PostScript-compatible (sometimes called a *PostScript clone*) interpreter developed by another company. After a somewhat rocky start, PostScript-clone printers have established themselves in the printer market.

PostScript printers are more expensive than their QuickDraw counterparts, although the price gap has narrowed over the years. How much you pay for a printer depends on a number of factors, including resolution and the amount of RAM (random-access memory) the printer has. Assess your printing needs (and budget) when you're considering these factors. If you'll be working on font- and graphics-intensive projects, you'll need a printer with enough RAM to process your job; 4MB is about the minimum amount of RAM you should have for font-intensive jobs. You can add RAM to most PostScript printers by installing RAM SIMMs (Single-Inline Memory Modules). If you'll be using your printer for final output, instead of sending your documents to a service bureau for high-resolution output, you should buy a printer with a resolution of at least 600 dpi; this resolution is adequate for projects such as flyers and newsletters, but I wouldn't set a book at 600 dpi (the text you're reading now was set at 1250 dpi at a service bureau).

PostScript printers have a set of PostScript fonts built into their ROM (read-only memory). These fonts are always available to you (see Chapter 4). When your document contains a font that's not built into the printer, that font is automatically sent to the printer—or *downloaded*—to the printer's RAM when you print the document. (Think of ROM as the printer's permanent memory, and RAM as a temporary memory that stores information for awhile, then discards it—sort of like *my* memory.)

You can *manually download* printer fonts as well. Many font vendors include a manual-downloading utility with the fonts they sell. Here's the icon for the downloading utility that's included with Adobe's fonts (other companies' icons may look different):

Downloader 5.0.4

Like automatically-downloaded fonts, manually-downloaded fonts are sent to a printer's RAM before a document is printed. Unlike automatically-downloaded fonts, which are periodically flushed from the printer's memory and reloaded again when needed, manually-downloaded fonts remain in memory until the printer is turned off. Because they stay in RAM, manually-loaded fonts print faster than automatically-downloaded ones; an application doesn't have to search for and dowload a font each time it's needed for printing. But because manually-downloaded fonts aren't cleared from memory after a document is printed, this technique limits the number of fonts that you can use at once. If you use a particular font throughout the day, you may find it more efficient to manually download the font, keeping it available in memory at all times.

Now let's look at the mechanics of two popular types of printers: ink-jet printers and laser printers.

Ink-Jet Printers

Ink-jet printers are popular because they're small, affordable, and produce good-looking output. These printers have an ink-filled cartridge that slides back and forth on a track, spraying tiny spurts of ink on a page at a resolution of 360 dpi. The output generally looks very crisp and clear (although the ink blurs a little when it hits the page), but you have to be careful not to smear the ink when you're handling a printed page.

Ink-jet printers fall into the "dumb" printers category, since they don't have the PostScript language built into them. They also fall into the inexpensive category, typically selling for around $300. If you need an inexpensive printer for home or office use—letters, reports, memos, and the like—an ink-jet printer may be just the thing. I wouldn't recommend this type of printer for any major publishing projects, however.

Laser Printers

It was a laser printer that started the desktop publishing revolution back in 1985. Apple's LaserWriter was a big hit, and helped put the Macintosh on the map. Various companies' laser printers differ in many respects—price, memory capacity, resolution, built-in font selection, and even the language they use to create text and graphics. But most laser printers share common printing components: laser beams, a rotating drum, and a fine black powder called toner. In many laser printers, a printing mechanism shoots a series of needle-thin pulses of laser light—300 or 600 per inch in many models—through a series of lenses and mirrors onto the surface of a rotating drum (reminds me of a Grateful Dead concert I saw back in '77...but I digress). Wherever a beam hits the drum, it creates an electrical charge that attracts the fine toner powder to the drum as it rolls by. As the drum continues to rotate, it encounters a sheet of paper. When the paper contacts the drum, the toner is fused to the paper by a combination of heat and pressure.

(*Note:* You can improve the appearance of your laser-printed output by using high-quality paper. I like the selection offered by Paper Direct (800/272-7377), which sells paper that's designed for laser printers.)

Save a Tree

Are you tired of that pesky test page your LaserWriter spews out every time you turn it on? If you want to save paper and toner, you can easily suppress the test page with the LaserWriter Utility program that comes with the printer. If you've misplaced your LaserWriter Utility, you can cancel the test page by pulling the LaserWriter's paper tray out about an inch before you turn on the printer. Turn on the printer and wait while it completes its initialization procedure (this usually takes a minute or so). Then, simply slide the tray back in and print your documents as usual.

At Your Service Bureau

At 300, or even 600 dots per inch, laser printers are fairly low on the resolutionary scale. (A number of 1200-dpi laser printers have recently become available, but many are still a bit expensive for most home or small-business users.) If you want to make the leap from near-typeset to typeset quality—and you don't have $30,00 to $80,00 or so to invest in a PostScript imagesetter—you'll need to take your document to a service bureau. A service bureau uses a high-resolution PostScript *imagesetter* (so called because it sets text and graphics) from a variety of manufacturers, including Agfa, Autologic, Linotype, and Monotype. These imagesetters offer high-resolution output that ranges from 1000 to 3000 dots per inch. Linotype's Linotronic L300, for example, offers a choice of 1270 or 2540 dpi. The difference between 300 and 1270 dots per inch may not sound that great to you, but look at the formula in terms of dots per square inch. At 300 dpi, a printer covers 90,000 dots per square inch. But an imagestter's 1270 dpi comes out to 1.6 million dots per square inch—about 18 times the resolution of a 300-dpi printer. And 2540-dpi output produces 6.45 million dots per square inch, which should be sufficient for just about any printing job.

Imagesetting service bureaus range from do-it-yourself outfits (you bring in your files and they sit you down at a Mac) to full-service outfits that offer everything from design consulting to desktop publishing classes. Appendix D provides a list of service bureaus, but it probably won't list all the

---

Raising Resolution

If you can't afford to have a large job printed at high resolution on an imagesetter, you can squeeze a little more resolution out of your 300-dpi laser printer simply by having your printshop photographically reduce your laser-printed output. For example, if your pages are reproduced at 78 percent instead of 100 percent, the size reduction effectively raises the resolution of the page from 300 dpi to 400 dpi. Fellow Peachpit Press author Daniel Will-Harris used this technique to set a 475-page book, which looks pretty good.

service bureaus in your area. If there are several service bureaus near you, it might pay to shop around until you find one that suits your needs; actually, the service bureau doesn't have to be in your immediate area—some bureaus accept files by modem. Look in your local phone book under "Desktop Publishing,""Typesetting," or "Printers" to find a listing of service bureaus near you, or—better yet—ask a friend, coworker, or member of your local Mac user group to recommend a good service bureau. If you have a small printing job—and some spare time in case something goes wrong—you might want to try a self-service outfit; they're generally cheaper than full-service operations, and you can walk out with your output in a short time (with any luck). If you're still a little intimidated by font management, however, you might be better off going to a full-service imagesetting bureau. If you end up doing so, here are some questions for you to ask a service bureau representative before you bring in your job:

• Does the service bureau charge by the hour or by the page? Most bureaus charge somewhere in the range of $5 to $10 per 8½-by-11-inch page, printed at 1200 dpi. The cost for printing at 2500 dpi can add an extra $2 to $4 per page, but unless your document contains halftones, you probably won't need to print at the higher resolution.

• Does the bureau charge overtime fees? Most text pages take less than five minutes to print. If a page takes longer than an amount of time specified by the service bureau (10 minutes in many cases), some bureaus add a per-minute charge to the per-page fee. Overtime charges can add up if your document includes numerous graphics, fonts, or PostScript effects.

• Does the bureau provide rush service? If so, what are the rates?

• Does it offer volume rates (for jobs of 50 pages or more, for example)?

• If you're working with a full-service bureau, are the employees familiar with the software you're using? If they say "Quark what?" when you tell them your brochure is laid out in QuarkXPress, you'd better look for another service bureau. Sooner or later you'll run into printing problems and need a troubleshooter who's familiar with your program. Most full-service bureaus (and most self-service bureaus, for that matter) have employees who are familiar with popular programs such as PageMaker and QuarkXPress.

• How should you set up your screen fonts? If you read Chapter 5, you're aware of the perils of font ID number conflicts. The service bureaus I've worked with use Suitcase or MasterJuggler to load their fonts, and suggested that I put all the screen fonts for my printing job in a single suitcase to avoid conflicts. (That wasn't practical for this book, which uses hundreds of fonts, but I placed the fonts in suitcases arranged by chapter, and brought in my whole project—QuarkXPress documents, fonts, and all—on a couple of SyQuest cartridges at their request.)

• Does the service bureau accept files via modem? Sending files by modem can save you time, but keep in mind that phone charges can add up. Also, telecommunications can be tricky. You may have to spend a good deal of time making sure your communications software works with theirs. Finally, you may want to send the bureau laser-printed page proofs so it can make sure its output matches yours.

Saving a File as PostScript

If your document doesn't print correctly on a service bureau's imagesetter, consider saving it as a PostScript file. System 7's Print dialog box lets you save a file as PostScript code with the click of a button. If you're using System 6, you must perform the following steps:

• Choose the Print command and press OK in the resulting dialog box.

• Immediately press ⌘-F.

• Look in your Mac's System Folder for a file named "PostScript 0."

Because the PostScript file records information about your fonts, the document should print just fine on the service bureau's imagesetter. (Check with your service bureau to make sure they'll accept documents submitted in PostScript format.)

The following tips can save you time and money, as well as spare you (and the service bureau staff) a lot of aggravation when you're working with a service bureau for the first time.

• The most imprtant thing to remember about imagesetters is this: The fact that your document prints out fine on a laser printer doesn't mean it's going to print successfully on a service bureau's imagesetter. In theory, a document should print equally well on various PostScript devices. But laser printers and imagesetters are different machines, and any number of printing glitches can occur. For example, several pages of this book came out fine on my LaserWriter at home, but inexplicably wouldn't print at the service bureau. (We eventually badgered them into printing by resaving the document, reloading the fonts, praying, and so on.)

• Always allow extra time to get rid of bugs in the printing process. Don't sashay into a service bureau at 3 o'clock and expect to walk out with a flawlessly printed 10-page document by 5. This warning is especially pertinent if it's your first trip to a service bureau.

• An imagesetter doesn't always behave like a laser printer. For example, most imagesetters can print all the way to the edge of a sheet of paper, while the LaserWriter's print area is restricted to a width of 8 inches on 8½-by-11-inch paper.

Another difference: Unlike the LaserWriter series and other printers, imagesetters don't offer a smoothing option for bitmapped graphics. If you want to smooth the jaggies, you can print your graphics on a LaserWriter and manually paste them into your publication.

Unlike the LaserWriter series, an imagesetter doesn't have Helvetica Narrow built into its ROM. You should use the Helvetica Condensed font instead.

• You'll save yourself and the people at your service bureau some trouble if you specify your printing needs in writing. Many service bureaus provide forms that ask you to indicate which program(s) you're using (including version numbers), which fonts you used, what output resolution you require, and so on. If your bureau doesn't provide a form, you can make yourself a form like the one shown in Figure 7.1, fill in the blanks for your job, and bring it with you to the service bureau.

Type e & Graphics

E & G Design • 415-555-8432

Date In: _____

Date Needed: _____

Filename: _____

Number of pages: _____

Program: _____

Fonts: _____

Resolution: _____

Notes: _____

_____

_____

FIGURE 7.1. Prepare a form like the one shown here before you take your document to a service bureau to be printed. (Before you go to the trouble of preparing your own, however, check with your bureau to see if they provide such a form.)

• If your document includes graphics in TIFF or EPS format, you may have to include the original TIFF or EPS files when you print the document. (Some programs allow you to embed the graphics files in your document, while others don't.) To be on the safe side, bring your TIFF and EPS files with you to the service bureau (it's easier to bring these files with you than to make a trip home to get them if they're needed). You may also need to bring the data file created by your page layout program.

• You should bring a printout from your laser printer to ensure that the service bureau's output matches yours. Proof the high-resolution output carefully against your laser-printer output, checking for incorrect fonts or fonts printed as Courier or as bitmaps.

• If you add special effects such as fill patterns or gray scales to a font, keep in mind that the grays you see on your laser-printer printout won't necessarily match the grays on your imagesetter output. With a resolution of only 300 or 600 dpi, the laser printer can only approximate the subtle gradations achieved by a high-resolution imagesetter. In many cases, a shade of gray will look lighter on an imagesetter printout than on a laser printer proof.

• If you have a complex page of text and graphics, you may be better off getting out your trusty razor blade and some glue and pasting in some elements by hand. Almost every page in this book was pasted up electronically, but a few had to be printed separately and pasted up by hand.

• Here's a final—and important—piece of advice. Don't be afraid to ask your service bureau representative questions. Even if you think a question is stupid, you're better off asking it than making a mistake that will cost you time and money. Service bureau operators are used to dealing with customers of all levels of expertise; they'd rather answer several questions early on than deal with printing snafus once you bring in your document.

8
Portable Documents

When you tell someone there are more than 20,000 digital fonts available, you're likely to get one of two responses: "Gee! That's swell!" or "Aaaaargh! Noooo!" (or words to that effect). The former response comes from the typical type fan, who is always happy to see new faces. The latter reaction comes from the poor wretch who has to send a document to someone electronically.

The trouble with computer fonts is that they don't travel along with a document. If you use Poppl-Pontifex and Smaragd (two of my favorite font names) in a document, then send the document to a colleague—either by modem or by mailing a disk—your colleague won't be able to print an accurate rendition of your document unless he or she has the same fonts. If the person on the receiving end doesn't have the right fonts, the document will print in a bitmapped font or in Courier, and formatting elements such as line breaks, leading, and column widths will differ from those in the original.

What can you do? You're not supposed to send the font files along with the document because, in most cases, your licensing agreement allows you to use your fonts on only a single printer or computer. One solution is to use one or more of the standard fonts that come with the Mac's System software (Times, Helvetica, or Bookman, for example). This solution makes for some pretty boring documents, however. Another solution is to use either *synthetic fonts* or a *portable-document program*. In this chapter we'll look at several solutions for getting your documents and the fonts they contain—or a reasonable facsimile—from point A to point B.

Synthetic Fonts

First, let's look at a couple of relatively inexpensive programs that create fonts from outline data. Each program takes a different approach to transferring font information when a document travels from one person to another.

Adobe Super ATM

Super ATM is an enhanced version of Adobe Type Manager (ATM), which was described in Chapter 4. Super ATM uses a process called *font substitution* to create a faux font that matches the metrics (character widths) and weight of the font in the original document.

Super ATM uses Adobe's Multiple Master font technology (Multiple Master fonts were also described in Chapter 4; briefly, they're fonts created from a set of master character outlines that can vary in width, weight, or other attributes) to generate a serif or sans serif font that matches, as closely as possible, the appearance of the original font. Let's say you send a friend a document you created in a page layout program using the Gill Sans Bold font. Your friend opens the document in his copy of the page layout program. If your friend has Gill Sans Bold installed, no problem; your friend's copy of Super ATM leaves well enough alone, and the document prints in Gill Sans Bold. If the friend doesn't have Gill Sans Bold, however, Super ATM creates a substitute sans serif font that matches the character widths and boldness of the original font you used. The substitute font won't look exactly like Gill Sans

Bold, but it will have the look and feel of the real font, allowing your friend to view and print a document that looks somewhat like the one you created—with line breaks, page breaks, kerning, and leading intact. If your friend wants to make some changes, he can edit the text.

In many cases, Super ATM produces a font that convincingly mimics the appearance of the original. Its generic serif and sans serif master outlines have their limits, however. Don't expect Super ATM to create a look-alike for your favorite grunge face or a highly stylized design like uncial or black-letter (it will at least replicate the metrics and formatting, however).

Super ATM's fonts aren't meant to replace real PostScript fonts. (You wouldn't want to use a substitute font in final output for a client, for example.) This program merely provides a convenient way to view and print a readable replica of a document—with formatting intact—if the recipient doesn't have the fonts used in the original.

FontChameleon

Like Super ATM, Ares Software's FontChameleon builds serif and sans serif fonts from a master outline file. But unlike SuperATM, FontChameleon creates faces that are, in many cases, virtually indistinguishable from the digital faces you'd buy from a vendor. The example below shows Adobe's Palatino (top) and Ares Serif 85 (bottom), which is similar to Palatino:

"I'll bring the hot dogs!" she said with relish.

"I'll bring the hot dogs!" she said with relish.

The fonts this amazing program creates are renditions of popular faces such as Avant Garde Gothic, Bembo, Bodoni, Bookman, Century Old Style, Franklin Gothic, Futura, Galliard, Garamond, Goudy Old Style, Helvetica, Janson, Melior, Palatino, Times, Univers, and others. In most cases, a number of weights and styles—including italic—are available.

FontChameleon uses files called *font descriptors* to mold its master outline into the characters of the requested font design. (Font descriptors are binary files, which means they are portable between Macintosh, DOS, Windows, and Unix systems.) FontChameleon uses the descriptor and the master outline to generate a PostScript or TrueType font, which can be installed and printed just like a font from Adobe, Bitstream, or any other digital-type vendor. Unlike a PostScript or TrueType font, which might be 40K or 50K in size, a font descriptor—essentially a "recipe" for creating a font from the master outline—takes up 5K or less, allowing you to fit hundreds of font descriptions on a floppy disk. If you want to send a document to a friend who also owns FontChameleon, you can send the font descriptors, rather than the fonts themselves, along with the document file, and your friend can use her copy of FontChameleon to construct the necessary fonts. Such a scheme saves not only disk space, but also time and money when sending files by modem.

The fonts created by FontChameleon are compatible with Adobe's font metrics. You can assign Adobe Font Metrics (AFM) files to font descriptors, ensuring that documents created with FontChameleon fonts have the same character spacing and line spacing as fonts in the Adobe Type Library. Therefore, if you create a document using FontChameleon's version of Melior, then print it at a service bureau that uses Adobe's Melior, the font metrics of the two documents will match.

You can use the set of font descriptors that come with FontChameleon, or modify the descriptors to create custom fonts. The program lets you alter character weight, width, slant, x-height, and tracking and save the result as a new font descriptor. You can also blend fonts to create hybrids, which can range from eye-catching novelties to aesthetic atrocities; if you're of a more practical bent, you can blend from one weight to another within the same family, creating, for example, a demibold weight. Unlike Adobe's Multiple Master fonts, which provide some constraints on character manipulation (in part to prevent amateur designers from running amok), FontChameleon lets you condense or extend the heck out of fonts.

The fonts generated by FontChameleon are inexpensive (a Starter Kit with 47 font designs costs around $50; additional font sets are available), remarkably faithful to the original designs, compact, and portable between platforms. So what's the catch? There's really no catch—just a few limitations.

FontChameleon's master outline, impressive though it may be, can only be stretched and molded so far. If you want a more exotic design—or simply a face that isn't in the program's font-descriptor repertoire—you'll have to purchase a traditional PostScript or TrueType font.

Apple has licensed Ares' Chameleon technology, so we may see it in future operating systems and printers.

Portable Documents

Another way to get font information from point A to point B is with portable documents. A number of applications can take documents created in a variety of applications and turn them into a common format that other people can read—even if they don't have the application or fonts that were used to create the original. You can think of a portable document as the electronic equivalent of a fax; a document that looks like the original can be viewed and printed by the recipient—but the text it contains is no longer "live," and can't be edited. Let's look at a few portable-document programs.

Adobe Acrobat

Adobe Acrobat lets you create documents in *Portable Document Format (PDF)*, a PostScript-based file format that works on Macintosh, DOS, Windows, and Unix platforms. Think of PDF as a high-fidelity snapshot of a document, including graphics and text. It's not just a bitmapped representation of the document, however, but a more sophisticated, outline-based representation that can be printed at any resolution.

A PDF document contains the names and metrics information for all the fonts in a document (both TrueType and PostScript fonts are supported). This information is called a *font descriptor*. Let's say you send someone an Acrobat file you've created using the ITC Galliard font. If the person on the receiving end has ITC Galliard installed, the actual font will be used when the document is printed. If Galliard is not available, a substitute font that simulates the appearance of Galliard will be created and rasterized by ATM or the TrueType rasterizer (see Chapter 4 if you're unfamiliar with these terms). Acrobat preserves spacing, stroke weight, and other characteristics of the original font, ensuring that the document will look pretty much like the original. As described earlier in this chapter for Super ATM, this scheme uses serif and sans serif Multiple Master font outlines to create synthetic versions of PostScript fonts.

But what if you want to use a decorative font? As you'll recall, that's where Super ATM fell down on the job, since its generic serif and sans serif outlines can't handle any exotic character shapes. That's where *embedded fonts* come in. Instead of including just the metrics information, you can include the actual font data into the PDF document. Embedded fonts take up more disk space than font descriptors (about 25K to 30K for an embedded font, versus about 1K for just the font metrics), but they ensure that a decent replica of the original font is produced.

Adobe Acrobat includes a program called Acrobat Reader, which allows you to view and print PDF documents. You can freely distibute Acrobat Reader to other users, allowing them to read your documents. Other Acrobat utilities let you search or annotate PDF files.

An enhanced version called Acrobat Pro includes all the features of Acrobat, plus a program called Acrobat Distiller, which converts files from graphics programs, page layout progams, and other programs into PDF files.

Acrobat is proving to be a handy tool for exchanging documents on online services. Why, just the other day I downloaded a PDF version of a tax-extension form from an online service, printed it on my laser printer with Acrobat Reader, filled it in, mailed it out, and put off paying my taxes for another few months. Now that's progress!

Common Ground

Common Ground, from Common Ground Software (formerly No Hands Software), is another portable-document program. Like Acrobat, Common Ground lets you send a portable document that the recipient can view and print on a Mac, DOS, Windows, or Unix platform, even if that person doesn't have the application or fonts that were used to create the original document. Common Ground works with both PostScript and TrueType fonts.

While Acrobat uses PostScript to create its documents, Common Ground uses its own file format, which is called DigitalPaper. Unlike Acrobat, Common Ground doesn't require you to run ATM (why anyone who uses

PostScript fonts on a Mac wouldn't use ATM is beyond me, but some users might opt to use only TrueType fonts, which don't require ATM).

You can create a document with Common Ground, or convert a document from virtually any application into a Common Ground document by simply dragging the document's icon onto Common Ground's AutoMaker icon. You can then send your file electronically, and the recipient can view and print it with a Common Ground Viewer. If you wish, you can embed a MiniViewer in the document, creating a completely self-contained portable document. Common Ground also lets you search documents, copy text or graphics (or prevent items from being copied or printed if you wish), and annotate a document.

The latest version of Common Ground uses Bitstream's *TrueDoc* portable-font technology, which reads Type 1 PostScript and TrueType character outlines, stores the curves that make up the characters' shapes, and generates hints, producing a high-fidelity version of the original fonts. Rather than imaging fonts at a fixed set of resolutions, as the earlier version did, the new Common Ground allows you to zoom in and view characters at any resolution, as well as print documents at any resolution.

While portable documents don't match the quality of the real thing, they provide a relatively painless way to send people something that looks like your original document, fonts and all. Like most new-ish technologies, portable-document applications will no doubt evolve. As more software developers incorporate portable-font solutions like Bitstream's TrueDoc and Ares Software's MiniFont (another technology that lets users embed Post-Script and TrueType fonts in documents) into their applications, document fidelity will improve and, with any luck, the "I don't have that font" blues will eventually fade away.

9

What Next?

Fonts, like everything else in the digital ecosystem, are constantly evolving. In the Mac's first decade, we saw a rapid progression from bitmapped fonts to PostScript, with TrueType—a subspecies of scalable outline fonts—cropping up a few years ago. With System 7.5, we saw the emergence of another subspecies of fonts: QuickDraw GX fonts. Although superior to their predecessors in many ways, GX fonts are struggling to survive in an environment that is not yet ready for them.

You may be surprised to see GX fonts covered in a "What Next?" chapter. After all, they've been around for some time. Yes, they exist. But they have not yet arrived. Read on, and you'll hear a tale of a technology that will either revolutionize digital typography or languish in obscurity, depending on which way the winds of politics and marketing blow.

QuickDraw GX Fonts

Most of this chapter is devoted to Apple's QuickDraw GX font technology. If you have System 7.5, you can get your hands on a set of GX fonts and experiment with them.

What Is a GX Font?

First, let's establish what this new type of type is—and is not. A QuickDraw GX font is an outline font that takes advantage of Apple's QuickDraw GX imaging model, which is included as an extension to System 7.5. QuickDraw GX is an enhanced version of QuickDraw (the Mac's set of built-in instructions for displaying text and graphics) that includes an expanded set of graphics routines and improvements in color matching, printing, document portability, and typography.

QuickDraw GX is *not* a new font format—a GX font can be in either TrueType or PostScript Type 1 format—but rather a new technology that lets type developers add functionality to fonts. (*Note:* Your old PostScript and TrueType fonts will still work when the GX extension is installed.)

The beauty of GX fonts is that typographic "intelligence" can be built into the font itself, rather than provided by the application in which the font is used. This allows even "productivity" applications, such as word processors and databases, to offer advanced typographic features—*if* the application has been revised to make it GX-aware.

In the current scheme of things, fonts are pretty much just collections of characters; what you do with them depends on the application you're using. With a word processor, you can specify type size, justification, leading, and so on. A page layout program gives you precise control over typographic features such as kerning and tracking, while a graphics program might let you skew or rotate text, shade a letter, thicken an outline, and so on. If you're a sophisticated type user, you might augment a typeface with an expert collection. If you want to customize features such as character width, weight, or optical scaling, you can buy a Multiple Master typeface.

On the other hand, QuickDraw GX lets font developers add typographic instructions that perform many of the functions just described. A GX font can contain information about features such as tracking, kerning, justification, and weight or width variations. In addition, the font can contain thousands of additional characters, including accents, symbols, ornaments, small caps, old style numerals, ligatures, and more. "Wait a minute!" you say, "My keyboard doesn't have enough keystroke combinations to let me type thousands of characters." That's part of a GX font's charm: you don't have to use keystroke combinations to type special characters such as fractions or ligatures. Instead, you can turn typographic variations on and off as needed in a menu or dialog box. For example, say you're typing the following sentence in your word processor, using the current, non-GX version of Adobe Garamond: "To add flavor to grilled chicken, add ¼ cup chopped garlic to the barbecue sauce and marinate for 30 to 45 minutes." If you read Chapters 1 and 2 of this book, you're familiar with the following problems and workarounds:

• The *T* and the *o* in *To* should be closer together. Too bad; your word processor doesn't support kerning.

• You'd like to use an "fl" ligature in *flavor*. You either type the ligature with the Shift-Option-5 keystroke combination (if you can remember it), use the program's Change command to convert every "f-l" letter combination to a ligature when the document is finished, or activate your page layout program's ligatures option, if it has one.

• You want to type "¼" as a fraction. You mess around with superscript numbers, different type sizes, and the Shift-Option-1 keystroke combination, which produces a slash that's suitable for fractions. Or you create custom fractions in Fontographer. Or you buy the Adobe Garamond Expert Collection font, which includes fractions.

• You'd prefer to use old style numerals for the "30" and "45," since they're more pleasing to the eye than numbers that don't fall below the baseline. You buy the Adobe Garamond Expert Collection, which includes old style numerals.

With the QuickDraw GX version of Adobe Garamond and a word processor that supported GX fonts, you could type the above sentence much more easily. You'd simply pull down a menu for Adobe Garamond GX, and select Ligatures, Fractions, and Oldstyle Numerals. As you typed *f* and then *l*, the *fl* ligature would automatically appear. As you typed 1, a slash, and 4, the font would automatically generate a fraction. Old style numerals would appear as well. If the font designer built a *T-o* kerning pair into the font, QuickDraw GX's Line Layout function would apply the specified kerning, even in a lowly word processor. As another plus, the *f* and the *l* in the ligature are recognized by the System as a separate *f* and *l*, so the word *flavor* will be intact—as opposed to *–avor*—if you change your text to a font that doesn't have that ligature.

Feature-Rich Fonts

GX font designers have the tools to add a broad range of typographic enhancements to their fonts. Here's an overview of the features that can be included in a GX font:

• *Thousands of characters per font.* Unlike today's fonts, which can include a maximum of 256 characters, a GX font can include up to 65,000 characters. To be more precise, a GX font can include up to 65,000 *glyphs*, or character representations. While you might think of the letter *s* as a single character, that *s* can be represented by any number of glyphs. Depending on what options are selected, pressing the S key on your keyboard could produce a lowercase letter, an uppercase one, a swash, or a small cap, for example. In each of these examples, a different glyph is invoked for the letter *s*.

While a GX font *can* include 65,000 glyphs, 400 to 600 glyphs is a more typical range for a roman alphabet. Of course, there's more to typography than the roman alphabet. The ability to place thousands of glyphs in a single font is a plus for creators of nonroman fonts such as kanji, which consists of several thousand symbols.

• *Automatic glyph substitution.* GX fonts go further than just adding alternate letter styles; the characters in GX fonts can be context-sensitive. An *s* at the end of a word could have a calligraphic flourish, for example, while an *s* in the middle of a word would not. Typing an *s* followed by a *t* could produce a ligature. As another example, with a font's Fractions option turned on, typing a number, then a slash, then another number would automatically generate a fraction.

Automatic glyph substitution can also be applied to nonroman text systems such as Arabic, in which the appearance of a character changes depending on its position with respect to other characters.

• *Kerning and tracking.* A type designer can place kerning and tracking instructions in a GX font. Since QuickDraw GX instructions operate at the System level, rather than the application level, this means that kerning and tracking can occur in any GX-aware application, rather than exclusively in high-end page layout programs.

• *Optical alignment.* In some cases, several lines of text can be vertically aligned along a margin, but appear crooked to the reader. A letter with a rounded edge, such as C, might be touching the same margin as a letter with a straight edge, such as R. Optical alignment moves the letters slightly so they appear to the eye to be aligned. A GX font can support optical alignment based on instructions included in the font.

Similarly, punctuation that falls at the end of a line, including hyphens, can leave a visual gap along the right margin. GX fonts can incorporate hanging punctuation, in which punctuation protrudes a minute distance over the margin, making the margin appear more even.

• *Live text as graphics.* In illustration programs such as Illustrator or FreeHand, you can stretch, slant, rotate, or skew text. Once you manipulate text in this way, however, it's no longer "live." You can't correct a typo or delete a word in a line without negating the effect that was applied. With QuickDraw GX fonts, you can apply effects to text while maintaining full text-editing functionality.

• *Variable style options.* QuickDraw GX fonts can support style variations similar to those of Adobe's Multiple Master fonts. For example, a GX font might allow the user to adjust style axes for width, weight, or optical scaling. Skia, one of the GX fonts included with System 7.5, allows the user to adjust character width and weight.

Not every GX font will include all of the features just described. In some cases, a font's design will dictate which features will be included. For example, a decorative face might not contain *fi* and *fl* ligatures, which are often found in traditional serif faces. Similarly, a modern sans serif design would probably have no call for swash characters, but such a face might contain a set of alternate capitals or other letter variations. In other cases, time or budget constraints might dictate how many characters a GX font will have; creating a GX font is much more labor-intensive than creating a traditional font.

What If They Gave a Font Technology and Nobody Came?

So, where are all the GX fonts? Well, that's the sad part of this story. Several font companies, including Adobe, ITC, Bitstream, and Linotype, have released GX fonts. But they're not exactly selling like hotcakes. While font fans were understandably excited about the potential of this new technology, software application developers were less enthused. One problem is the lack of cross-platform compatibility. While TrueType fonts are currently supported by the Macintosh and Windows operating systems, no such cross-platform capability exists for QuickDraw GX fonts, since QuickDraw is an imaging architecture unique to the Macintosh. Although many font developers have made it clear to Apple that they want cross-platform compatibility, it's unclear what—if anything—can be done to accomplish that. Microsoft has shown no inclination to support GX font technology in its Windows platform.

So far, only a few programs—notably Manhattan Graphics' Ready-SetGo page layout program and Pixar's Typestry type-effects program—fully support GX fonts.

Apple's System 7.5 includes four GX fonts: Hoefler, Apple Chancery, Skia, and Tekton Plus. You can install these fonts, if you wish, when you install the System software. Unfortunately, that's about all you can do with them. Unless you use one of the programs just mentioned (or another program that supports GX fonts), your GX fonts will look and act like any other font—you won't be able to see their additional characters and capabilities. So you can get a look at some of the special characteristics of the GX fonts that come with System 7.5, they're previewed on the following pages.

• *Hoefler.* Designed by Jonathan Hoefler, this family includes Hoefler Regular, Black, Italic, and Black Italic, as well as Hoefler Ornaments. The fonts include old style numerals, inferior and superior numbers and letters, fractions, ligatures, engraved characters, small caps, and ornaments.

WORK

"Anyone can do any amount of work, provided it isn't the work he's supposed to be doing at that moment."

— Robert Benchley

• *Apple Chancery.* Designed by Charles Bigelow and Kris Holmes, this lovely font is based on handwriting scripts developed during the Renaissance. It has four design levels featuring different serifs, ascenders, descenders, and swashes. It includes old style numerals, inferior and superior numbers and letters, fractions, ligatures, and fleurons.

You spotted snakes with double tongue,
Thorny hedgehogs, be not seen;
Newts and blind-worms, do no wrong,
Come not near our fairy queen.

• *Skia*. This stylish sans serif face by Matthew Carter offers variable weight and width axes. It includes old style numerals, inferior and superior numbers and letters, fractions, and ligatures.

"Diets?" she said.
"My dear, I have tried them all and have had no luck whatsoever.
Alas! Nothing seems to work.
I am more thinned against than thinning."

• *Tekton Plus*. Based on David Siegel's popular Tekton, Tekton Plus is a PostScript Type 1 GX font released by Adobe. It includes accented characters, small caps, ligatures, superior and inferior numbers, fractions, and swashes.

Dear Levi:

You are cordially invited to join us for an evening of poetry and song at the Corn Palace in Mitchell, South Dakota. The fabulous Korn Kings will be playing on Wednesday, September 28, at 7 P.M.

How to Install and Use GX Fonts

If you want to use QuickDraw GX fonts, you need a Mac with a minimum configuration of a 68020 processor; 5MB of RAM (8MB is suggested) with System 7.1, 8MB of RAM with System 7.5, and 16MB of RAM with System 7.5 on a Power Mac; and Apple's QuickDraw GX extension (included with System 7.5; also available from vendors who license the extension for inclusion with their products). GX fonts will work in a limited capacity with current applications, but to take advantage of alternate characters and other GX functions, you'll need applications that are GX-aware.

To install QuickDraw GX and the GX fonts that are included with System 7.5, you run an installer program. This program automatically installs the QuickDraw GX extension and the Hoefler Text and Ornaments, Apple Chancery, Skia, and Tekton Plus fonts. The program also installs ATM GX, Adobe's GX-savvy version of Adobe Type Manager.

If you have existing TrueType fonts installed, they'll work under QuickDraw GX. If you have existing PostScript Type 1 fonts installed, the installer will convert them to a form that will work under QuickDraw GX. During the installation process, a message says "Enabling Type 1 fonts." When you look in your Fonts folder, you'll see a new entity: a single suitcase icon that holds both the screen and printer components of a PostScript font. (Your old PostScript fonts are archived in a separate folder, in case you need them later. If you decide to remove QuickDraw GX, don't forget to reinstall your PostScript fonts by dragging their icons into the Fonts folder.)

The enabling process just described works only on PostScript fonts that are installed in the Fonts folder. If you use a font-management utility such as Suitcase—or if you need to install PostScript fonts after you've installed the GX extension—you must run a Type 1 font enabler from Adobe that's included with System 7.5.

To install a new GX font, you simply drag it into the System Folder as you would any other font.

PostScript fonts that are enabled to operate under QuickDraw GX will work just like they used to under your previous System setup. They will not magically acquire any GX font characteristics such as additional characters; these must be provided by a font designer when a GX font is made.

Once your GX fonts are installed, open an application that supports GX fonts (if you have one), select a GX font, and check the attributes you want to use (ligatures, swash characters, different script styles, old style numerals, and so on). When you start typing, the characteristics you selected will be applied on the fly.

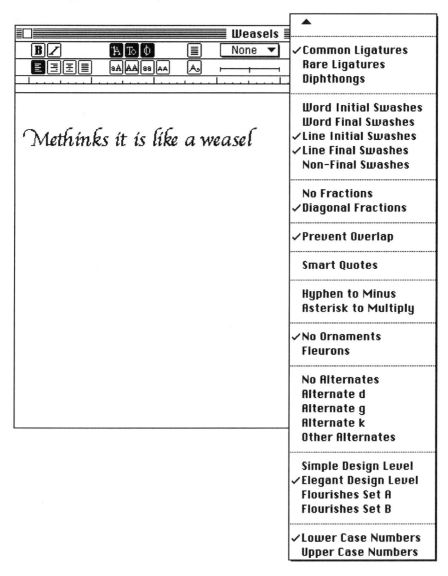

Fonts of the Future

I don't know whether QuickDraw GX fonts will ever catch on. I hope so; these fonts far outshine their non-GX counterparts when it comes to sophisticated typographic features. If QuickDraw GX *per se* doesn't pan out, I'd be willing to bet that a similar font technology that offers the same kind of enhancements will someday become established.

While I'm making predictions, I'll venture a few more. Some of these are educated guesses, based on talks with industry experts and observations of current trends. Others are, perhaps, wishful thinking. Here are some trends I expect to see:

‣ *A simpler installation procedure.* As you read in Chapter 5, font installation has gotten much easier since the days of the Font/DA Mover. I think it will become easier still as the Mac's operating system evolves. Installing fonts by clicking a single button should be possible (as it is in some software-installation utilities today).

Also, I wouldn't be surprised if PostScript fonts became easier to handle; QuickDraw GX has shown us that it's possible to consolidate the screen and printer fonts that make up a PostScript font (Tekton Plus is a Type 1 PostScript GX font that resides in a single icon). We may see single-icon PostScript fonts in the future.

‣ *More online font sales.* Companies like Treacyfaces, Alphabets Inc., and Monotype already let customers order their fonts via online services. As online commerce becomes more accepted (and people stop worrying about sending their credit card numbers out into cyberspace), I suspect more and more companies will let you log on, order a font, and instantly download it to your computer.

‣ *An increasing reliance on portable documents and synthesized fonts.* As you saw in the last chapter, portable-document technologies allow font information to travel along with a document. As people increasingly rely on modems to transfer information, we'll have to figure out how to reliably get font information from point A to point B.

• *Better-looking fonts on the Internet.* If the masses can rise up in revolt when the flavor of their favorite cola is altered, I don't see why they can't make some noise about the dismal, hard-to-read fonts one sees on the World Wide Web. I hope this situation will be corrected before we all go blind from reading obliqued Times at tiny point sizes.

New technologies such as Bitstream's TrueDoc will enable software developers to create browsers and other programs that retain the look and feel of fonts in documents published on the World Wide Web.

• *Better, cheaper printers.* If the current trend continues, you can expect to see printer resolution going up and printer prices going down. These days, 600-dpi laser printers are becoming more popular (and more affordable), and many 1200-dpi printers will soon be within financial reach of individuals and small businesses.

Whatever happens in the coming years, you can be sure that digital font technology won't stagnate. Fonts have become too important a part of the Macintosh environment to be left behind as other parts of the system are enhanced to keep up with the times. 🐾

A
Vendor
Information

This appendix lists companies that sell fonts, font utilities, and other programs mentioned in this book. If you see some faces in this book that you like in the samples printed throughout this book, you should contact the appropriate vendors and ask for their catalogs.

Another way to keep up-to-date on the latest fonts is to check out the World Wide Web or a commercial online service. Some popular online services are listed here.

Fonts

Adobe Systems Inc.
1585 Charleston Rd.
P.O. Box 7900
Mountain View, CA 94309-7900
415/961-4400; 800/445-8787;
Internet: http://www.adobe.com/
Text, display, decorative, pictorial,
foreign language
$29.95–$275 per package

Agfa Division, Bayer Corp.
100 Challenger Rd.
Ridgefield Park, NJ 07660-2199
201/440-0111; 800/424-8973
Text, display, decorative
$29–$59 per font

Alphabets, Inc.
P.O. Box 5448
Evanston, IL 60204-5448
708/328-2733; 800/326-8973;
fax 708/328-1922
Internet: info@alphabets.com
CompuServe: 73306,2703
Text, display, decorative, pictorial
$34.95–$74.95 per font

Autologic
1050 Rancho Conejo Blvd.
Thousand Oaks, CA 91320
805/498-9611; 800/457-8973;
fax 805/498-7099
Internet: mtoft@autologic.com
Text, display, decorative
$23–$40 per font

Bear Rock Technologies
4140 Mother Lode Drive #100
Shingle Springs, CA 95682-8038
916/672-0244; 800/232-7625;
fax 916/672-1103
Bar code
$95–$395 per package

Bersearch Information Services
26160 Edelweiss Circle
Evergreen, CO 80439
303/674-8875; 800/851-0289;
fax 303/674-1850
America Online: Bersearch
Internet: bersearch@mcimail.com
Cyrillic
$49

Bitstream Inc.
215 First St.
Cambridge, MA 02142
617/497-6222; 800/522-3668;
fax 617/868-0784
Internet: http://www.bitstream.com
Text, display, decorative, pictorial
$20 per font

Blue Sky Research
534 S.W. Third Ave.
Portland, OR 97204
503/222-9571; 800/622-8398;
fax 503/222-1643
Internet: sales@bluesky.com
Text, math symbols (for TeX)
$99–$149

Carter & Cone Type Inc.
2155 Massachusetts Ave.
Cambridge, MA 02140
617/576-0398; 800/952-2129;
fax 617/354-4146
Text, display, decorative
$40–$60 per font; $75–$150 per package

Casady & Greene, Inc.
22734 Portola Dr.
Salinas, CA 93908-1119
408/484-9228; 800/359-4920;
fax 408/484-9218
Internet: sales@casadyg.com
*Text, display, decorative, foreign language,
music notation*
$40–$60 per package

Castle Systems Design
1306 Lincoln Ave.
San Rafael, CA 94901-2105
415/459-6495
America Online: jcastle
Display, decorative, text
$39 per font

Davka Corp.
7074 N. Western Ave.
Chicago, IL 60645
312/465-4070; 800/621-8227;
fax 312/262-9298
Hebrew
$25–$40 per font

DS Design
1157 Executive Circle, Suite D
Cary, NC 27511
919/319-1770; 800/745-4037;
fax 919/460-5983
America Online: dsd soft
Internet:
http://www.dsdesign.com/dsdesign/
Childrens' drawings and handwriting
$55 per package

DVM Publications
P.O. Box 399
Thorofare, NJ 08086
609/853-5580 (phone and fax)
America Online: splsa
Musical notation
$24.95–$39.95 plus $3 shipping

Eastern Languages
39 E. 300 North Street
Provo, UT 84606
801/377-4558; fax 801/377-2200
Foreign language
$149–$249 per package

Ecological Linguistics
P.O. Box 15156
Washington, DC 20003
202/546-5862
America Online: ecoling
Foreign language
$45–$80 per family (send 9- by 12-inch
SASE with 95¢ postage for catalog)

Judith Sutcliffe: The Electric Typographer
501 First Ave.
P.O. Box 224
Audubon, IA 50025-0224
805/966-7563
Display, decorative, handwriting, pictorial
$45–$79.95 per package

EmDash
P.O. Box 8256
Northfield, IL 60093
708/441-6699
Text, display, pictorial
$20 per font

Emigre
4475 D St.
Sacramento, CA 95819
916/451-4344; 800/944-9021;
fax 916/451-4351
Internet: http://www.emigre.com
Text, display, decorative
$59–$95 per package

FontBank Inc.
2620 Central St.
Evanston, IL 60201
708/328-7370; fax 708/328-7491
Internet: jerry@jworld.com
Display, decorative
$19.95–$49.95

The Font Bureau, Inc.
175 Newbury St.
Boston, MA 02116
617/423-8770; fax 617/423-8771
America Online: fontbureau
Text, display, decorative
$40 per font; site license $300

FontHaus Inc.
1375 Kings Highway E.
Fairfield, CT 06430
203/367-1993; 800/942-9110;
fax 203/367-1860
America Online: fonthaus
Text, display, decorative, pictorial
(FontHaus offers faces from numerous
type developers, as well as custom
FontHaus designs)
$29 and up per font

FontShop USA Inc.
47 W. Polk St., #100–310
Chicago, IL 60605
800/897-3872; fax 312/360-1997
Text, display, decorative, pictorial
(FontShop offers faces from numerous
type developers, as well as custom
FontShop designs)
$39–$319

Font World, Inc.
2021 Scottsville Rd.
Rochester, NY 14623-2021
716/235-6861; fax 716/235-6950
Text, foreign language, custom font software
$25–$1500

Galápagos Design Group
256 Great Road, Suite 15
Littleton, MA 01460-1916
508/952-6200; fax 508/952-6260
Text, display, decorative, handwriting
$59 per font

Handcraftedfonts Company
P.O. Box 14013
Philadelphia, PA 19122
215/922-5584; fax 215/922-7709
America Online: jonathan45
Pictorial
$35 per font

Image Club Graphics, Inc.
729 24th Avenue S.E.
Calgary, Alberta
T2G 5K8 Canada
403/262-8008; 800/661-9410 (US);
fax 403/261-7013
America Online: imageclub/
CompuServe: 72560,2323
Internet:
http://www.adobe.com/imageclub
Text, display, decorative, pictorial
$19–$150 per font

ITC Fonts
866 Second Ave.
New York, NY 10017
212/371-0699 (NY); 800/425-3882;
fax 212/752-4752
Internet: hgrey@interport.net
Text, display, decorative
$29 per font

Lanston Type
P.O. Box 60
Mount Stewart
Prince Edward Island
COA 1T0 Canada
902/676-2835; 800/478-8973;
fax 902/676-2393
Text, display
$39–$360 per font; $75–$295 per fam.

LaserMaster Corp.
6900 Shady Oak Rd.
Eden Prairie, MN 55344
612/943-8286; 800/947-8880
Internet: support@lmt.mn.org
Text, display, decorative
$295 per 100-font volume (2 vols. $550;
3 vols. $825)

Letraset USA
40 Eisenhower Dr.
Paramus, NJ 07653
201/845-6100; 800/343-8973;
fax 201/845-5047
Display, decorative, pictorial
$39.95–$89.95 per font

Letter Perfect
P.O. Box 785
Gig Harbor, WA 98335
206/851-5158 (phone and fax);
800/929-1951
America Online: ltdesign
Display, decorative
$39 per face

Linguist's Software, Inc.
P.O. Box 580
Edmonds, WA 98020-0580
206/775-1130; fax 206/771-5911
CompuServe: 75507,1157
Foreign language, math
$99.95 per font

Linotype-Hell Company
425 Oser Avenue
Hauppauge, NY 11788
800/633-1900 (US);
800/366-3735 (Canada);
fax 516/434-2720
Text, display, decorative, pictorial, foreign lang.
$75–$275 per family

Monotype Typography Inc.
150 S. Wacker Drive, Suite 2630
Chicago, IL 60606
312/855-1440; 800/666-6897;
fax 312/855-9475
Internet: sales@monotypeusa.com
Text, display, decorative, pictorial, borders
$25–$195

NEC Technologies, Inc.
1414 Massachussetts Avenue
Boxborough, MA 01719
508/264-8000; 800/366-3632
Adobe Library on CD ROM
Prices vary

Nisus Software, Inc.
107 South Cedros Avenue
P.O. Box 1300
Solana Beach, CA 92075
619/481-1477; 800/890-3030;
fax 619/481-6154
Internet: info@nisus-soft.com
Math equations, circuit diagrams
$49 per package

Pacific Rim Connections, Inc.
1838 El Camino Real, Suite 219
Burlingame, CA 94010
415/697-0911; fax 415/697-9439
Internet: pacrim@sirius.com
Foreign language
$99–$3000

Page Studio Graphics
3175 N. Price Road, Suite 1050
Chandler, AZ 85224
602/839-2763 (phone and fax)
Pictorial
$29–$165

Phil's Fonts, Inc.
14605 Sturtevant Road
Silver Springs, MD 20905
301/879-0601; 800/424-2977;
fax 301/879-0606
(Phil's offers faces from numerous type
developers)
Text, display, decorative
Prices vary

Precision Type
47 Mall Dr.
Commack, NY 11725-5703
516/864-0167; 800/248-3668;
fax 516/543-5721
(Precision Type offers faces from
numerous type developers)
Text, display, decorative, pictorial
$19–$49 per font

Prepress Direct
11 Mount Pleasant Ave.
East Hanover, NJ 07936
201/887-8000 ext. 999 (NJ);
800/443-6600 (US, except NJ)
Text, display, decorative
$45–$370 per family

RoadRunner Computing
P.O. Box 21635
Baton Rouge, LA 70894
504/928-0780; fax 504/928-0802
CompuServe: 76436,2426
Keycap symbols
$49 per package

Signature Software
489 N. 8th Street, Suite 201
Hood River, OR 97031
503/386-3221; 800/925-8840;
fax 503/386-3229
Internet: sigsoft@netcom.com
Will make font from your handwriting
$49.95–$299.95

Stone Type Foundry Inc.
626 Middlefield Road
Palo Alto, CA 94301
415/324-1870; fax 415/324-1783
Text, display
$69–$149

T-26
361 West Chestnut, First Floor
Chicago, IL 60610
312/787-8973; fax 312/649-0376
America Online: T26Font
Text, display, decorative, weird
$49–$69 per font

TPS Electronics
2495 Old Middlefield Way
Mountain View, CA 94043
415/988-0141; fax 415/988-0289
Bar code
$50–$219 per package

Treacyfaces, Inc.
P.O. Box 26036
West Haven, CT 06516-8036
203/389-7037; fax 203/389-7039
CompuServe: 74041,3336 (info and
ordering: go dtponline)
Text, display, specialty
$49–$130 per package

URW America, Inc.
4 Manchester Street
Nashua, NH 03060
603/882-7445; fax 603/882-7210
Text, display, decorative
$45 per font

Typeface Catalogs & Reference Books

The Electronic Type Catalog
by Steve Byers
Bantam Books/ITC
$34.95

FontBook
FontShop USA Inc.
47 W. Polk St., #100–310
Chicago, IL 60605
800/897-3872; fax 312/360-1997
$89 (2-volume set)

Font Sampler Catalog
HyperActive Software
5226 W. Nokomis Parkway
Minneapolis, MN 55417
612/724-1596
(Each volume shows 100 samples of freeware and shareware fonts)
$15 per volume; $45 for 4 volumes

Precision Type Font Reference Guide
Precision Type
47 Mall Dr.
Commack, NY 11725-5703
516/864-0167; 800/248-3668;
fax 516/543-5721
$39.95

U&lc
ITC Fonts
866 Second Ave.
New York, NY 10017
212/371-0699 (NY); 800/425-3882;
fax 212/752-4752
$5 per issue

x-height
c/o FontHaus Inc.
1375 Kings Highway E.
Fairfield, CT 06430
203/367-1993; 800/942-9110;
fax 203/367-1860
$7 per issue plus $3 shipping

Font Creation/Editing Programs

FontChameleon
Ares Software Corporation
565 Pilgrim Drive, Suite A
Foster City, CA 94404
415/578-9090; 800/783-2737;
fax 415/378-8999
America Online: ARESSW
CompuServe: 70253,3164
$295 (Starter Kit $55)

FontMonger
Ares Software Corporation
565 Pilgrim Drive, Suite A
Foster City, CA 94404
415/578-9090; 800/783-2737;
fax 415/378-8999
America Online: ARESSW
CompuServe: 70253,3164
$149

Fontographer

Macromedia Inc.
600 Townsend Street
San Francisco, CA 94103
415/252-2000; 800/945-4061
Internet: http://www.macromedia.com
$495

Ikarus-M

URW America, Inc.
4 Manchester Street
Nashua, NH 03060
603/882-7445; fax 603/882-7210
$598

Font Special Effects Programs

Envelopes

Letraset USA
40 Eisenhower Dr.
Paramus, NJ 07653
210/845-6100; 800/343-8973;
fax 201/845-5047
$199 (program plus 200 plug-ins);
$99 (program plus 58 plug-ins)

LetraStudio

Letraset USA
40 Eisenhower Dr.
Paramus, NJ 07653
210/845-6100; 800/343-8973;
fax 201/845-5047
$249

Pixar Typestry 2

Pixar
1001 W. Cutting Blvd.
Richmond, CA 94804
510/236-4000; 800/888-9856
America Online: pixartech
$299

StrataType 3d

Strata
2 W, Saint George Blvd., Suite 2100
Saint George, UT 84770
801/628-5218; 800/678-7282;
fax 801/628-9756
America Online: strata 3d
$199

TypeStyler

Brøderbund Software
500 Redwood Blvd., P.O. Box 6121
Novato, CA 94948-6121
415/382-4400; 800/521-6263;
fax 415/382-4419
$129.95

Type Twister

Adobe Systems Inc.
1585 Charleston Rd.
P.O. Box 7900
Mountain View, CA 94309-7900
415/961-4400; 800/445-8787
Internet: http://www.adobe.com/
$29.95

Utilities

Adobe Acrobat

Adobe Systems, Inc.
1585 Charleston Rd.
P.O. Box 7900
Mountain View, CA 94309-7900
415/961-4400; 800/344-8335;
fax 415/960-0886
Internet: http://www.adobe.com/
$195 (Acrobat Exchange);
$595 (Acrobat Pro)

Adobe Type Manager (ATM)

Adobe Systems Inc.
1585 Charleston Rd.
P.O. Box 7900
Mountain View, CA 94309-7900
415/961-4400; 800/445-8787
Internet: http://www.adobe.com/
$65

Adobe Type Reunion

Adobe Systems Inc.
1585 Charleston Rd.
P.O. Box 7900
Mountain View, CA 94309-7900
415/961-4400; 800/445-8787
Internet: http://www.adobe.com/
$65

Agfa TypeChart

Agfa Division, Bayer Corp.
100 Challenger Rd.
Ridgefield Park, NJ 07660-2199
201/440-0111; 800/424-8973
$99

BigCaps

Dubl-Click Software Corp.
20310 Empire Ave., Suite A102
Bend, OR 97701-5713
503/317-0355; fax 503/317/0430
America Online: DublClick
Internet: http://www.dublclick.com
$69.95 (MenuFonts package; includes
BigCaps)

Captivate

Mainstay
591-A Constitution Avenue
Camarillo, CA 93012
805/484-9400; 800/484-9817;
fax 805/484-9428
America Online: Mainstay1
CompuServe: 76004,1525
$89.95

Common Ground

Common Ground Software Inc.
303 Twin Dolphin Drive, Suite 420
Redwood City, CA 94065
415/802-5800; fax 415/593-6868
Internet:
hhtp://www.commonground.com
$189

theFONDler

Rascal Software
25223 Wheeler Road
Newhall, CA 91321
805/255-6823; fax 805/255-9691
CompuServe: 71604,3213
805/255-6823; fax 805/255-9291
$69.95

FontHopper
Ares Software Corporation
565 Pilgrim Drive, Suite A
Foster City, CA 94404
415/578-9090; 800/783-2737;
fax 415/378-8999
America Online: ARESSW
CompuServe: 70253,3164
$149

Fontina
Eastgate Systems
134 Main Street
Watertown, MA 02172
617/924-9044; 800/562-1638
Internet: http://www.eastgate.com
$69.95

FontMixer
150 S. Wacker Drive, Suite 2630
Chicago, IL 60606
312/855-1440; 800/666-6897;
fax 312/855-9475
Internet: sales@monotypeusa.com
$79

FontMonger
Ares Software Corporation
565 Pilgrim Drive, Suite A
Foster City, CA 94404
415/578-9090; 800/783-2737
fax 415/378-8999
America Online: ARESSW
CompuServe: 70253,3164
$149

LetrTuck
EDCO Services, Inc.
4107 Gunn Highway
Tampa, FL 33624
813/962-7800; 800/523-8973
$99; Pro Version $199

MacQWERTY
107 South Cedros Avenue
P.O. Box 1300
Solana Beach, CA 92075
619/481-1477; 800/890-3030;
fax 619/481-6154
Internet: info@nisus-soft.com
$45

MasterJuggler
Alsoft, Inc.
P.O. Box 927
Spring, TX 77383-0927
713/353-4090; 800/257-6381;
fax 713/353-9868
$69.95

MathType
Design Science, Inc.
4028 Broadway
Long Beach, CA 90803
310/433-0685; 800/827-0685;
fax 310/433-6969
Internet:
http://www.mathtype.com/mathtype/
$199

MenuFonts
Dubl-Click Software Corp.
20310 Empire Ave., Suite A102
Bend, OR 97701-5713
503/317-0355; fax 503/317/0430
America Online: DublClick
Internet: http://www.dublclick.com
$69.95

QuicKeys
CE Software, Inc.
P.O. Box 65580
West Des Moines, IA 50265
515/221-1801; 800/523-7638;
fax 515/221-1806
$119

Suitcase
Symantec Corp.
175 West Broadway
Eugene, OR 97401
503/333-6054; 800/441-7234;
fax 503/334-7400
CompuServe: go symantec
$79

Super ATM
Adobe Systems, Inc.
1585 Charleston Rd.
P.O. Box 7900
Mountain View, CA 94309-7900
415/961-4400; 800/344-8335;
fax 415/960-0886
Internet: http://www.adobe.com/
$99

the TypeBook
Rascal Software
25223 Wheeler Road
Newhall, CA 91321
805/255-6823; fax 805/255-9691
CompuServe: 71604,3213
805/255-6823; fax 805/255-9291
$49.95

TypeTamer
Impossible Software, Inc.
P.O. Box 52710
Irvine, CA 92619-2710
714/470-4800; fax 714/470-4740
America Online: typetamer
$59.95

Page Layout Programs

PageMaker
Adobe Systems, Inc.
1585 Charleston Rd.
P.O. Box 7900
Mountain View, CA 94309-7900
415/961-4400; 800/344-8335;
fax 415/960-0886
Internet: http://www.adobe.com/
$895

QuarkXPress
Quark, Inc.
1800 Grant Street
Denver, CO 80203
303/894-8888; 800/788-7835;
fax 303/894-3399
$895

ReadySetGo
Manhattan Graphics
250 E. Hartsdale Ave.
Hartsdale, NY 10530
914/725-2048; 800/572-6533;
fax 914/725-2450
America Online: RSG
$395

PostScript Graphics Programs

Adobe Illustrator
Adobe Systems Inc.
1585 Charleston Rd.
P.O. Box 7900
Mountain View, CA 94309-7900
415/961-4400; 800/445-8787
Internet: http://www.adobe.com/
$99

Macromedia FreeHand
Macromedia Inc.
600 Townsend Street
San Francisco, CA 94103
415/252-2000; 800/945-4061
Internet: http://www.macromedia.com
$595

Word Processors

MacWrite Pro
Claris Corporation
5201 Patrick Henry Dr.
Santa Clara, CA 95052
408/727-8227; 800/325-2747
$49

Microsoft Word
Microsoft Corporation
1 Microsoft Way
Redmond, WA 98052-6393
206/882-8080; 800/426-9400;
fax 206/635-6100
$339

Nisus Writer
107 South Cedros Avenue
P.O. Box 1300
Solana Beach, CA 92075
619/481-1477; 800/890-3030;
fax 619/481-6154
Internet: info@nisus-soft.com
$149

Novell (WordPerfect)
Novell
1555 North Technology Way
Orem, UT 84057-2399
801/225-5000; fax 801/728-5077
$189

WriteNow
Softkey International Inc.
1 Athenaeum Street
Cambridge, MA 02142
617/494-1200; 800/227-5609;
fax 617/494-0067
$55.95

Online Services

America Online

8619 Westwood Center Drive
Vienna, VA 22182
703/448-8700; 800/827-6364
Internet: http://www.blue.aol.com
$9.95 per mo. (includes 5 hours of
connect time; $2.95 per additional hour)

CompuServe

P.O. Box 20212
5000 Arlington Centre Blvd.
Columbus, OH 43220
614/457-8600; 800/524-3388
Internet: http://www.compuserve.com
$9.95 per mo. (includes 5 hours of
connect time; $2.95 per additional hour)

User Groups

Rather than list all the Mac user groups
here, I'll just list two nationally active
groups. For information on user groups
in your area, call Apple at 800/538-9696,
extension 500.

BMUG (Berkeley Mac Users Group)

1442A Walnut Street, Suite 62
Berkeley, CA 94709-1496
510/549-2684; fax 510/849-9026;
BBS 510/849-2684
America Online: bmug1
CompuServe: 73237,501
Internet: http://www.bmug.org

The Boston Computer Society (BCS)

1972 Massachusetts Avenue
Cambridge, MA 02140
617/864-1700; fax 617/864-3501;
BBS 617/864-3375
Internet: http://www.bcs.org

B

Specialty Faces

A selection of specialty fonts is listed here. For information on the vendors listed here, see Appendix A.

Bar Code

Bear Rock, TPS Electronics

Borders

Adobe, Agfa, Linotype, Monotype

Chess

Adobe, Ecological Linguistics

Crossword Puzzle

Treacyfaces

OCR

Adobe, FontShop

Musical Notation

Adobe, Casady & Greene, DVM

Pictorial

Adobe, Agfa, Alphabets Inc., Electric Typographer, Image Club, Letraset, Linotype-Hell, Monotype, Page Studio Graphics

Initial Caps

Adobe, Electric Typographer, Image Club, Lanston Type

Keyboard Layouts

Casady & Greene, Page Studio Graphics, Roadrunner

Math Symbols

Adobe, Blue Sky Research, Linguist's Software, NisusSoftware

C

Foreign Language Faces

This appendix lists companies that sell foreign-language fonts. For vendor information, see Appendix A.

Note: If you don't see the language you're looking for here, contact Ecological Linguistics or Linguist's Software. Both companies offer extensive collections of foreign-language fonts.

Arabic

Ecological Linguistics, Font World, Linguist's Software

Burmese

Ecological Linguistics

Cambodian

Ecological Linguistics, Linguist's Software

Cyrillic

Adobe, Bersearch, Casady & Greene, Ecological Linguistics, Linguist's Software

Greek

Font World, Ecological Linguistics, Linguist's Software

Hebrew

Font World, Ecological Linguistics, Linguist's Software

Hindi

Linguist's Software

Japanese

Adobe, Ecological Linguistics, Linguist's Software, Pacific Rim Connections

Korean

Ecological Linguistics, Linguist's Software

Laotian

Ecological Linguistics, Linguist's Software

Tibetan

Ecological Linguistics, Linguist's Software

Thai

Ecological Linguistics, Linguist's Software

Vietnamese

Linguist's Software

D
Imagesetting Service Bureaus

This appendix lists imagesetting service bureaus in the United States and Canada. The bureaus listed here are members of the International Digital Imaging Association, which is made up of digital imaging professionals in 45 countries. (If you'd like more information on the IDIA, call 910/854-5697.)

This is by no means an exhaustive list, but it may help you find a service bureau in your area. If you're connected to the online world, you can find a directory of Adobe-authorized service bureaus at http://www.adobe.com/ on the World Wide Web, or in the Adobe Forum on America Online. Alternatively, you can look in your phone book under Desktop Publishing, Printers, or Typesetting.

USA

Alaska

Anchorage

Visible Ink Inc.
P.O. Box 103035
Anchorage, AK 99510
907/562-3825; fax 907/563-8405

Alabama

Birmingham

Birmingham Blue Print
3000 Third Avenue South
Birmingham, AL 35233
205/323-1563; fax 205/324-6980

The Graphic Zone, Inc.
10 Office Park Circle #100
Birmingham, AL 35223
205/870-5300; fax 205/870-5307

Mobile

Mobile Graphics Inc.
157 Dexter
Mobile, AL 36604
334/476-7400; fax 334/479-1376

Arkansas

Little Rock

Spectrum Graphics
824 West 7th Street
Little Rock, AR 72201
501/375-7732; fax 501/372-4769

Arizona

Phoenix

Central Graphics, Inc.
1610 E. Osborn Road
Phoenix, AZ 85016
602/207-3000; fax 602/207-3050

California

Brea

Graphic Design Services, Inc.
515 West Lambert Road
Brea, CA 92621
714/529-7003; fax 714/529-1382

Carmel

World Graphics, Inc.
P.O. Box 223490
Carmel, CA 93922
408/625-6301; fax 408/625-8674

Claremont

HIGHPOINT
131 Spring Street Center
Claremont, CA 91711
909/625-7785: fax 909/625-0894

Costa Mesa

The Typesetting Room
150 Paularino Avenue, #150
Costa Mesa, CA 92626
714/549-3902; fax 714/557-7991

Culver City

RPI
3960 Ince Blvd, #200
Culver City, CA 90232
310/838-9966; fax 310/838-9936

Foster City

Applied Graphics Technologies
110 Marsh Dr., #105
Foster City, CA 94404
415/578-8333; fax 415/578-0599

Fremont

Grand Junction Networks
47281 Bayside Parkway
Fremont, CA 94538
510/252-0726; fax 510/252-0915

Long Beach

Versa Type, Inc.
249 East Ocean Blvd., #504
Long Beach, CA 90802
310/432-4086; fax 310/437-0754

Los Angeles

Adage Graphics
8632 S. Sepulveda Blvd., #100
Los Angeles, CA 90045
310/216-2828; fax 310/417-3026

G2 Graphic Service Inc.
7014 Sunset Blvd.
Los Angeles, CA 90028
213/467-7828; fax 213/469-6966

L.A. Fonts Typography
8800 Venice Blvd.
Los Angeles, CA 90034
310/204-2777; fax 310/204-2637

Westlight
2223 South Carmelina Avenue
Los Angeles, CA 90064
800/622-2028; fax 310/820-2687

WestPro Graphics
4552 West Colorado Blvd.
Los Angeles, CA 90039
818/247-7030; fax 818/243-4135

ZZYZX Visual Systems
949 North Highland
Los Angeles, CA 90038
213/856-5260; fax 213/856-5270

Milpitas

Abel Graphics
60 S. Abel Street
Milpitas, CA 95035
408/263-4412; fax 408/263-3755

Palo Alto

The Typemasters
575 High Street
Palo Alto, CA 94301
415/329-8973; Fax 415/329-1246

Petaluma

Petaluma Imagesetting
1340 Commerce Street
Petaluma, CA 94954
707/769-1115; Fax 707/769-1116

Rancho Cordova

InfoMania
11492 Sunrise Gold Circle
Rancho Cordova, CA 95742
916/852-5900; fax 916/852-8956

Riverside

Riverside Blueprint
4295 Main Street
Riverside, CA 92502
909/686-0530; fax 909/683-8454

Sacramento

Ferrari Color
2574 21st Street
Sacramento, CA 95818
916/455-8224; fax 916/455-0308

San Diego

Color Works, Graphic Repro. Center
9833 Pacific Heights, Blvd., #H
San Diego, CA 92121
619/558-4638; fax 619/558-3604

San Francisco

BPS Reprographic Services
149 2nd Street
San Francisco, CA 94105
415/495-8700; fax 415/495-2542

MasterType
747 Front Street #202
San Francisco, CA 94111
415/781-8973; fax 415/781-7465

Octagon Graphics
665 Third Street, Suite 430
San Francisco, CA 94107
415/777-9889; fax 415/777-0259

Omnicomp
99 Green St.
San Francisco, CA 94111
415/398-3377; fax 415/781-4010

Top Copy & S. Park Digital Graphics
1401 Market St.
San Francisco, CA 94103
415/553-8611; fax 415/553-8605

San Luis Obispo

Direct Imaging
874 Unit B Via Esteban
San Luis Obispo, CA 93401
805/543-4624; fax 805/543-4632

San Rafael

California Graphics
1100 Third Street
San Rafael, CA 94901
415/454-3494; fax 415/457-8922

Strahm Printing
3060 Kerner Blvd.
San Rafael, CA 94901
415/459-5409; fax 415/459-7701

Santa Barbara

Graphic Traffic
1528 State Street
Santa Barbara, CA 93101
805/965-2372; fax805/966-3160

Partners Imaging Services
1727 State Street
Santa Barbara, CA 93101
805/966-3977; fax 805/966-6178

Torrance

Midnight Media
2421 West 205th, D-203
Torrance, CA 90501
310/787-7651; fax 310/787-7652

Walser's
22850 Hawthorne Blvd.
Torrance, CA 90505-3671
310/373-4330; fax 310/375-1027

Van Nuys

Eureka!
16934 Saticoy St.
Van Nuys, CA 91406
818/609-0702; fax 818/609-7356

Ventura

Graphic Traffic
4277 Transport St. #D
Ventura, CA 93003
805/650-9807; fax 805/650-9824

Visalia

Illustrated Word
1500 S Mooney Blvd, Suite 7
Visalia, CA 93277
209/738-8911; fax 209/738-5871

Walnut Creek

PageWorks
1777 Oakland Boulevard, Suite 101
Walnut Creek, CA 94596
510/945-1908; fax 510/945-0029

Colorado

Aspen

SLIDEMASTER
305-D Airport Business Center
Aspen, CO 81611
303/925-8082; fax 303/925-8949

Colorado Springs

A G P
218 East Cache La Poudre
Colorado Springs, CO 80903
719/632-8142; fax 719/632-8143

Denver

Allied Reprographics
4040 Fox Street
Denver, CO 80216
303/458-7074; fax 303/455-8167

Lineaux, Inc.
1626 Franklin Street
Denver, CO 80218
303/333-5466; fax 303/388-7437

Greeley

Kendall Printing Company
P.O. Box 5080
Greeley, CO 80631
303/330-8895; fax 303/330-1412

Connecticut

New Haven

Phoenix Press
Box 347
New Haven, CT 06513
203/498-1055; fax 203/498-1057

North Haven

Northeast Graphics
291 State Street
North Haven, CT 06473
203/288-2468; fax 203/248-6478

Prospect

Outback Computer Graphics
16 Waterbury Road
Prospect, CT 06712
203/758-5253; fax 203/758-6847

Shelton

Image Graphics Recording Ctr.
917 Bridgeport Avenue
Shelton, CT 06484
203/926-0100; fax 203/926-9705

Wallingford

Typehouse, Inc.
65 N. Plains Industrial Rd.
Wallingford, CT 06492
203/284-8737; fax 203/284-1868

Westport

Image Works
49 Richmondville Avenue
Westport, CT 06880
203/226-7611; fax 203/226-8700

District of Columbia

Washington

ALG Electronic Publishing Center
1101 30th Street, Suite 100
Washingt
on, DC 20007   202/342-
2100; fax 202/298-6776

Design Imaging
1730 M St. NW, Suite 505
Washington, DC 20036
202/296-3799; fax 202/296-3796

Delaware

Wilmington

Firenze & Company, Inc.
300 Cornell Dr, Suite A-2
Wilmington, DE 19801
302/571-8973; fax 302/571-0897

Alabama

Jacksonville

Paramount Miller Graphics
5299 St. Augustine Road
Jacksonville, FL 32207
904/448-1701; fax 904/448-1711

Reddi-Arts
1037 Hendricks Avenue
Jacksonville, FL 32207
904/398-316; fax 904/396-9261

Miami

Applied Imaging
5190 NW 167th Street, #110
Miami, FL 33014
305/626-0408; fax 305/626-0410

ImagExpress Corporation
7953 NW 53rd Street
Miami, FL 33166
305/477-3000; fax 305/477-2426

T Square Express
998 West Flagler Street
Miami, FL 33130
305/324-1234 ; fax 305/324-8040

Orlando

Digital Graphics
617 N. Magnolia
Orlando, FL 32801
407/425-4824; fax 407/839-0975

Pensacola

Typemasters of Pensacola
2803 E. Cervantes Street
Pensacola, FL 32503
904/438-6010; 904/435-2503

Riviera Beach

Graphics Illustrated Inc.
1500 Australian Avenue
Riviera Beach, FL 33404
407/848-8989; fax 407/863-5531

Tampa

Hillsboro Printing
2442 Mississippi Avenue
Tampa, FL 33629
813/251-2401; fax 813/251-0831

West Palm Beach

Final Proof, Inc.
1750 N. Florida Mango-303
West Palm Beach, FL 33409
407/684-9434; fax 407/684-0196

Georgia

Atlanta

America's Performance Group
2841 Akers Mill Road
Atlanta, GA 30339
404/951-9500; fax 404/933-9072

Digital Connectivity Inc.
250 William Street, #1200
Atlanta, GA 30303
404/522-0220; fax 404/522-9142

Decatur

American Color
5305 Snapfinger Woods Drive
Decatur, GA 30035
404/981-5305; fax 404/987-4197

Church Street Type & Pub.
124 Church Street
Decatur, GA 30030
404/373-5360; fax 404/371-0833

Kennesaw

Compoz Design Imaging
425 E. Barrett Parkway, C-3
Kennesaw, GA 30144
404/426-1409; fax 404/426-1579

Tucker

Copy Preparation
2200 Northlake Parkway, Suite 355
Tucker, GA 30084
404/939-2002; fax 404/939-5638

Hawaii

Honolulu

HonBlue, Inc.
501 Sumner St #3B1
Honolulu, HI 96817
808/531-4611; fax 808/531-2977

Kailua

Island Instant Printing, Inc.
305 Hahani Street
Kailua, HI 96734
808/261-8515; fax 808/261-9958

Iowa

Davenport

Typecraft, Inc.
3528 Jersey Ridge Road
Davenport, IA 52807
319/355-2500; fax 319/355-0624

Des Moines

Waddell's Computer Graphic Center
1125 High Street
Des Moines   IA   50309
515/282-0000   515/282-8777

Idaho

Boise

Typestyle, Inc.
513 S. Eighth Street
Boise, ID 83702
208/342-6563; fax 208/342-6594

Illinois

Bensenville

Micro Link Solutions
205 W. Grand, #123
Bensenville, IL 60106
708/860-1661; fax 708/860-1672

PagePath Technologies, Inc.
611 North Busse Road
Bensenville, IL 60106
708/616-0131; fax 708/616-0440

Chicago

Award Graphics
208 South Jefferson
Chicago, IL 60661
312/263-6002; fax 312/236-1807

InfoComm
213 W. Institute Place, #604
Chicago, IL 60610
312/751-1220; fax 312/751-1051

LaSalle Copy Service, Inc.
300 S. Wacker, Suite LL
Chicago, IL 60606
312/341-1443; fax 312/341-0150

PicturePlace, Inc.
55 West Burton Place
Chicago, IL 60610
708-406-9666; fax 708-406-8332

Publishers ImageSet, Inc.
5272 North Elston
Chicag, IL 60630
312/283-3340; fax 312/283-3514

Des Plaines

J. A. Sheahan & Co., Inc.
2590 Devon, #107
Des Plaines, IL 60018
708/298-2510; 708/298-2513

Lisle

Graphics Plus, Inc.
1808 Ogden Avenue
Lisle, IL 60532
708/968-9073; fax 708/963-7887

Northbrook

Publishing Technologies
400 Skokie Blvd., #550
Northbrook, IL 60062
708/498-5633; fax 708/498-5989

Vision Art, Inc.
3300B Commercial Avenue
Northbrook, IL 60062
708/272-1902; fax 708/272-8940

Park Ridge

Typographics Plus, Inc.
780 Busse Highway
Park Ridge, IL 60068
708/292-8973; fax 708/292-8977

Rolling Meadows

A to Z Type & Graphics
1805 Hicks Road
Rolling Meadows, IL 60008
708/776-0300; fax 708/776-0249

Vernon Hills

FX Reprographics
1001 Butterfield Road
Vernon Hills, IL 60061
708/816-6022; fax 708/816-6028

Indiana

Columbus

Pentzer Printing, Inc.
P.O. Box 981
Columbus, IN 47202
812/372-2896; fax 812/372-2901

Elkhart

Dec-O-Art, Inc.
29150 Lexington Park Drive North
Elkhart, IN 46514
219/294-6451; fax 219/295-6534

Markley Enterprises, Inc.
800 Lillian Street
Elkhart, IN 46516
219/295-4195; fax 219/522-2230

Fort Wayne

Fast Print, Inc.
3050 East State Boulevard
Fort Wayne, IN 46805
219/484-5487; fax 219482-8531

Indianapolis

Firehouse Image Center
1030 E. Washington Street
Indianapolis, IN 46202
317/236-1747; fax 317/236-0464

Mishawaka

COLORIP Imaging Center,
Division of Makielski, Inc.
3838 N. Main Street
Mishawaka, IN 46545-3110
219/259-2500; fax 219/259-2900

Kentucky

Louisville

Publishers Press, Inc.
P. O. Box 37500
Louisville, KY 40233
502/543-2251; fax 502/543-4700

Massachussetts

Burlington

Strato Reprographix, Inc.
62 Middlesex Turnpike
Burlington, MA 01803
617/273-1530; fax 617/272-7687

Canton

ABC Publications, Inc.
770 Dedham Street
Canton, MA 02021
617/575-9915; fax 617/575-9445

Hanover

Image Resolutions, Inc.
105 Webster Street, Unit 6
Hanover, MA 02339
617/871-8300; fax 617/871-8322

Maryland

Bethesda

Litho Composition Services
4401 East-West Highway
Bethesda, MD 20814
310/657-2990; fax 301/656-8907

Lanham

Van Cortlandt Press, Inc.
10123 Senate Drive
Lanham, MD 20706
301/577-7377; fax 301/459-7768

White Plains

Automated Graphic Systems
4590 Graphics Drive
White Plains, MD 20695
301/843-1800; fax 301/843-6339

Maine

Camden

High Resolution, Inc.
87 Elm Street
Camden, ME 04843
207/236-3777; fax 207/236-2500

Michigan

Brighton

Digital Displays, Inc.
11154 Guyn Drive
Brighton, MI 48116
810/229-9042; fax 810/347-8894

Grand Rapids

Digital Video Services
6025 South Division
Grand Rapids, MI 49548
616/534-3222; fax 616/534-7576

Okemos

Infinity Graphics
2277 Science Parkway
Okemos, MI 48864
517/349-4635; fax 517/349-7608

Saginaw

Dornbos Press, Inc.
1131 East Genesee Street
Saginaw, MI 48607
517/755-2116; fax 517/755-2120

Southgate

Electronic Type & Color
One Heritage Place, # 130
Southgate, MI 48195
313/246-0133; fax 313/282-2907

Minnesota

Bloomington

Control Graphics
6509 Cecelia Circle
Bloomington, MN 55439
612/942-9900; fax 612/942-6820

Edina

Digital Imaging & Design
7346 Ohms Lane
Edina, MN 55439
612/832-9433; fax 612/835-2353

Minneapolis

Creative Visuals, Inc.
731 Harding Street N.E.
Minneapolis, MN 55413
612/378-1621; fax 612/378-1367

Electric Images
430 1st Ave. North, Suite 230
Minneapolis, MN 55401
612/340-9536; fax 612/340-9222

Management Graphics USA
1401 East 79th Street
Minneapolis, MN 55425
612/854-1220; fax 612/851-6159

Photographic Specialties 1718
Washington Avenue North
Minneapolis, MN 55411
612/522-7741; fax 612/522-1934

New Hope

GS Graphics Inc.
5601 Boone Avenue, North
New Hope, MN 55428
612/533-2275; fax 612/533-0932

Saint Louis Park

ASAP, Inc.
3000 France Avenue South
St. Louis Park, MN 55416
612/926-4735; fax 612/926-9814

Saint Paul

Source, Inc.
2000 Energy Park Dr.
St. Paul, MN 55108
612/646-4422; fax 612/646-3480

Missouri

Kansas City

Custom Color Corporation
300 West 19th Terrace
Kansas City, MO 64108
816/474-3200; fax 816/221-1921

Fontastik Inc.
911 Main St., Suite 1717
Kansas City, MO 64105
816/474-4366; fax 816/474-4389

Saint Louis

Color Express Ltd.
1015 Washington, Suite 200
St. Louis, MO 63101
314/421-6744; fax 314/421-6749

The Composing Room, Inc.,
2208 S. Vandeventer
St. Louis, MO 63110
314/773-2400; fax 314/773-2699

Montana

Stevensville

PrintLink
3972A Highway 93 North
Stevensville, MT 59870
406/777-2773; fax 406/777-2406

North Carolina

Asheville

Montage Productions
P.O. Box 9121
Asheville, NC 28815
704/299-4103; fax 704/299-1828

Durham

Azalea Graphics
P. O. Box 15494
Durham, NC 27704
919/286-2091; fax 919/286-4466

Greensboro

DTP, Inc.
5601 Roanne Way, Suite 605
Greensboro, NC 27409
910/855-0400; fax 910/632-0200

DTP, Inc.
5601 Roanne Way, Suite 605
Greensboro, NC 27409
910/855-0400; fax 910/632-0200

Hickory

TLC Advertising, Inc.
110 Third St., NE
Hickory, NC 28601
704/322-2750; fax 704/324-8293

Raleigh

Image Associates
4909 Windy Hill Drive
Raleigh, NC 27609
919/876-6400; fax 919/876-7064

Leico, Inc.
501 Washington Street
Raleigh, NC 27605
919/821-7800; fax 919/821-7883

New Jersey

East Rutherford

TBC Color Imaging, Inc.
200 Murray Hill Parkway
East Rutherford, NJ 07073
201/896-4760; fax 201/939-4416

Englewood

ACCM Communications
155 North Dean Street
Englewood, NJ 07631
201/569-2028; fax 201/569-7487

Harrison

R.O.P. Digitek Corp.
501 Bergen St.
Harrison, NJ 07029
201/482-8000; fax 201/482-4821

Maywood

Brook Litho, Inc.
230 West Passaic Street
Maywood, NJ 07607
201/845-5656; fax 201/845-3322

Princeton

L & B of Princeton
27 Wall Street
Princeton, NJ 08540
609/683-7888; fax 609/497-9779

New Mexico

Santa Fe

The Paper Tiger
1248 San Pelipe
Sante Fe, NM 87501
505/983-2839; fax 505/982-6412

Nevada

Reno

Nevada Typesetting
75 Caliente Street
Reno, NV 89509
702/329-1225; fax 702/329-9458

Reno Typographers
427 Ridge Street
Reno, NV 89509
702/322-7366; fax 702/322-9312

New York

Albany

Associated Graphic Services
8 Corporate Circle
Albany, NY 12203
518/456-6789; fax 518/456-6846

Brooklyn

Mendelsohn Press
738 Lefferts Ave.
Brooklyn, NY 11203
718/467-1957; fax 718/778-5918

Buffalo

Computer Generation
910 Main Street
Buffalo, NY 14202
716/884-8900; fax 716/884-3943

ImageCore Ltd.
525 Hertel Avenue
Buffalo, NY 14207-0647
716/871-1348; fax 716/871-1477

New York City

Boro Typographers
49 East 21st Street
New York, NY 10010
212/475-7850; fax 212/228-6537

Chroma Copy
423 W. 55th Street, 6th Floor
New York, NY 10019
212/399-2420; fax 212/582-4107

Frey Imaging
902 Broadway
New York, NY 10010
212/477-0300; fax 212/982-5470

Graphic Systems
33 West 17th Street
New York; NY 10010
212/242-8787; fax 212/627-5153

Integrated Imaging Center
526 W. 26th Street
New York, NY 10001
212/366-6672; fax 212 /366-6725

LinoGraphics Corporations
20 West 20th Street
New York, NY 10011
212/727-3070; fax 212/727-3792

Quadratone
115 West 45th Street
New York, NY 10036
212/764-1393; fax 212/764-0985

RSVP
120 West 44th Street, #504
New York, NY 10036
212/719-2922; fax 212/719-2976

Studio Chrome Labs, Inc.
36 West 25th Street, 9th Floor
New York, NY 10010
212/989-6767; fax 212/989-6785

Scarsdale

EPI Graphics
720 White Plains Road
Scarsdale, NY 10583
914/472-0000; fax 914/472-0008

Syracuse

Graphics Workshop
1005 W. Fayette Street
Syracuse, NY 13204
315/422-8115; fax 315/479-6153

Ohio

Akron

CarPec Graphics
221 Beaver Street
Akron, OH 44304
216/434-2288; fax 216/434-8562

Cincinnati

Berman Printing Company
1441 Western
Cincinnati, OH 45214
513/421-1162; fax 513/421-2102

Precision Digital Images, Inc.
700 West Pete Rose Way
Cincinnati, OH 45203
513/784-1555; fax 513/784-1517

Cleveland

A.C. Color Lab, Inc.
2310 Superior Avenue
Cleveland, OH 44114
216/621-4575; fax 216/241-7400

DISC 1740 Chester Avenue
Cleveland, OH 44114
216/771-1040; fax 216/771-3029

Columbus

Harlan Type
1107 Dublin Road
Columbus, OH 43215
614/486-9641; fax 614/486-4355

S.E.P.S. 872 Freeway Drive N,
Building 11
Columbus, OH 43229
614/431-0102; fax 614/431-0226

Dayton

Kramer Graphics
1616 Mardon Drive
Dayton, OH 45432
513/426-6118; fax 513/426-3019

North Olmstead

Mister Jiffy Instant Printing
27529 Lorain Road
North Olmsted, OH 44070
216/777-7100; fax 216/777-7535

Solon

KSK Color Lab
32300 Aurora Road
Solon, OH 44139
216/248-0208; fax 216/248-1233

Toledo

H.O.T. Graphic Services
19 North Erie
Toledo, OH 43624
419/242-7000; fax 419/242-3299

Metzger's PrePress, Inc.
305 Tenth Street
Toledo, OH 43624
419/241-7195; fax 419/255-3299

Youngstown

Youngstown Litho
380 Victoria Road
Youngstown, OH 44515
216/793-2471; fax 216/793-8471

Oklahoma

Tulsa

PennWell Publishing and Printing
1421 S. Sheridan
Tulsa, OK 74112
918/835-3161; fax 918/831-9475

Oregon

Beaverton

Phoenix Digital PrePress
1600 NW 167th Place, # 320
Beaverton, OR 97006
503/629-0587; fax 503/690-6690

Eugene

E & D Graphic Services, Inc.
1176 W. 7th Avenue
Eugene, OR 97402
503/683-2657; fax 503/683-6184

Portland

Economy Prepress & Imagesetting
8032 East Burnside St.
Portland, OR 97215-1549
503/255-4113; fax 503/256-3851

Pennsylvania

Akron

Tapsco
309 Colonial Drive, Box 131
Akron, PA 17501
717/859-2006; fax 717/859-3702

Boyertown

Desktop Technologies, Inc.
P.O. Box 80, County Line Road
Boyertown, PA 19512
215/367-7599; fax 215/367-5881

Fort Washington

International Computaprint
475 Virginia Drive
Fort Washington, PA 19034
215/641-6000; fax 215/641-6176

Langhorne

Bucks County Type & Design
832 Town Center Drive
Langhorne, PA 19047
215/757-3600; fax 215/757-3838

Mechanicsburg

SpectraComp
5170 East Trindle Road
Mechanicsburg, PA 17055
717/697-8600; fax 717/691-0433

Media

Michael Typography Inc.
415 East Baltimore Pike
Media, PA 19063
610/565-1683; fax 610/891-9566

Philadelphia

Today's Graphics, Inc.
1341 North Delaware, #100
Philadelphia, PA 19125
215/634-6200; fax 215/634-6619

Pittsburgh

Herrmann Printing & Litho, Inc.
1709 Douglas Dr.
Pittsburgh, PA 15221
412/243-2374; fax 412/731-2268

New Image Press
4433 Howley Street
Pittsburgh, fax PA 15224
412/683-1300; fax 412/683-1390

TDS Prepress
2652 Library Road
Pittsburgh, PA 15234
412/884-8077; fax 412/884-9077

Whitehall

Photo Fountain
2180 MacArthur Road
Whitehall, PA 18052
610/776-6520; fax 610/776-6524

Rhode Island

Providence

Faces Typography, Inc.
222 Atwells Ave.
Providence, RI 02903
401/273-4455; fax 401/273-4471

Prime Graphics
12 Bassett Street
Providence, RI 02903
401/455-0650; fax 401/455-0651

South Carolina

Bluffton

Village Graphics, Inc.
P.O. Box 707
Bluffton, SC 29910
803/842-6869; fax 803/842-6869

Spartanburg

Copac, Inc.
195 Davis Chapel Rd.
Spartanburg, SC 29318
803/579-4458; fax 803/579-2820

Tennessee

Blountville

Bryant Label Co.
2240 Hwy 75
Blountville, TN 37617
615/323-5440; fax 615/323-6671

Chattanooga

The Type Shop, Inc.
737 McCallie Avenue
Chattanooga, TN 37403
615/266-4545; fax 615/266-7020

Collegedale

The College Press
P.O. Box 400
Collegedale, TN 37315
615/396-2164; fax 615/238-3546

Johnson City

Interstate Graphics
3208 Hanover Road
Johnson City, TN 37604
615/282-1511; fax 615/282-0452

Memphis

Hanson Graphics
3086 Bellbrook Drive
Memphis, TN 38116
901/396-4350; fax 901/398-2717

Nashville

ColorCopy, Inc.
1804 Hayes Street
Nashville, TN 37203
615/321-5740; fax 615/320-9600

Texas

Austin

Miller Blueprint Company
501 West Sixth Street
Austin, TX 78701
512/478-8793; fax 512/474-7099

Dallas

Dallas Photolab, Inc.
3942 Irving Blvd.
Dallas, TX 75247
214/630-4351; fax 214/630-1997

Graphics Group
2820 Taylor St.
Dallas, TX 75226
214/749-2222; fax 214/749-2252

El Paso

RJ Typesetters
2717 E. Missouri
El Paso, TX 79903
915/565-4696; fax 915/565-0430

McAllen

Texas Data Systems
P.O. Box 1358
McAllen, TX 78501
512/682-6091; fax 512/631-4244

Plano

Plano Type & Graphics
1412 14th St.
Plano, TX 75074
214/881-1689; fax 214/423-5134

San Antonio

New Century Graphics
100 W. Olmos, Suite 104
San Antonio, TX 78212
210/829-7515; fax 210/829-7546

Utah

Orem

Lettersetters
836 South State Street
Orem, UT 84058
801/224-6990; fax 801/224-1784

Virginia

Alexandria

VIP Systems, Inc.
1423 Powhatan Street, Suite 7
Alexandria, VA 22314
703/548-2164; fax 703/548-9851

Glen Allen

Graphics Gallery of Virginia
4443 Cox Road
Glen Allen, VA 23060
804/270-5300; fax 804/747-7237

Lynchburg

The Design Group
311 Rivermont Avenue
Lynchburg, VA 24505
804/528-4665; fax 804/847-0036

Richmond

Lewis Creative Technologies
900 West Leigh Street
Richmond, VA 23220
804/648-2000; fax 804/644-3502

Roanoke

Moody Graphics, Inc.
1113 Piedmont Street
Roanoke, VA 24014
703/427-3127; fax 703/427-3120

Vermont

Burlington

Stereotype
266 Pine Street
Burlington, VT 05401
802/864-5495; fax 802/864-6408

Washington

Bellevue

Typesetter Plus
1813 130th Avenue NE, #210
Bellevue, WA 98005
206/883-3337; fax 206/885-6415

Olympia

Designers Service Bureau, Inc.
122 N. Capitol Way
Olympia, WA 98501
206/943-7964; fax 206/943-6685

Seattle

Digicolor
1300 Dexter Ave. N. #130
Seattle, WA 98109
206/284-2198; fax 206/285-9664

Ivey Seright International
424 8th Avenue, North
Seattle, WA 98109
206/623-8113; fax 206/467-6297

Wizywig, Inc.
3151 Elliott Ave. # 310
Seattle, WA 98121
206/283-3069; fax 206/282-1383

Spokane

EM Space, Inc.
19 W. Pacific
Spokane, WA 99204
509/747-1901; fax 509/747-3045

Tacoma

Graphic Services, Inc.
1101 South Fawcett, Suite 100
Tacoma, WA 98402
206/627-8495; fax 206/272-5184

Wisconsin

Lake Geneva

TSR, Inc.
P.O. Box 756
Lake Geneva, WI 53147
414/248-3625; fax 414/248-0389

Madison

Images Unlimited
2918 Bryant Road
Madison, WI 53713
608/273-8588; fax 608/273-3718

Madison Reprographics
P.O. Box 55193
Madison, WI 53705
608/836-8890; fax 608/836-8860

Port-to-Print, Inc.
2851 Index Road
Madison, WI 53713
800/236-4887; fax 608/273-4896

Milwaukee

General Graphics Corp.
400 S. 5th St.
Milwaukee, WI 53204
414/276-4246; fax 414/276-7488

Polomar Color Reproductions
541 North Broadway
Milwaukee, WI 53202
414/765-9229; fax 414/272-3282

New Berlin

American Color Systems
16645 W. Greenfield Avenue
New Berlin, WI 53151
414/786-9648; fax 414/786-9037

Wauwatosa

City Press, Inc.
7400 West State Street
Wauwatosa, WI 53213
414/774-7400; fax 414/774-9410

Canada

Alberta

Calgary

Creative Thinking Imaging
210, 2750-22 Street N.E.
Calgary, Alberta T2E 7L9
403/291-6414; fax 403/291-6408

Edmonton

Megatron Electric
11915 69th Street
Edmonton, Alberta T5B 1S4
403/479-4303; fax 403/479-7207

British Columbia

Vancouver

Stellar Graphics LTD
400 - 510 West Hastings
Vancouver, BC V6B 1L8
604/688-7835; fax 604/688-7833

Victoria

Alston Graphic Services Ltd.
200 Esquimalt Rd.
Victoria, BC V9A 3K9
604/382-4291; fax 604/382-3931

Ontario

Hamilton

Stirling Print and Creative Services
374 King Street East
Hamilton, Ontario L8N 1C3
416/525-5467; fax 416/529-5215

London

Bogdan Graphics, Inc.
344 Ridout St., South
London, Ontario N6C 3Z5
519/438-9003; fax 519/438-0236

Toronto

Clarity Colour, Inc.
138 Huron Street
Toronto, Ontario M5T 2B2
416/340-0333; fax 416/340-9309

Management Graphics, Inc.
20 Martin Ross Avenue
Toronto, Ontario M3J 2K8
416/667-8877; fax 416/667-7145

Rhino Imaging, Inc.
65 George Street
Toronto, Ontario M5A 4L8
416/366-5466; fax 416/366-3275

E

Typeface Listing

This appendix lists more than 2500 typefaces, from more than a dozen vendors (vendor addresses and phone numbers are listed in Appendix A). Text, decorative, and display faces are listed. The faces are listed alphabetically by family name; space restrictions prevent me from listing each style and weight of every family. When a typeface family includes multiple styles and/or weights, only the family name is listed. If a type foundry's name is part of the typeface name (ITC Galliard, for instance), the face is alphabetized under its name, with the foundry name after it in parentheses (Galliard (ITC) in this example). New typefaces appear every day, but this list will give you a solid starting point if you're searching for a particular face. For the latest information, contact the font vendors listed in Appendix A.

Note: Many of the faces listed here are available from Precision Type, which offers a useful catalog that includes thousands of typeface samples.

A

American Classic . . . . Agfa
American Text . . . . Bitstream, FontShop
American Typewriter (ITC) . . Adobe, Agfa, Bitstream, FontHaus, FontShop, Image
      Club, Linotype, Monotype, URW
American Uncial . . . . FontHaus, Image Club, URW
    American Uncial Initials . . . . URW
Americana . . . Adobe, Agfa, Bitstream, FontHaus, FontShop, Image Club, Linotype,
      Monotype
Amerigo (Bitstream) . . . . Bitstream, FontShop
Amethyst Script . . . . FontHaus
Amigo . . . . Adobe, Agfa, FontHaus, FontShop, Linotype, Monotype
Amoeba (FF) . . . . FontShop
Amoebia . . . . FontHaus
Amphora . . . . FontShop, T-26
Amsterdam Garamont . . . . FontShop
Andrich Minerva . . . . Image Club
Angie (FF) . . . . FontShop
Angro . . . . FontHaus, FontShop
Anna (ITC) . . . . Adobe, Agfa, FontHaus, FontShop, Image Club, ITC, Linotype,
      Monotype, URW
      ITC Anna Small Caps . . . . URW
      ITC Anna GX . . . . ITC
Annlie Extra Bold . . . . FontHaus, URW
Antikva Margaret . . . . Image Club
Antiqua
      URW Antiqua . . . . URW
      URW Antiqua Small Caps . . . . URW
Antique
      Antique Condensed . . . . Agfa, FontHaus, FontShop
      Antique No. 3 . . . . FontShop
      Antique Roman . . . . Agfa, FontShop
Antique Olive . . . . Adobe, Agfa, FontHaus, FontShop, Image Club, Linotype,
      Monotype, URW
      Antique Olive DisCaps . . . . URW
      Antique Olive Nord PosterType . . . . URW
Antorff . . . . Page Studio
Anzeigen Grotesk . . . . FontHaus
Apolline . . . . Agfa, FontShop
Apollo . . . . Adobe, Agfa, FontHaus, FontShop, Linotype, Monotype
    Apollo Expert Collection . . . . Adobe, Agfa, FontHaus, FontShop, Linotype,
      Monotype
Aquarius . . . . Agfa, FontShop
Aquinas (Letraset) . . . . Letraset
Aquitaine Initials . . . . Image Club, Letraset

Arab Brushstroke . . . . URW
Arabia Felix . . . . Electric Typographer
Arbitrary . . . . Emigre
Arcadia . . . . Adobe, Agfa, FontHaus, FontShop, Linotype, Monotype
Architext . . . . EmDash
Architype
    Architype Bayer . . . . FontHaus
    Architype Bill . . . . FontHaus
    Architype Renner . . . . FontHaus
    Architype Tschichold . . . . FontHaus
    Architype Van der Leck . . . . FontHaus
    Architype Van Doesburg . . . . FontHaus
Ardent (TF) . . . . FontHaus, Treacyfaces
Arepo . . . . Agfa, FontShop
Ariadne . . . . Adobe, Agfa, Linotype, Monotype
Arial . . . . FontShop
Aritus . . . . URW
Armada . . . . Font Bureau, FontHaus
    TF Armada, FontHaus, FontShop, Treacyfaces
Arnold Böcklin . . . . Adobe, Agfa, FontHaus, FontShop, Linotype, Monotype, URW
    Arnold Böcklin Initials . . . . URW
Arquitectura . . . . Image Club
Arriba (Letraset) . . . . Letraset
Arrow . . . . Image Club
    TF Arrow . . . . FontHaus, FontShop, Treacyfaces
Arrus (Bitstream) . . . . Bitstream, FontShop
Arsis . . . . FontHaus
Art Deco . . . . FontShop
Art World . . . . FontShop
Arta . . . . Agfa, FontShop
Artisan Roman . . . . Agfa, FontShop
Artiste . . . . FontShop, Letraset
Artistik . . . . Agfa
Arwen . . . . Agfa, FontShop
Ashley
    Ashley Crawford . . . . Agfa, FontShop
    Ashley Inline . . . . Agfa
    Ashley Script . . . . Adobe, Agfa, FontHaus, FontShop, Linotype, Monotype
Ashtabula . . . . FontHaus
Asphalt Black . . . . Agfa, FontShop
Assuri (FF) . . . . FontShop
Aster
    New Aster . . . . Adobe, Agfa, FontHaus, FontShop, Linotype, Monotype
Athenaeum . . . . Agfa, FontShop

Athenaeum (continued)

    Athenaeum Initials . . . . Agfa

Atlanta (FF) . . . . FontShop

Atlas . . . . FontHaus

Aubette Architype . . . . Agfa, FontShop

Augius Open. . . . . URW

Augustea (Letraset) . . . . Letraset

Aura . . . . FontShop

Aurea . . . . Image Club

Aurelia . . . . FontHaus, FontShop

Aurelius . . . . FontHaus, T-26

Aureus Uncial. . . . . Agfa, FontShop

Auriol . . . . Adobe, Agfa, FontHaus, FontShop, Linotype, Monotype

Aurora. . . . . Bitstream, FontShop

AutoSuggestion (F) . . . . FontShop

Autotrace (FF) . . . . FontShop

Avalon. . . . . Agfa, FontShop

Avant Garde

    ITC Avant Garde Alternative Characters . . . . URW

    ITC Avant Garde Gothic . . . . . . Adobe, Agfa, Bitstream, FontHaus, FontShop,
        Image Club, Linotype, Monotype, URW

    ITC Avant Garde Gothic GX . . . . Linotype

Avenida (Letraset) . . . . Letraset

Avenir . . . . Adobe, Agfa, FontHaus, FontShop, Linotype, Monotype

Avian (TF) . . . . FontHaus, FontShop, Treacyfaces

B

Baccarat (TF) . . . . FontHaus, FontShop, Treacyfaces

Backspacer . . . . Emigre

Backstitch . . . . Page Studio

Badloc . . . . Image Club

BadTimes (A*I) . . . . Alphabets Inc., FontHaus

BadTyp . . . . Font Bureau, FontHaus

Bahnhof . . . . FontHaus

Baker Signet. . . . . Adobe, Agfa, Bitstream, FontHaus, FontShop, Image Club,
    Linotype, Monotype

Balance (FF) . . . . FontShop

Ballmer . . . . Agfa, FontShop

Balloon . . . . Bitstream, FontHaus, FontShop, Image Club, URW

    Balloon PosterType. . . . . URW

    Balloon Small Caps. . . . . URW

Balmoral . . . . FontHaus, FontShop, Image Club, Letraset, URW
Baluster . . . . FontHaus, T-26
Balzano . . . . Adobe, Agfa, FontHaus, FontShop, Linotype, Monotype
Bamboo . . . . Image Club
Banco. . . . . Adobe, FontShop, Image Club
Bang (Letraset) . . . . Letraset
Bank
    Bank Gothic . . . . Bitstream, FontShop
    Bank Script . . . . URW
Barbedor. . . . . FontHaus, URW
    Barbedor DisCaps. . . . . URW
    Barbedor Small Caps . . . . URW
Barcelona (ITC) . . . . Image Club, FontHaus, FontShop
Barclay Open . . . . Agfa, FontShop
Barcode . . . . Font Bureau, FontHaus
Barmeno. . . . . Adobe, Agfa, FontHaus, FontShop, Linotype, Monotype
Barnum
    PL Barnum . . . . Agfa, FontShop
    P.T. Barnum . . . . Bitstream, FontShop, Image Club
Basilea . . . . Image Club
Basilia . . . . Agfa, FontShop
    Basilia Compress. . . . . URW
Basilica . . . . FontShop
Baskerville. . . . . Bitstream, FontShop
    Baskerville Expert. . . . . FontShop
    Baskerville No. 2. . . . . Bitstream, FontShop
    Baskerville Old Face . . . . FontHaus, FontShop, URW
    Baskerville Old Face DisCaps . . . . URW
    Baskerville Old Face Small Caps . . . . URW
    Berthold Baskerville . . Adobe, Agfa, FontHaus, FontShop, Linotype, Monotype
    Fry's Baskerville. . . . . Bitstream
    ITC New Baskerville . . . . Adobe, Agfa, Bitstream, FontHaus, FontShop,
        Linotype, Monotype
    ITC New Baskerville Small Caps & Old Style Figures . . . . Adobe, Agfa,
        FontHaus, FontShop, Linotype, Monotype
    Monotype Baskerville . . . . Monotype
Basque. . . . . Agfa
Bauhaus (ITC) . . . . Adobe, Agfa, Bitstream, FontHaus, FontShop, Image Club,
    Linotype, Monotype, URW
    ITC Bauhaus PosterType. . . . . URW
    ITC Bauhaus Round . . . . URW
Bayer Type Architype. . . . . Agfa, FontShop
Becka Script (Letraset). . . . . FontShop, Letraset

Beesknees (ITC) . . . . Adobe, Agfa, FontHaus, FontShop, Image Club, Linotype, Monotype, URW

    ITC Beesknees Poster Type, URW

    ITC Beesknees Small Caps, URW

Behemoth (PL) . . . . Agfa, FontShop

Belizio . . . . Font Bureau, FontHaus

Bell . . . . FontShop

    Bell Centennial . . . . . . Adobe, Agfa, Bitstream, FontHaus, FontShop, Linotype, Monotype

    Bell Gothic . . . . Adobe, Agfa, Bitstream, FontHaus, FontShop, Linotype, Monotype

Bellevue . . . . Adobe, Agfa, FontHaus, FontShop, Linotype, Monotype

Belshaw . . . . FontHaus

    Belshaw Compress . . . . URW

    Belshaw Initials . . . . URW

Belucian . . . . Font Bureau, FontHaus, FontShop

Belwe . . . . Adobe, Agfa, Bitstream, FontHaus, FontHaus, FontShop, Linotype, Monotype

    Belwe Mono . . . . Letraset

    Belwe Round . . . . URW

    Belwe Stencil . . . . URW

Bembo . . . . Adobe, Agfa, FontShop, Linotype, Monotype

    Bembo Expert Collection . . . . . . Adobe, Agfa, FontHaus, FontShop, Linotype, Monotype

    Bembo Schoolbook . . . . FontShop, Monotype

    Bembo Titling . . . . FontShop, Monotype

Bemtus . . . . URW

BenedictUncial (A*I) . . . . Alphabets Inc.

Benguiat

    ITC Benguiat . . . . . Adobe, Agfa, Bitstream, FontHaus, FontShop, Image Club, Linotype, Monotype

    ITC Benguiat Gothic . . . . Adobe, Agfa, Bitstream, FontHaus, FontShop, Image Club, Linotype . . . . Monotype

    PL Benguiat Frisky . . . . Agfa, FontShop

Beosans

    Beosans Hard (FF) . . . . FontShop

    Beosans Soft (FF) . . . . FontShop

Beowolf Serif (FF) . . . . FontShop

Bergell (Letraset) . . . . FontShop, Letraset

Berkeley Oldstyle (ITC) . . . . . . Adobe, Agfa, Bitstream, FontHaus, FontShop, Image Club, Linotype, Monotype, URW

Berlin Sans . . . . Font Bureau, FontHaus

Berliner Grotesk . . . Adobe, Agfa, FontHaus, FontShop, Linotype, Monotype, URW

    Berliner Grotesk Antique . . . . URW

Binny Old Style . . . . FontShop, Monotype
Birch . . . . Adobe, Agfa, FontHaus, FontShop, Linotype, Monotype
Birdlegs . . . . FontHaus
Bison . . . . FontShop
Bisque . . . . Image Club
Bistro (TF) . . . . FontHaus, FontShop, Treacyfaces
Bitmax (Letraset) . . . . Letraset
Black . . . . FontHaus
Black Rocks . . . . Electric Typographer
Black Tents . . . . Electric Typographer
Blackfriar . . . . FontHaus
Blackletter 686 . . . . Bitstream, FontShop
Blackmoor (Letraset) . . . . Letraset
Blackoak . . . . FontShop
Blado Italic . . . . FontShop, Monotype
Blast-O-Rama T-26
Blaze (ITC) . . . . ITC, FontShop
Blind Date . . . . FontHaus
Blippo . . . . Bitstream
    Blippo Black . . . . FontHaus, FontShop, URW
    Blippo Black PosterType . . . . URW
    Blippo Black Round . . . . URW
    Blippo Stencil . . . . URW
Blizzard . . . . URW
Block . . . . FontShop, URW
    Block Berthold . . . . . . Adobe, Agfa, FontHaus, FontShop, Linotype, Monotype
    Block Gothic . . . . FontHaus
Blocks . . . . Agfa, FontShop
Blueprint . . . . Monotype
Bluntz (Letraset) . . . . Letraset
Blur (FF) . . . . FontShop
Boca Raton . . . . Image Club
Bodega
    Bodega Sans . . . . Font Bureau, FontHaus, FontShop
    Bodega Serif . . . . Font Bureau, FontHaus, FontShop
Bodoni . . . . Adobe, Agfa, Bitstream, FontHaus, FontShop, Image Club, Lanston
    Type, Linotype, Monotype
    Bauer Bodoni . . . . Adobe, Agfa, Bitstream, FontHaus, FontShop, Linotype,
    Monotype, URW
    Bauer Bodoni DisCaps . . . . URW
    Bauer Bodoni Small Caps . . . . URW
    Bauer Bodoni Small Caps & Old Style Figures . . . . Adobe, Agfa, FontHaus,
    FontShop
    Bauer Bodoni Titling . . . . Bitstream

Bodoni (continued)

Berthold Bodoni Antiqua . . . . Adobe, Agfa, FontHaus, FontShop

Berthold Bodoni Antiqua Expert Collection. . . . . Adobe, Agfa, FontHaus, FontShop, Linotype, Monotype

Berthold Bodoni Old Face . . . . . . Adobe, Agfa, FontHaus, FontShop, Linotype, Monotype

Berthold Bodoni Old Face Expert CollectionAdobe, Agfa, FontHaus, FontShop, Linotype, Monotype

Bodoni 26 . . . . FontHaus, FontShop

Bodoni Antiqua . . . . URW

Bodoni Antiqua Compress . . . . URW

Bodoni Antiqua Small Caps . . . . URW

Bodoni Campanile . . . . FontShop

Bodoni FB . . . . Font Bureau, FontHaus

Bodoni Highlight . . . . Image Club

Bodoni Nr. 1 . . . . FontHaus

Bodoni No. 2 Compress . . . . URW

Bodoni No. 2 Ultra . . . . URW

Bodoni No. 175 . . . . FontShop

Bodoni Stencil . . . . URW

BodoniEF . . . . FontHaus

FF Bodoni Classic . . . . FontShop

FF Bodoni Classic Chancery . . . . FontShop

FF Bodoni Shaded Initials . . . . FontShop

ITC Bodoni 6 . . . . FontHaus, FontShop, ITC

ITC Bodoni 12 . . . . FontHaus, FontShop, ITC

ITC Bodoni 72 . . . . FontHaus, FontShop, ITC

Monotype Bodoni . . . . FontShop, Monotype

Poster Bodoni . . . . Adobe, Agfa, Bitstream, FontHaus, FontShop, Image Club, Linotype, Monotype

WTC Our Bodoni . . . . Agfa, FontShop

Boink . . . . Letraset

Bolide Script . . . . FontHaus

Bolt (ITC) . . . . Bitstream, FontHaus, FontShop

Book Jacket . . . . Image Club

Bookman . . . . FontShop

Bookman Headline . . . . FontShop

ITC Bookman . . . . Adobe, Agfa, Bitstream, FontHaus, FontShop, Image Club, Linotype, Monotype, URW

ITC Bookman GX . . . . Linotype

ITC Bookman Contour . . . . Image Club

ITC Bookman Outline . . . . Image Club

ITC Bookman Swash . . . . URW

C

Calisto . . . . FontShop
Calligraphic
    Calligraphic 421 . . . . Bitstream, FontShop
    Calligraphic 810 . . . . Bitstream, FontShop
Calligraphica. . . . . URW
Calvert. . . . . Adobe, Agfa, FontHaus, FontShop, Linotype, Monotype
Camelia . . . . Image Club
Camellia (Letraset) . . . . FontHaus
Cameo . . . . FontHaus
Campaign (Letraset) . . . . Image Club, Letraset
Campus . . . . FontShop
Can you...? (F) . . . . FontShop
Cancellaresca Script (Letraset). . . . . Letraset
Candice (Letraset) . . . . FontHaus, URW
Candida . . . . Adobe, Agfa, Bitstream, FontHaus, FontShop, Linotype, Monotype
    Candida Stencil. . . . . URW
Cantoria . . . . Adobe, Agfa, FontHaus, FontShop, Linotype, Monotype
Capone. . . . . FontHaus, FontShop
    Capone Light. . . . . Agfa
Card Cameo . . . . FontShop
Cargo . . . . URW
Carlton (Letraset) . . . . Letraset
Carmela. . . . . Agfa, FontShop
Carmina (Bitstream) . . . . Bitstream, FontShop
Carmine Tango. . . . . Agfa, FontShop
Carnival T-26
Carolina . . . . Adobe
Carolus
    Carolus Magnus (FF) . . . . FontShop
    Carolus Roman . . . . Image Club
Carousel (Letraset) . . . . FontHaus
Carpenter . . . . FontHaus, Image Club
Carplate . . . . FontShop
Cartier. . . . . Agfa, FontShop
Cartoon . . . . Image Club
Carumba . . . . Letraset
Carver . . . . Image Club
Cascade Script . . . . Adobe, Agfa, FontHaus, FontShop,, Linotype, Monotype
Caslon
    Adobe Caslon . . . . Adobe, Agfa, FontHaus, FontShop, Linotype, Monotype
    Adobe Caslon Expert Collection. . . . . Adobe, Agfa, FontHaus, FontShop,
        Linotype, Monotype
    Berthold Caslon Book . . . . .Adobe, Agfa, FontHaus, FontShop, Linotype,
        Monotype

Cavolfiore (FF). . . . . FontShop
Caxton . . . . Adobe, Agfa, Bitstream, FontHaus, FontShop, Letraset, Linotype, Monotype
Celeste (FF) . . . . FontShop
Celestia. . . . . FontHaus
    Celestia Antiqua. . . . . FontHaus
Centaur . . . . Adobe, Agfa, FontHaus, FontShop, Linotype, Monotype
    Centaur Expert Collection, ...Adobe, Agfa, FontHaus, FontShop, Linotype, Monotype
Centennial (Linotype) . . . . Adobe, Agfa, FontHaus, FontShop, Linotype, Monotype
    Linotype Centennial Small Caps & Old Style Figures. . Adobe, Agfa, FontHaus, FontShop, Linotype, Monotype
Century
    Century 725 . . . . Bitstream, FontShop
    Century 731 . . . . Bitstream, FontShop
    Century 751 . . . . Bitstream
    Century 751 . . . . Bitstream, FontShop
    Century Expanded . . . Adobe, Agfa, Bitstream, FontHaus, FontShop, Linotype, Monotype, URW
    Century Old Style. . . . . Adobe, Bitstream, FontHaus, FontShop, ImageClub,Linotype,Monotype, URW
    Century Old Style DisCaps . . . . URW
    Century Old Style Small Caps. . . . . URW
    Century Schoolbook . . . . . Bitstream, FontHaus, FontShop, Image Club, URW
    Century Schoolbook Monospace. . . . . Bitstream
    FB Century, Font Bureau, FontHaus
    ITC Century . . . . . . Adobe, Agfa, Bitstream, FontHaus, FontShop, Image Club, Linotype, Monotype
    ITC Century Condensed. . . . . . . Adobe, Agfa, Bitstream, FontHaus, FontShop, Image Club, Linotype, Monotype
    ITC Century Handtooled . . . . Adobe, Agfa, FontHaus, Image Club, ITC, Linotype, Monotype
    Monotype Century Old Style . . . . Monotype
    New Century Schoolbook . . . . . . Adobe, Agfa, FontHaus, FontShop, Linotype, Monotype
    New Century Schoolbook GX, Linotype
Cerigo (ITC). . . . . Adobe, Agfa, FontHaus, FontShop, Linotype, Monotype
    ITC Cerigo Small Caps . . . . URW
    ITC Cerigo Swash & Alternative Characters . . . . FontHaus, URW
Challenge (Letraset). . . . . Letraset
Champagne . . . . Image Club
Champers (Letraset). . . . . FontShop, Letraset
Chaotiqua (A*I) . . . . Alphabets Inc.
Chaplin . . . . Agfa, FontShop

Cooper

    Bitstream Cooper . . . . Bitstream, FontShop

    Bitstream Cooper Black . . . . Bitstream, FontShop

    Cooper Antique . . . . URW

    Cooper Black . . . . . . Adobe, Agfa, FontHaus, FontShop, Image Club, Linotype,
        Monotype, URW

    Cooper Black PosterType . . . . URW

    Cooper PosterFH . . . . FontHaus

    Cooper Stencil . . . . URW

Copal . . . . Adobe, Agfa, FontHaus, FontShop, Linotype, Monotype

Copperplate . . . . FontHaus, URW

    Copperplate Gothic . . . . . Adobe, Agfa, Bitstream, FontHaus, FontShop, Image
        Club, Linotype, Monotype

    Copperplate Gothic Condensed . . . . Bitstream

Copperplate Script . . . . Castle, FontHaus

Coptek . . . . Letraset

Corinthian . . . . Letraset, URW

Corona . . . . Adobe, Agfa, FontHaus, FontShop, Linotype, Monotype

Coronet . . . . Agfa, FontShop, Monotype

Corsiva . . . . Monotype

Cortez . . . . FontHaus

    Cortez Alternative Characters . . . . URW

Corvallis . . . . Agfa, FontShop

    Corvallis Sans . . . . Agfa, FontShop

Corvinus Skyline . . . . FontHaus, Image Club

Cosmos . . . . Adobe, Agfa, FontHaus, FontShop, Linotype, Monotype

Cottonwood . . . . Adobe, Agfa, FontHaus, FontShop, Linotype, Monotype

Countdown (Letraset) . . . . FontHaus

    Countdown Compress . . . . URW

Courier . . . . FontShop, URW

    Courier 10 Pitch . . . . Bitstream

    Courier GX . . . . Linotype

    Monotype Courier Twelve . . . . Monotype

Craft (FF) . . . . FontShop

Crane, Agfa . . . . FontShop

Crash (F) . . . . FontShop

CrashBangWallop (FF) . . . . FontShop

Craw Modern . . . . FontHaus, Image Club

Cremona . . . . Adobe, Agfa, FontHaus, FontShop, Linotype, Monotype

Cresci Rotunda . . . . Agfa, FontShop

Criblé (FF) . . . . FontShop

Crillee (Letraset) . . . . Bitstream, FontHaus, FontShop, Letraset, URW

Croissant . . . . FontHaus, URW

Crucible . . . . FontHaus

D

Delphin . . . . . Adobe, Agfa, FontHaus, FontShop, Image Club, Linotype, Monotype
    Delphian Open . . . . Agfa, FontShop
Delta Jaeger . . . . Adobe, Agfa, FontHaus, FontShop, Linotype, Monotype
Demian . . . . Letraset, FontShop
Democratica . . . . Emigre
Demonstrator. . . . . FontHaus
Demos . . . . FontHaus, FontShop
Derek Italic. . . . . Agfa, FontShop
De Stijl. . . . . Letter Perfect
DeVinne (CG) . . . . Agfa, FontShop
Devit. . . . . FontHaus, T-26
Dex Gothic Stencil. . . . . URW
Dextor . . . . FontHaus
    Dextor Black Round. . . . . URW
    Dextor Black Small Caps . . . . URW
    Dextor Initials. . . . . URW
    Dextor Small Caps . . . . URW
Diamanti . . . . FontHaus
Didi (ITC) . . . . FontHaus, Image Club
Didot (Linotype) . . . . Adobe, Agfa, FontHaus, FontShop, Linotype, Monotype
    Didot Display. . . . . FontHaus
Dierama
    ITC Dierama, FontHaus
    TF Dierama, Treacyfaces
Dig (FF) . . . . FontShop
Digi Grotesk . . . . FontHaus
DigiAntiquaEF . . . . FontHaus
Digit . . . . Page Studio
Digital . . . . Image Club
Digitek (Letraset) . . . . Letraset
Din 1451 . . . . FontHaus
DIN . . . . FontShop
    DIN Schriften . . . . Adobe, Agfa, FontHaus, FontShop, Linotype, Monotype
Dingaling. . . . . Image Club
Dinitials (ITC) . . . . FontShop, ITC
Dino (A*I) . . . . Alphabets Inc.
Diotima. . . . . Adobe, Agfa, FontHaus, FontShop, Linotype, Monotype
    Diotima Small Caps & Old Style Figures. . . Adobe, Agfa, FontHaus, FontShop,
        Linotype, Monotype
Dirty (FF). . . . . FontShop
Diskus. . . . . URW
Disturbance (FF) . . . . FontShop
Dog (FF) . . . . FontShop

E

Equinox (Letraset) . . . . Image Club, Letraset
Eras (ITC) . . . . Adobe, Agfa, Bitstream, FontHaus, FontShop, FontShop, Image
    Club, Linotype, Monotype
    ITC Eras Outline . . . . Bitstream, FontShop, Image Club
    ITC ITC Eras PosterType . . . . URW
    Eras Ultra . . . . URW
Erazure . . . . FontHaus
Erbar . . . . Agfa
    Erbar Condensed . . . . FontShop, Linotype
Erikrighthand (FF) . . . . FontShop
Esagerate (FF) . . . . FontShop
Escalido T-26
Esprit (ITC) . . . . Adobe, Agfa, FontHaus, FontShop, Image Club, Linotype,
    Monotype, URW
    ITC Esprit Caps . . . . URW
    ITC Esprit Small Caps . . . . FontShop, URW
Estro . . . . FontShop, Image Club
Etruscan . . . . Letraset, FontShop
Euphoria T-26
Euro Technic . . . . Image Club
Eurocrat . . . . FontShop
Europa
    Europa 022 . . . . FontHaus
    Europa Bold (TC) . . . . Agfa, FontShop
    Europa Grotesque Nr. 2 . . . . FontHaus
Eurostile, Adobe, Agfa, FontHaus, FontShop, Linotype, Monotype, URW
    Eurostile DisCaps . . . . URW
    Eurostile Small Caps . . . . URW
    Eurostile Stencil . . . . URW
Eva Antiqua . . . . FontHaus
Ex Ponto . . . . Adobe, Agfa, FontHaus, FontShop, Linotype, Monotype
Excelsior . . . . Adobe, Agfa, FontHaus, FontShop, Linotype, Monotype
Exocet . . . . Emigre
Exotic . . . . Bitstream
Extra (FF) . . . . FontShop

F

Fairfield . . . . Adobe, Agfa, FontHaus, FontShop, Linotype, Monotype
Fajita . . . . Image Club
Falstaff . . . . Adobe, Agfa, FontHaus, FontShop, Linotype, Monotype
Fanatique . . . . FontHaus

Franklin Gothic
 ATF Franklin Gothic . . . . FontShop
 Franklin Gothic . . . . . . Adobe, Agfa, Bitstream, FontHaus, FontShop, Linotype,
  Monotype
 Franklin Gothic Caps . . . . URW
 ITC Franklin Gothic . . . . . Adobe, Agfa, Bitstream, FontHaus, FontShop, Image
  Club, Linotype, Monotype, URW
 ITC Franklin Gothic Small Caps . . . . URW
FranklySpoken (A*I) . . . . Alphabets Inc.
Freakshow T-26
FreeBe . . . . FontHaus, T-26
FreeDom . . . . FontHaus, T-26
Freeform
 Freeform 710 . . . . Bitstream, FontShop
 Freeform 721 . . . . Bitstream, FontShop
Freehand
 Freehand 471 . . . . Bitstream, FontShop
 Freehand 521 . . . . Bitstream, FontShop
 Freehand 575 . . . . Bitstream, FontShop
 Freehand 591 . . . . Bitstream
Freestyle Script . . . . Adobe, Agfa, FontHaus, FontShop, Letraset, Linotype,
  Monotype, URW
French Letters . . . . FontHaus
French Script . . . . Agfa, Monotype
Friday (FF) . . . . FontShop
Friz Quadrata . . . . FontHaus, FontShop
 ITC Friz Quadrata . . . . . . Adobe, Agfa, Bitstream, FontHaus, FontShop, Image
  Club, ITC, Linotype, Monotype, URW
 ITC Friz Quadrata Small Caps . . . . URW
Frontiera (CG) . . . . Agfa
Frutiger . . . . Adobe, Agfa, FontHaus, FontShop, Linotype, Monotype
Frutus . . . . URW
Fudoni . . . . FontShop
Fulham Road . . . . FontHaus
Fur Round . . . . FontShop, T-26
Fusion (A*I) . . . . Alphabets Inc.
Futura . . . . Adobe, Agfa, Bitstream, FontHaus, FontShop, Image Club, Linotype,
  Monotype, URW
 Bauer Futura Ultra Bold . . . . Castle
 Futura Black . . . . Agfa, Bitstream, FontHaus, FontShop
 Futura Black Initials . . . . URW
 Futura Caps . . . . URW
 Futura DisCaps . . . . URW
 Futura Display, FontHaus . . . . URW

Futura (continued)

G

Garamond (continued)

    Berthold Garamond Expert Collection .... Adobe, Agfa, FontHaus, FontShop, Linotype, Monotype

    Classical Garamond .... Bitstream

    Elegant Garamond .... Bitstream

    Garamond (ITC) .. Adobe, Agfa, Bitstream, FontHaus, FontShop, Image Club, Linotype, Monotype, URW

    Garamond Antiqua.. Agfa

    Garamond FB................................... Font Bureau, FontHaus

    Garamond No. 1 .... FontHaus

    Garamond No. 2 Caps .... URW

    Garamond No. 2 DisCaps .... URW

    Garamond No. 2 Small Caps .... URW

    Garamond No. 3 ..... Adobe, Agfa, FontHaus, FontShop, Linotype, Monotype

    Garamond No. 3 Small Caps & Old Style Figures .... Adobe, Agfa, FontHaus, FontShop, Linotype, Monotype

    Garamond No. 5 .... FontHaus

    Garamond No. 5 Swash .... URW

    Granjon ... Adobe, Agfa, Bitstream, FontHaus, FontShop, Linotype, Monotype

    ITC Garamond.... Adobe, Agfa, Bitstream, FontHaus, FontShop, Image Club, Linotype, Monotype, URW

    ITC Garamond Condensed .... Adobe, Agfa, FontHaus, FontHaus, FontShop, Image Club, Linotype, Monotype

    ITC Garamond Handtooled .... Adobe, Agfa, FontHaus, FontShop, Image Club, ITC, Linotype, Monotype

    ITC Garamond Narrow .... Adobe, Agfa, Bitstream, FontHaus, FontShop, Linotype, Monotype

    Italian Garamond .... Bitstream

    Monotype Garamond .... FontShop, Monotype

    Old Claude.................................. FontHaus, Letter Perfect

    Original Garamond .... Bitstream

    Simoncini Garamond .... Adobe, Agfa, FontHaus, FontShop, Linotype, Monotype

    Stempel Garamond ... Adobe, Agfa, FontHaus, FontShop, Linotype, Monotype

    Stempel Garamond Small Caps & Old Style Figures............ Adobe, Agfa, FontHaus, FontShop, Linotype, Monotype

    URW Garamond Stencil .... URW

Garamont (Amsterdam) .... FontShop

Garbage T-26

Garth Graphic.......... Adobe, Agfa, FontHaus, FontShop, Linotype, Monotype

Gary (TF) .... FontHaus, FontShop, Treacyfaces

Gazette .... Adobe, Agfa, FontHaus, FontShop, Linotype, Monotype

Gendarme.. EmDash

Gentle Sans .... Image Club

H

Helvetica (continued)
    Helvetica Rounded . . . Adobe, Agfa, FontHaus, FontShop, Linotype, Monotype
    Neue Helvetica . . . . . . Adobe, Agfa, FontHaus, FontShop, Linotype, Monotype
Herald Gothic . . . . Font Bureau, FontHaus
Heraldus . . . . FontShop
    Heraldus Extra Bold . . . . FontHaus
Herculanum . . . . Adobe, Agfa, FontHaus, FontShop, Linotype, Monotype
Hermes . . . . Agfa, FontShop
Hibiscus . . . . Electric Typographer
Highlander (ITC) . . . Adobe, Agfa, FontHaus, FontShop, ITC, Linotype, Monotype
    ITC Highlander GX . . . . ITC
    ITC Highlander Small Caps . . . . URW
Highlight (Letraset) . . . . FontHaus, FontShop, Letraset
Highway Gothic . . . . Page Studio
Hindenburg . . . . Agfa, FontShop
Hip (FF) . . . . FontShop
HipHop . . . . Font Bureau, FontHaus
    HipHop Inline . . . . Font Bureau, FontHaus
Hiroshige . . . . Adobe, Agfa, FontHaus, FontShop, Monotype
    Hiroshige Sans, ... Monotype, URW
Hobo . . . . Adobe, Agfa, Bitstream, FontHaus, FontShop, Image Club, Linotype,
    Monotype, URW
    Hobo Initials . . . . URW
Hoffman . . . . Font Bureau, FontHaus
Hogarth Script . . . . FontHaus, FontShop, URW
Holland
    Holland Seminar . . . . Agfa, FontShop
    Holland Title . . . . Agfa, FontShop
Hollander . . . . FontHaus, FontShop
Hollandse Mediaeval . . . . Agfa, FontShop
Hollyweird (Letraset) . . . . Letraset
Hollywood Deco . . . . FontHaus
Honda (ITC) . . . . FontHaus, Image Club
Honeyspot (TF) . . . . FontHaus, FontShop, Treacyfaces
Horatio . . . . FontHaus
Horizon . . . . Bitstream
Horley Old Style . . . . Adobe, Agfa, FontHaus, FontShop, Linotype, Monotype
Horndon (Letraset) . . . . FontHaus
    Horndon Initials . . . . URW
Hôtelmoderne (TF) . . . . FontHaus, FontShop, Treacyfaces
    TF Hôtelmoderne Calligraphic . . . . FontShop, Treacyfaces
    TF Hôtelmoderne Serif . . . . FontHaus, Treacyfaces
Hrabanus . . . . Agfa, FontShop

Humanist
    FF Humanist . . . . FontShop
    Humanist 521 . . . . Bitstream
    Humanist 531 . . . . Bitstream
    Humanist 777 . . . . Bitstream
    Humanist 970 . . . . Bitstream, FontShop
    Humanist Slabserif 712 . . . . Bitstream, FontShop
Hurry . . . . EmDash
Huxley . . . . Bitstream, FontShop, Image Club
    TF Huxley High . . . . FontHaus, FontShop, Treacyfaces
    TF Huxley Low . . . . FontHaus, FontShop, Treacyfaces

I

Ice Age . . . . URW
Ideal Gothic . . . . FontHaus
Ignatius (Letraset) . . . . FontShop, Image Club, Letraset
Image Club . . . . Image Club
Imago (Berthold . . . . Adobe, Agfa, FontHaus, FontShop, Linotype, Monotype
Impact . . . . Adobe, Agfa, FontHaus, FontShop, Linotype, Monotype
Impakt (Letraset) . . . . Letraset
Imperial . . . . Bitstream, FontShop
Impress . . . . Bitstream, FontShop
Impressum . . . . Adobe, Agfa, FontHaus, FontShop, Linotype, Monotype, URW
    Impressum Caps . . . . URW
    Impressum DisCaps . . . . URW
    Impressum Small Caps . . . . URW
Imprimeur . . . . FontHaus
Imprint . . . . FontShop, Monotype
Improv . . . . Image Club
Impuls . . . . Bitstream, FontShop
In Tegel (F) . . . . FontShop
Incised 901 . . . . Bitstream
Industria . . . . Adobe, Agfa, FontHaus, FontShop, Linotype, Monotype
Industrial 736 . . . . Bitstream
Indy Italic (Letraset) . . . . Letraset
Inflex Bold . . . . Adobe, Agfa, FontHaus, FontShop, Linotype, Monotype
Informal
    Informal 011 . . . . Bitstream
    Informal Black . . . . Agfa, FontShop
    Informal Roman (Letraset) . . . . Letraset
Innercity (FF) . . . . FontShop

J

K

L

M

N

Novarese (ITC)... Adobe, Agfa, Bitstream, FontHaus, FontShop, Image Club, Linotype, Monotype
Nueva.................... Adobe, Agfa, FontHaus, FontShop, Linotype, Monotype
Numskill.................................... Font Bureau, FontHaus
Nuptial Script .... Adobe, Agfa, Bitstream,FontHaus, FontShop, Linotype, Monotype
Nutcracker .... Font Bureau, FontHaus

O

Oak Graphic...................................... URW
Oakland .... Emigre, FontShop
Obedience (F) .... FontShop
Obelisk.................................. Lanston Type
Obelisk No. 2577 .... FontShop
Oblong .... Emigre, FontShop
Ocean Sans .... Monotype
OCR ....
    OCR-A .... Adobe, Agfa, FontHaus, FontShop, Linotype, Monotype
    OCR-A SB .... FontHaus
    OCR-B.............. Adobe, Agfa, FontHaus, FontShop, Linotype, Monotype
    OCR-F (FF) .... FontShop
Octavian................. Adobe, Agfa, FontHaus, FontShop, Linotype, Monotype
Octopuss (Letraset) .... FontHaus, URW
    Letraset Octopuss PosterType .... URW
    Letraset Octopuss Shaded........................ FontHaus
Odessa (Letraset).......................... FontShop, Letraset
Odin.................................. FontHaus, URW
    Odin Initials.................................. URW
    Odin PosterType .... URW
    Odin Round.................................. URW
Officina
    ITC Officina Sans .... Adobe, Agfa, FontHaus, FontShop, ITC, Linotype, Monotype
    ITC Officina Serif .... Adobe, Agfa, FontHaus, FontShop, ITC, Linotype, Monotype
Oklahoma
    URW Oklahoma Compress................................. URW
    URW Oklahoma Stencil .... URW
Old Claude .... FontHaus, Letter Perfect
Old Dreadful No. 7........................... Bitstream, FontShop
Old English .... Agfa, FontHaus, Letraset
    Monotype Old English Text........................... FontShop, Monotype

P

Placard . . . . FontShop, Monotype
Plak . . . . Linotype
Plantin . . . . Adobe, Agfa, FontHaus, FontShop, Linotype, Monotype
   News Plantin . . . . FontShop, Monotype
   Plantin Expert Collection . . . . Adobe, Agfa, FontHaus, FontShop, Linotype,
      Monotype
Platelet . . . . Emigre
Playbill. Bitstream, FontHaus, FontShop, Image Club, URW
   Playbill Antique. . . . . URW
Plaza . . . . FontShop, Letraset, URW
   Plaza Cameo . . . . URW
   Plaza Poster Type. . . . . URW
   Plaza Round . . . . URW
   Plaza Small Caps. . . . . URW
   Plaza Swash . . . . URW
Pleasure Bold Shaded (Letraset) . . . . FontShop, Letraset
PMN Caecilia . . . . Adobe, Agfa, FontHaus, FontShop, Linotype, Monotype
PMN Caecilia Small Caps & Old Style Figures . . . . Adobe, Agfa, FontHaus, FontShop,
      Linotype, Monotype
Pneuma (Letraset) . . . . FontShop, Letraset
Poetica . . . . Adobe, Agfa, FontHaus, FontShop, Linotype, Monotype
   Poetica Supplement . . . . Adobe, Agfa, FontHaus, FontShop, Linotype, Monotype
Poetry . . . . Agfa, FontShop
Poggio Bookhand . . . . Agfa, FontHaus, FontShop, Linotype, Monotype
Pointille . . . . Image Club
Polaris (TF) . . . . FontHaus, FontShop, Treacyfaces
Poliphilus Roman. . . . . FontShop, Monotype
Polka. . . . . FontShop
Pompeii Capitals . . . . Agfa, FontShop
Pompeijana. . . . . Adobe, Agfa, FontHaus, FontShop, Linotype, Monotype
Ponderosa. . . . . Adobe, Agfa, FontHaus, FontShop, Linotype, Monotype
Pop (FF). . . . . FontShop
Poplar . . . . Adobe, Agfa, FontHaus, FontShop, Linotype, Monotype
Poppl-Laudatio . . . . Adobe, Agfa, FontHaus, FontShop, Linotype, Monotype
   Poppl-Laudatio Condensed. . . . . Adobe, Agfa, FontHaus, FontShop, Linotype,
      Monotype
Poppl-Pontifex. . . . . Adobe, Agfa, FontHaus, FontShop, Linotype, Monotype
   Poppl-Pontifex Expert Collection . . . Adobe, Agfa, FontHaus, FontShop, Linotype,
      Monotype
Poppl-Residenz . . . . Adobe, Agfa, FontHaus, FontShop, Linotype, Monotype
Populist Control (F) . . . . FontShop
Populist Exclaim (F) . . . . FontShop
Populist Shout (F) . . . . FontShop

Q

Quadraat (FF) . . . . FontShop
Quadrus (Letraset) . . . . Letraset
Quaint . . . . Image Club
    Quaint Roman . . . . Agfa
Quake . . . . Adobe
Quanta (A*I) . . . . Alphabets Inc., FontHaus
Quartet . . . . Emigre
    Quartet Small Caps . . . . Emigre
Quartz . . . . FontHaus, URW
QuasiModo (A*I) . . . . Alphabets Inc.
Quay
    ITC Quay Sans . . . . FontHaus, FontShop, URW
    ITC Quay Small Caps . . . . URW
Queen Dido Extrabold (TF) . . . . FontHaus, FontShop, Treacyfaces
Queensbury . . . . FontHaus
Quentin . . . . FontHaus
Quercus . . . . FontHaus
Quicksans
    Quicksans Accurate . . . . Image Club
    Quicksans Fast . . . . Image Club
Quicktype . . . . FontHaus
    Quicktype Sans . . . . FontHaus
Quill
    FF Quill . . . . FontShop
    Quill Script, Agfa
Quirinus . . . . Agfa, FontShop
Quixley (Letraset) . . . . FontShop, Letraset
Quorum (ITC) . . . Adobe, Agfa, Bitstream, FontHaus, FontShop, Image Club, Linotype,
    Monotype

R

Rabbit Ears . . . . FontHaus
Raceway . . . . Font Bureau, FontShop
Radiant . . . . FontHaus, FontShop, Image Club
    Radiant Bold Extra Condensed . . . . Agfa, Castle
Rage . . . . FontShop, Letraset, URW
Ragtime (Letraset) . . . . Letraset

Raincheck (TF) . . . . FontHaus, FontShop, Treacyfaces
Raleigh . . . . Adobe, Agfa, Bitstream, FontHaus, FontShop, Linotype, Monotype
    ATF Raleigh Gothic . . . . FontHaus
Ramiz . . . . FontHaus, T-26
Ramsey . . . . Agfa, FontShop
Randomun . . . . FontHaus, T-26
Ransahoff . . . . FontHaus
Raphael . . . . Agfa, FontShop
Rapier (Letraset) . . . . FontShop, Letraset
Ravie . . . . Font Bureau, FontHaus
Reactor (F) . . . . FontShop
Refracta (Letraset) . . . . Letraset
Regatta Condensed (Letraset) . . . . Letraset
Regency Gothic . . . . FontShop
Regent . . . . FontHausRegular Joe, FontHaus
Reiner Script . . . . Font Bureau, FontHaus
Rekord (FF) . . . . FontShop
Relief . . . . Image Club
Religion (F) . . . . FontShop
Remedy . . . . Emigre
Renault . . . . FontHaus, FontShop, URW
Renner Bold Architype . . . . Agfa, FontShop
Renoir (TF) . . . . FontHaus, FontShop, Treacyfaces
Reporter . . . . FontShop, Image Club
    Reporter No. 2, ... Adobe, Agfa, FontHaus, FontShop, Linotype, Monotype
Republik
    Republik Sans . . . . Image Club
    Republik Serif . . . . Image Club
Retablo . . . . FontHaus
Retro . . . . Letraset
Revival
Revival 555 . . . . Bitstream
Revival 565 . . . . Bitstream, FontShop
Revolution T-26
Revolver (FF) . . . . FontShop
Revue . . . . . . Adobe, Agfa, Bitstream, FontHaus, FontShop, Linotype, Monotype, URW
    Revue PosterType . . . . URW
    Revue Round . . . . URW
Rialto
    Rialto Antique . . . . URW
    Rialto Stenci . . . . URW
Ribbon 131 . . . . Bitstream
Ringworld . . . . FontHaus
Rio FontHaus

Rubylith . . . . FontHaus
Rudolf . . . . Castle
Rudolph Koch . . . . FontHaus
Ruling Script Two . . . . Adobe, Agfa, FontHaus, FontShop, Linotype, Monotype
Runa Serif . . . . Agfa, FontShop
Rundfunk, (Letraset) . . . . Letraset
Runic
     Monotype Runic . . . . Monotype
     Runic Condensed . . . . . . Adobe, Agfa, FontHaus, FontShop, Linotype, Monotype
Russell Oblique (A*I) . . . . Alphabets Inc.
Russell Square . . . . Adobe, Agfa, FontHaus, FontShop, Linotype, Monotype
Rusticana . . . . Adobe, Agfa, FontHaus, FontShop, Linotype, Monotype
Ruzicka Freehand . . . . Adobe, Agfa, FontHaus, FontShop, Linotype, Monotype
     Ruzicka Freehand Small Caps & Old Style Figures . . . . Adobe, Agfa, FontHaus,
     FontShop, Linotype, Monotype

S

Sabbath Black . . . . Emigre
Sabius . . . . URW
Sabius Caps . . . . URW
Sabon . . . . Adobe, Agfa, FontHaus, FontShop, Linotype, Monotype
     Sabon Small Caps & Old Style Figures . . . . Adobe, Agfa, FontHaus, FontShop,
     Linotype, Monotype
Sackers Antique Roman . . . . Agfa, FontShop
Sackers Classic Roman . . . . Agfa, FontShop
Sackers English Script . . . . Agfa, FontShop
Sackers Gothic . . . . Agfa, FontShop
Sackers Square Gothic . . . . Agfa, FontShop
Saginaw (TF) . . . . FontHaus, FontShop, Treacyfaces
Sallando Italic . . . . Agfa, FontShop
Salto . . . . Image Club
Salut . . . . Agfa, FontShop
SamSans . . . . Font Bureau, FontHaus
San Marco . . . . Adobe, Agfa, FontHaus, FontShop, Linotype, Monotype
Sans No. 1 . . . . Agfa, FontShop
Santa Barbara . . . . Electric Typographer
Santa Fe . . . . Letraset
SantoDomingo (F) . . . . FontShop
Sanvito . . . . Adobe, Agfa, FontHaus, FontShop, Linotype, Monotype
Sassafras . . . . Monotype, URW

Sassoon
    Sassoon Primary . . . . Adobe, Agfa, FontHaus, FontShop, Linotype, Monotype
    Sassoon Sans . . . . FontShop, Monotype
Saturday (FF) . . . . FontShop
Savage . . . . Image Club
Savoye (Letraset) . . . . Letraset
Sayer
    Sayer Interview . . . . FontShop
    Sayer Script . . . . FontShop
    Sayer Spiritual . . . . FontShop
Scala (FF). . . . . FontShop
Scala Sans (FF) . . . . FontShop
Scamp. . . . . Font Bureau, FontHaus, FontShop
Scanning . . . . Image Club
Schablone. . . . . FontHaus
Schadow. . . . . Bitstream, FontShop
Schampel Black. . . . . Electric Typographer
Scherzo. . . . . Agfa, FontShop
Schmelvetica (FF) . . . . FontShop
Schneidler . . . . Bitstream, FontHaus, FontShop
    Schneidler Initials . . . . Castle, FontHaus
    Schneidler Mediaeval . . . . Agfa, URW
    Stempel Schneidler . . . . . Adobe, Agfa, FontHaus, FontShop, Linotype, Monotype
Schoensperger (FF). . . . . FontShop
Schreibmaschine. . . . . FontHaus, FontShop
Schrift (F) . . . . FontShop
Schulbuch (FF) . . . . FontShop
Schulschrift (FF) . . . . FontShop
Schwere . . . . FontHaus
Schwitters Architype. . . . . Agfa, FontShop
Scorpio T-26
Scotch Roman (Monotype) . . Adobe, Agfa, FontHaus, FontShop, Linotype, Monotype
Scotford Uncial. . . . . Image Club
Scotty. . . . . FontHaus, T-26
Scratch . . . . Letraset, FontShop, T-26
    FF Scratch . . . . FontShop
Scratched Out (F) . . . . FontShop
Scrawl. T-26
Screen Matrix (FF) . . . . FontShop
Scriba (letraset). . . . . Letraset
Scribble (FF) . . . . FontShop
Script
    BertholdScript. . . . . Adobe, Agfa, FontHaus, FontShop, Linotype, Monotype
    Monotype Script . . . . Monotype

Script (continued)

    Monotype Script Bold . . Adobe, Agfa, FontHaus, FontShop, Linotype, Monotype

    Sackers Script . . . . Agfa, FontShop

    Script 12 Pitch, Bitstream, FontShop

Scriptease (Letraset) . . . . Letraset

Scriptek (Letraset) . . . . Letraset

Scripture . . . . FontHaus

Scruff (Letraset) . . . . Letraset, FontShop

Seagull . . . . Bitstream, FontShop

Searsucker . . . . Agfa, FontShop

Section Bold . . . . Agfa, FontShop

Senator . . . . Emigre, FontShop

Senza . . . . FontHaus

Serene . . . . FontHaus

Serif Gothic (ITC) . . . . Adobe, Agfa, Bitstream, FontHaus, FontShop, Image Club,
    Linotype, Monotype

    ITC Serif Gothic Bold Outline . . . . Adobe, Agfa, Bitstream, FontHaus, FontShop,
    Linotype, Monotype

Serifa . . . . . Adobe, Agfa, Bitstream, FontHaus, FontShop, Linotype, Monotype, URW

Serlio . . . . Adobe, Agfa, FontHaus, FontShop, Linotype, Monotype

Serpentine, Adobe, Agfa, FontHaus, FontShop, Image Club,, Linotype, Monotype, URW

Serpentine Compress . . . . URW

Shannon . . . . Adobe, Agfa, FontHaus, FontShop,, Linotype, Monotype

    Shannon Premier . . . . FontShop

Shatter (Letraset) . . . . Letraset

Shelley . . . . Adobe, Agfa, Bitstream, FontHaus, FontShop,, Linotype, Monotype

Shimano . . . . Font Bureau, FontShop

Sho . . . . Adobe, Agfa, FontHaus, FontShop,, Linotype, Monotype

Shotgun . . . . Bitstream, FontShop

Showboat . . . . FontHaus

Showcard

    Showcard Gothic . . . . Font Bureau, FontHaus

    Showcard Moderne . . . . Agfa, FontShop

Siena

    Siena Black . . . . Agfa, FontShop

    TF Siena . . . . FontHaus, FontShop, Treacyfaces

Sierra . . . . FontHaus, FontShop

Signaler . . . . FontHaus

Signature . . . . Agfa, FontShop, Image Club

Silhouette . . . . FontShop, Letter Perfect

Silica . . . . FontHaus, Stone

Simper (TF) . . . . FontHaus, Treacyfaces

Sinaloa . . . . Agfa, FontShop, Image Club, Letraset, URW

    Sinaloa Initials . . . . URW

Sinaloa (continued)

    Sinaloa Small Cap . . . . URW

Singer (FF) . . . . FontShop

Sitcom . . . . FontHaus

Six Pack . . . . FontHaus

Skid Row (Letraset) . . . . Letraset

Skidoos . . . . URW

Skidoos PosterType . . . . URW

Skreetch T-26

Skylark (ITC) . . . . FontShop, ITC

Skyline . . . . Font Bureau, FontHaus

Slender . . . . FontHaus

Slimbach (ITC . . . . Adobe, Agfa, FontHaus, FontShop, Image Club, Linotype,
    Monotype, URW

    ITC Slimbach Caps . . . . URW

    ITC Slimbach Small Caps . . . . FontShop, URW

Slimline . . . . FontHaus

Slipstream (Letraset) . . . . FontShop, Letraset

Slogan . . . . FontHaus, FontShop, URW

Sloop . . . . Font Bureau, FontHaus

Smack . . . . Letraset

Smaragd . . . . Adobe, Agfa, FontHaus, FontShop, Linotype, Monotype

Smile . . . . Image Club

Smudger . . . . Letraset

Snap (ITC) . . . . FontShop, ITC

Snell . . . . Bitstream

    Snell Roundhand . . . . . . Adobe, Agfa, FontHaus, FontShop, Linotype, Monotype

Snow Caps . . . . Bitstream

Snydor (ITC) . . . . URW

    ITC Snydor Caps . . . . URW

Sonic . . . . Bitstream

Sophia . . . . Carter & Cone, FontHaus

Souvenir (ITC) . . . Adobe, Agfa, Bitstream, FontHaus, FontShop, Image Club, Linotype,
    Monotype, URW

    ITC Souvenir Bold Outline . . . . Bitstream

    Souvenir Gothic . . . . Agfa, FontShop

Space . . . . Bitstream

Spartan

    Monotype Spartan . . . . FontShop, Monotype

    Spartan Classified . . . . . . Adobe, Agfa, FontHaus, FontShop, Linotype, Monotype

Spectrum . . . . Adobe, Agfa, FontHaus, FontShop, Linotype, Monotype

    Spectrum Expert Collection . . . . Adobe, Agfa, FontHaus, FontShop, Linotype,
    Monotype

Stone (ITC)

    ITC Stone Informal . . . . Adobe, Agfa, FontHaus, FontShop, Image Club, Linotype, Monotype, Stone Type Foundry, URW

    ITC Stone Informal Small Caps . . . . FontShop, URW

    ITC Stone Print . . . . FontHaus, Stone Type Foundry

    ITC Stone Sans . . . . Adobe, Agfa, FontHaus, FontShop, Image Club, Linotype, Monotype, Stone Type Foundry

    ITC Stone Sans Small Caps . . . . FontShop, URW

    ITC Stone Serif . . . . Adobe, Agfa, FontHaus, FontShop, Image Club, Linotype, Monotype, Stone Type Foundry, URW

    ITC Stone Serif Small Caps . . . . FontShop, URW

Stone Age . . . . Bitstream

Stop . . . . FontHaus, URW

    Stop Round . . . . URW

    Stop Small Caps . . . . URW

Story . . . . EmDash

Stratford . . . . Agfa, FontShop

Stratosphere . . . . FontHaus

Streamline . . . . Agfa, FontShop

Strobo . . . . Letraset

Studio Script (ITC) . . . . FontHaus, FontShop, Image Club

    ITC Studio Script Alternative Character . . . . URW

    ITC Studio Script GX . . . . ITC

Stuyvesant . . . . Bitstream, Image Club

Stylus . . . . Bitstream

Stymie . . . . Bitstream, FontHaus, FontShop, URW

    Stymie DisCaps . . . . URW

    Stymie Small Caps . . . . URW

Suburban . . . . Emigre

Subway . . . . FontHaus

Sully Jonquieres . . . . FontShop

Sunday (FF) . . . . FontShop

Superba . . . . FontHaus

Superstar . . . . FontHaus, FontShop, Letraset, URW

    Superstar Initials . . . . URW

    Superstar Shaded . . . . FontHaus

Swift . . . . FontHaus, FontShop

Swing Bold . . . . FontShop, Monotype

Swiss

    Swiss 721 . . . . Bitstream

    Swiss 911 . . . . Bitstream

    Swiss 921 . . . . Bitstream

    Swiss 924 . . . . Bitstream, FontShop

Syllogon . . . . Image Club

Symbol (ITC) .... Adobe, Agfa, Bitstream, FontHaus, FontShop, Image Club, Linotype, Monotype, URW
    ITC Symbol Small Caps .... FontShop, URW
Symphonie.. FontHaus
Symphony (CG)... Agfa
Symposia... Agfa
Synchro (Letraset) .... Letraset
Synchron .... FontHaus
Syndor (ITC) .... FontHaus
    ITC Syndor Small Caps...................................... URW
Syntax................... Adobe, Agfa, FontHaus, FontShop, Linotype, Monotype
System X3 .... Agfa, FontShop
Szene (A*I) .... Alphabets Inc.

T

T H Alphabet Soup.. Image Club
Tagged .... FontShop, T-26
Tagliente .... Electric Typographer, FontShop
Tango .... Bitstream
Tannäuser .... Letraset
Tape Type (F) .... FontShop
Tarquinius (FF) .... FontShop
Tarragon .... URW
Tasse .... Font Bureau, FontHaus
Tattoo .... FontHaus, T-26
Teatro (FF) .... FontShop
Technique .... FontHaus
Teknik (Letraset)............................. FontShop, Letraset
Tekton .... Adobe, Agfa, FontHaus, FontShop, Linotype, Monotype
    Tekton GX .... Adobe, Agfa, FontHaus, FontShop, Linotype, Monotype
Telegram (Letraset) .... Letraset
Tema... T-26
    Tema Cantante T-26
Template Gothic .... Emigre, FontShop
Tempo .... Linotype
    Tempo Heavy Condensed .... Adobe, Agfa, FontHaus, FontShop, Linotype, Monotype
Tempto Open Face .... FontHaus
Terminal.. FontShop, T-26
Textype... FontShop
Thalia Italic .... Agfa, FontShop

Thane Gash. . . . . FontShop, T-26
TheMix (FF) . . . . FontShop
TheSans (FF) . . . . FontShop
TheSerif (FF) . . . . FontShop
Thompson Quillscript . . . . FontShop
Thor. . . . . Image Club
Throhand. . . . . Agfa, FontShop
Thunderbird. . . . . Bitstream, Image Club, FontHaus, FontShop, URW
Tiepolo (ITC). . . Adobe, Agfa, FontHaus, FontShop, Image Club, Linotype, Monotype,
        URW
        ITC Tiepolo Small Caps . . . . URW
Tiffany (ITC) . . . . Adobe, Agfa, Bitstream, FontHaus, FontShop, Image Club, Linotype,
        Monotype
Tiger Rag. . . . . Letraset
Tigerteeth . . . . Image Club
Time In Hell . . . . FontShop, T-26
Timeles. . . . . FontHaus
Times . . . . Adobe, Agfa, FontHaus, FontShop, Linotype, Monotype
        CG Times. . . . . Agfa
        Times Europa . . . . Adobe, Agfa, FontHaus, FontShop, Linotype, Monotype
        Times GX . . . . Linotype
        Times Headline. . . . . FontShop
        Times Modern . . . . FontHaus
        Times New Roman. . . . . . Adobe, Agfa, FontHaus, FontShop, Linotype, Monotype
        Times New Roman Small Caps & Old Style Figures . . . . . . Adobe, Agfa,FontHaus,
            FontShop, Linotype, Monotype
        Times Nr. 1 . . . . FontHaus
        Times Small Caps & Old Style Figure . . . . Adobe, Agfa, FontHaus, FontShop,
            Linotype, Monotype
        Times Ten . . . . Adobe, Agfa, FontHaus, FontShop, Linotype, Monotype
        Times Ten Small Caps & Old Style Figures . . . Adobe, Agfa, FontHaus, FontShop,
            Linotype, Monotype
Tiranti Solid (Letraset) . . . . Letraset
Titanic Condensed . . . . FontHaus
Toc (FF). . . . . FontShop
Today Sans Serif. . . . . FontHaus, FontShop
Tokay . . . . FontHaus
Tokyo (FF). . . . . FontShop
Tom's Roman (ITC) . . . . Bitstream, FontShop
TomBoy, FontShop . . . . Letter Perfect
Too Much . . . . Image Club
Tool Cities . . . . FontHaus
Torino Modern . . . . FontHaus
Torino Open (PL). . . . . Agfa, FontShop

Typewriter
    Typewriter . . . . FontShop, Monotype
    Old Typewriter . . . . FontHaus
    Typewriter Elite . . . . Monotype
    Typewriter Gothic . . . . Monotype
Typo Upright . . . . Bitstream
Tyson (FF) . . . . FontShop
Tzigane . . . . FontShop

U

Uck'N Pretty (F) . . . . FontShop
Ulissa . . . . Monotype
Ultra Condensed
    Ultra Condensed Sans . . . . Image Club
    Ultra Condensed Serif . . . . Image Club
Ulysses (Letraset) . . . . FontShop, Letraset
Umbra . . . . Adobe, Bitstream, FontHaus, FontShop, Linotype, Monotype
Uncial . . . . Agfa
Unica . . . . FontShop
Uniform . . . . Image Club
Union T-26
    Union Round One . . . . FontHaus
UniTronica (A*I) . . . . Alphabets Inc., FontHaus
Unitus . . . . URW
Univers . . . . Adobe, FontHaus, FontShop
    Univers Deco . . . . Castle
Universal . . . . Emigre, FontShop
University
    University Antique . . . . URW
    University Roman . . . . . . Adobe, Agfa, Bitstream, FontHaus, FontShop, Image Club,
        Letraset, Linotype, Monotype, URW
    University Swash . . . . URW
UpStart . . . . EmDash
Usherwood (ITC) . . . . Adobe, Agfa, FontHaus, FontShop, Image Club, Linotype,
        Monotype, URW
Utopia . . . . Adobe, Agfa, FontHaus, FontShop, Linotype, Monotype
    Utopia Expert Collection . . . . Adobe, Agfa, FontHaus, FontShop, Linotype,
        Monotype

V

W

X

Y

Z

Glossary

Ascender A stroke of a lowercase letter such as *d* or *b* that extends above the body of the letter.

ASCII American Standard Code for Information Interchange. A numbering scheme used by computers to denote characters and control commands. ASCII numbers 32 through 255 are used for printing characters.

Baseline An invisible line on which characters sit. In some typefaces, rounded characters such as *e* and *o* dip slightly below the baseline in order to visually line up with the other characters.

Bitmap A grid of dots, or *pixels*, that make up characters or graphics on a computer screen. The Mac displays black characters on a white background to simulate the appearance of a printed page.

Black-letter type (Also called Gothic, Old English, or Textura) An antique style of type based on the angular calligraphy of thirteenth-century German scribes.

Body copy (Also called body type) Text, generally set at 9 to 12 points, used for long passages of reading matter.

Bracketed serif A serif that is linked to a character with a curved bowl, rather than a right angle (vs. *square* or *slab serifs*).

Built-in font A set of characters that resides permanently in a printer's memory.

Cap height The height of a face's capital letters. In many faces, the capitals are shorter than the ascenders.

Center justified *See* Justified type.

Color The overall shade of gray perceived when a reader scans a block of type. The uniform color of a page can be disrupted by uneven word or letter spacing. Adding or subtracting leading affects color as well.

Condensed (Also called Narrow or Compressed) A typeface with characters that are narrower than those of the corresponding roman face, but retain the original face's cap height. Condensed faces can be created by hand or produced on a computer.

Counterform The space surrounded by closed letters such as *b* or *e*.

CPP (Characters per pica) A calculation used in copyfitting, the process of determining the correct type size

and leading to fill a predetermined area. The easiest way to determine CPP is to measure the width, in points, of a face's lowercase alphabet and divide that number by 342.

Decorative typeface A stylized typeface that's intended to catch the reader's attention. Decorative faces run the gamut from script to computer-esque, and are used in applications where readability isn't as important as grabbing attention or setting a mood.

Descender A stroke of a lowercase letter such as *g* or *y* that drops below the body of the letter.

Diacritic An accent or mark placed on a letter to indicate a particular pronunciation. Common diacritical marks are the acute accent (é), grave accent (è), umlaut (ü), circumflex (î), tilde (ñ), and cedilla (ç).

Dingbats Ornamental typographic elements such as stars, arrows, pointing hands, and so on. Used for decorative touches, highlights, and borders.

Display face A typeface designed to be set at relatively large sizes (usually 18 points and up) and used in titles, headlines, signs, and the like.

DPI Dots per inch. The resolution of a computer screen (the Mac's screen resolution is 72 dpi) or an output device such as a laser printer or imagesetter.

Downloadable font A font that can be temporarily stored in a printer's memory, printed, and flushed from memory when the job is done (vs. built-in fonts, which reside permanently in the printer).

Drop cap A large capital letter, placed at the beginning of a chapter or paragraph, that drops into the surrounding text.

Egyptian (Also called *slab serif* or *square serif*) A type style characterized by strong, uniform strokes and thick, square serifs. This style originated in France after Napoleon's return from Egypt.

Ellipsis A character made up of three periods. Ellipses are used to indicate an omission; often used when portions of quoted matter are omitted.

Family A group of typefaces that share a common design but differ in stylistic attributes such as weight or character width. A typical family consists of roman, bold, italic, and bold-italic faces.

Em A relative unit of measure equal to a face's point size. (An em is 10 points wide when a face is set at 10 points, for example.) Called an *em* because it's usually the width of a face's widest letter, the uppercase *M*. An em dash is one em wide.

En A relative unit of measure equal to half of a face's point size. An en dash is one en wide.

Extended (Also called Expanded) A typeface in which the letters are stretched horizontally while retaining their original height. An extended face can be created by hand or produced on a computer.

Font In digital typography, the data that describes the complete character set for a given typeface.

Gothic Another name for *sans serif* type. (Also occasionally used to signify *black-letter* type.)

Grotesque Another name for *sans serif* type.

Hot-metal typesetting A form of typesetting in which lines of characters are arranged in a matrix and cast in a molten lead alloy.

Initial cap A large capital letter, often decorative, placed at the beginning of a chapter, paragraph, section, or the like.

Inline A decorative type style in which a solid letterform is placed within an outlined letter.

Italic A slanted variation of a roman typeface, designed to complement the roman face's letterforms. Italics were originally modeled after handwritten script or calligraphy.

Justified type (Also called Center justified) Lines of text that line up at both the left and right margins. Often letterspacing as well as word spacing is adjusted to even out line lengths when text is justified.

Kerning Adjusting the space between letter pairs accommodate the varying shapes of letters and produce the appearance of consistent letter spacing. PostScript typefaces have built-in kerning pairs, but you may need to manually adjust kerning when type is set at a large size, which makes gaps more noticeable.

Leading The vertical distance between lines of type, from baseline to baseline, measured in points. Leading is expressed as a face's point size, followed by the baseline-to-baseline measurement (for example, "10/12" for 10-point type with 2 points of leading). The term derives from thin strips of lead placed between lines in the days of hot-metal typesetting.

Letterspacing The space between each letter in a word. Some programs add space between each letter to fill out a line when text is center-justified.

Ligature A special character made up of two or more characters. Many PostScript typefaces include the ligatures fi, fl, œ, and æ.

Line spacing *See* Leading.

Lowercase (Also called Minuscules) Small letters of a typeface (*a, b, c,* etc.). The term comes from the typesetting tradition of storing small letters in the lower part of a printer's typecase.

Modern A type style characterized by extreme contrast between thick and thin strokes, square serifs, and a strong vertical stress.

Monospaced type Type in which all characters are of the same width, as in a typewriter face (vs. *proportionally spaced* type).

Oblique A slanted version of a roman typeface. Some oblique faces are created by type designers, while others are produced with computer commands.

OCR face A typeface designed to be read by an optical character recognition device.

Old Style A type style characterized by small variations in stroke width, bracketed serifs, and a diagonal stress. Old Style numbers often extend below a face's baseline.

Outline font A computer font made up of curves that can be scaled to any size before being printed. Since outline fonts are scalable, only one set of outlines needs to be created for a given typeface.

Pi font A set of special characters for a particular profession or discipline. Examples of pi fonts include mathematical symbols, cartographic symbols, monetary symbols, fractions, or custom characters.

Pica A typographic unit of measurement equal to 12 points, or approximately 0.166 inches.

Pixel (From picture element) A square or rectangular dot that is the smallest unit displayed on a computer screen (the Mac displays 72 pixels per inch). Selected pixels in a grid are turned on or off to create characters or graphics.

Point A typographic unit of measurement equal to approximately $1/72$ inch (actually 0.1383 inches). A face's point size is the distance from the top of its ascenders to the bottom of its descenders.

PostScript A language developed by Adobe Systems to describe pages of scalable text and graphics. PostScript is built into Apple's LaserWriter printers and numerous other laser printers and imagesetters.

Printer font (for PostScript fonts) A set of scalable outlines for a given character set. Some printer fonts are built into laser printers and imagesetters, while others can be temporarily downloaded to the device for a particular printing job.

Proportionally spaced type A typeface in which character widths vary (vs. *monospaced type*, in which all characters of a face are the same width). In a proportionally spaced face, an *i* is narrower than an *m*, for example.

Ragged right Lines of type that line up at the left margin, but not the right margin.

RAM (Random Access Memory) Temporary storage space in a computer or printer that is used to store data, including fonts. Unlike information in ROM, information in RAM disappears when a device is turned off.

Reversed type White characters set on a dark background.

RIP (Raster Image Processor) A device that converts computer instructions (PostScript, in the case of the Mac) into bitmaps that are output by a printer or imagesetter.

ROM (Read-Only Memory) Permanent memory that is built into a computer or printer and used to store data (including fonts) shared by all programs.

Roman A style of type characterized by upright, as opposed to slanted characters. Called Plain in Mac font menus.

Sans serif face (also called *Gothic* or *Grotesque*) A typeface with no embellishments (serifs) at the ends of strokes. Sans serif faces are often composed of characters with little variation in stroke width.

Screen font The bitmapped characters that appear on the monitor when you type. For optimum readability, screen fonts must be installed in all the sizes you intend to use.

Serif face A typeface with small counterstrokes at the end of each main stroke. Serifs help the eye tie the letters of a word together.

Slab serif *See* Egyptian.

Small caps A set of capital letters that match the x-height and letter width of a given typeface and size. Small caps can be created by a type designer or produced by software.

Solid leading *Leading* equal to the point size of the type being used (for example, 12-point type set on 12 points of lead). Most digital typefaces have a little extra space built in so ascenders and descenders of adjoining lines don't touch when type is set solid.

Square serif *See* Egyptian.

Stress The vertical, horizontal, or diagonal emphasis of a letter stroke.

Text face   A typeface designed to be readable in long passages. Text faces are usually set at sizes from 9 to 12 points.

Tracking   The overall letterspacing in a passage of text. Some programs let you adjust tracking to tighten up a face that looks too airy, or to add space to even out lines of display type.

Transitional   A type style that forms a transition between Old Style and Modern faces. Characterized by moderate variation in stroke weight, smoothly-joined serifs, and a nearly vertical stress.

Typeface   A complete set of characters, punctuation, and symbols that share a common design.

Typeface family   *See* Family.

Uncial   A calligraphic typestyle that combines the attributes of uppercase and lowercase letters, rounding the normally straight lines of the capitals. The name comes from the Latin uncus, crooked.

Uppercase   Capital letters of a typeface (*A*, *B*, *C*, etc.). The term comes from the typesetting tradition of storing capital letters in the upper part of a printer's typecase.

Weight   Variation in a face's stroke width. Some typeface families include several weights, which can range from extralight to ultrabold. Common weights are light, regular, demibold or semibold, bold, and ultrabold (also called heavy or black).

Word spacing   The amount of space between each word in a line of text. Word spacing is automatically adjusted to even out lines in justified text.

X-height   The height of a face's lowercase letters. The lowercase *x* is measured because in most faces it sits squarely on the baseline and has no ascenders or descenders. X-height affects a face's perceived size; faces with large x-heights look bigger than faces with small ones.

Index

Index